IMAGES
of America

BEAUFORT COUNTY
NORTH CAROLINA

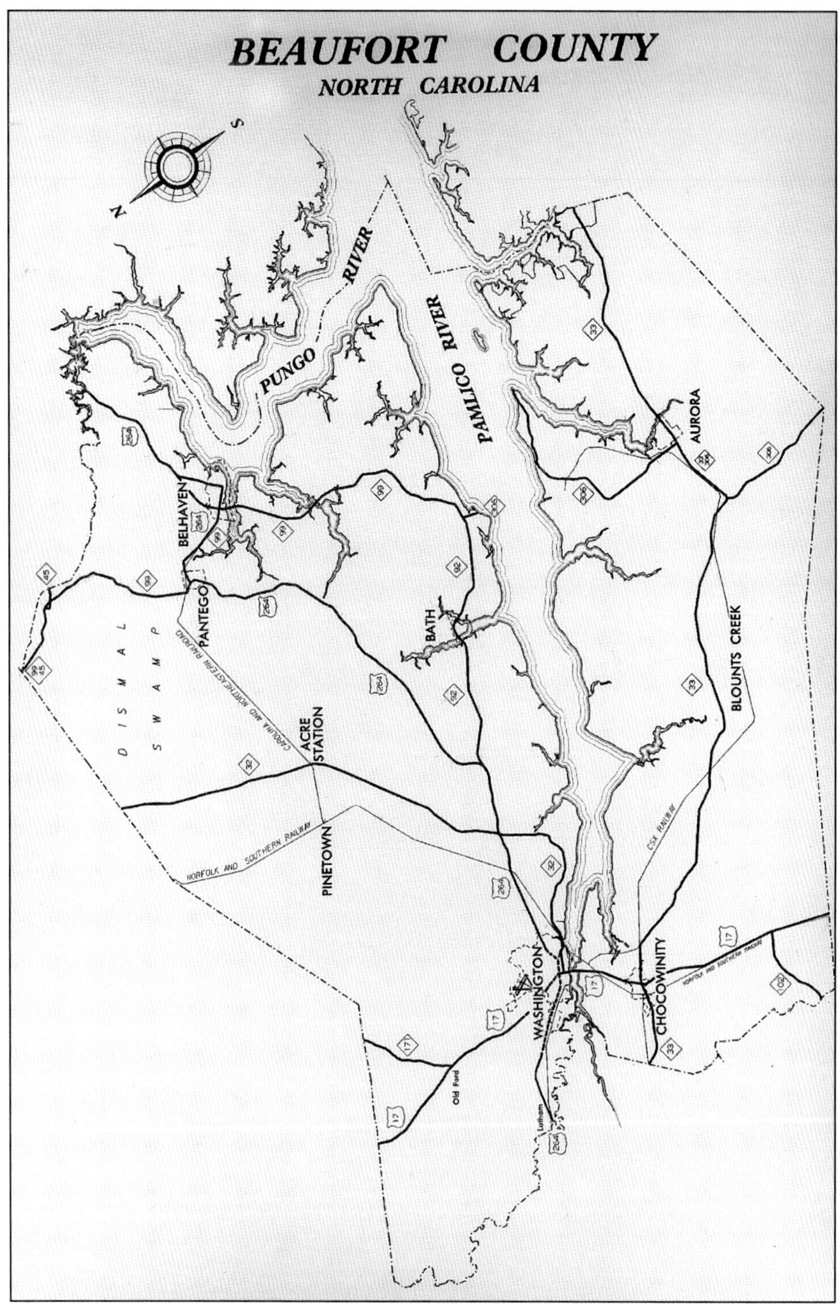

This map of Beaufort County was prepared by the NC Department of Transportation, Survey Unit, and drawn by Ryan Beacham.

On the cover: This scene is thought to depict crab or net fishing boats at the Belhaven Town Dock in the 1920s. The white house in the background was the Keaton home, and to the right was the Jordon home. (Courtesy of W. Mayo.)

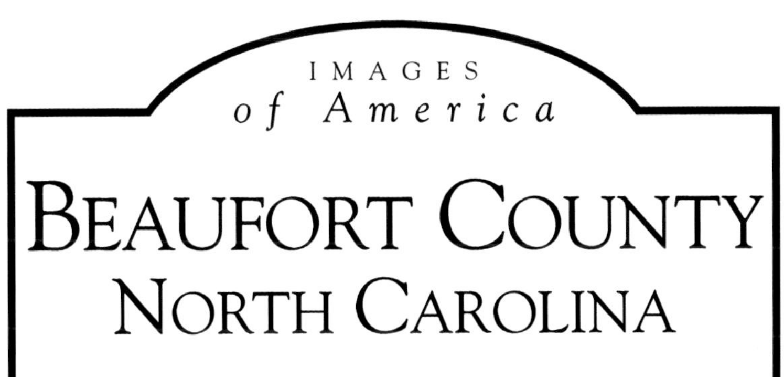

Louis Van Camp

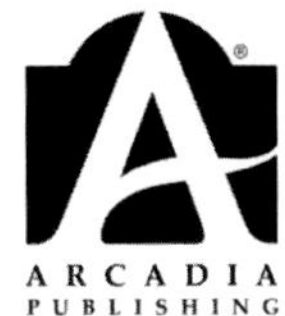

ISBN 978-0-7385-0661-6

Published by Arcadia Publishing
Charleston, South Carolina

Printed in the United States of America

Library of Congress Catalog Card Number: 00-108141

For all general information contact Arcadia Publishing at:
Telephone 843-853-2070
Fax 843-853-0044
E-Mail sales@arcadiapublishing.com
For customer service and orders:
Toll-Free 1-888-313-2665

Visit us on the Internet at www.arcadiapublishing.com

This book is dedicated to all the wonderful people of Beaufort County who strive to preserve the past while building for the future.

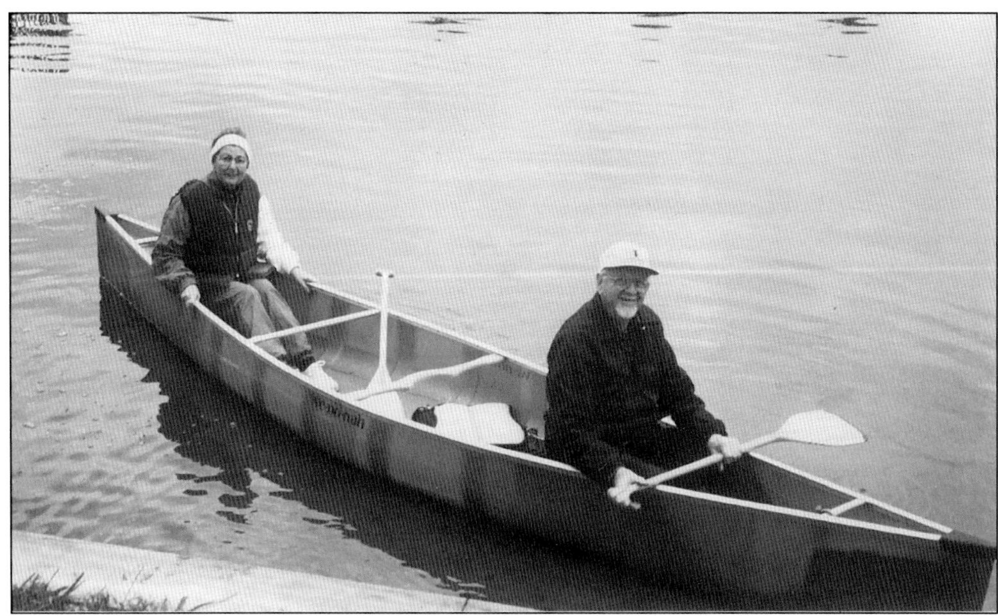

Author Louis Van Camp and his wife, Vera, of Washington, North Carolina are seen enjoying some water time on Blount's Creek while visiting their good friends Dave and Mary George Hocevar at their Bay Harbor, Chocowinity home. (Photo by Mary George Hocevar.)

Contents

Acknowledgments

A documentary about the people of a nation, a state, or a county can only be as interesting as the area and the people themselves. The story works only if the people of that area contribute their family pictures and stories, and this book matured because so many Beaufort County residents were willing to do just that. To this end I have chosen to acknowledge your contributions by including a credit line for each picture you have supplied. To all of you I say thank you. I hope you enjoy the way I have chosen to present your family genealogy and the way I have interpreted your stories. I found your stories very interesting, and my only regret is that I had to condense many of them to fit the layout. Thank you one and all for contributing to this pictorial history of Beaufort County.

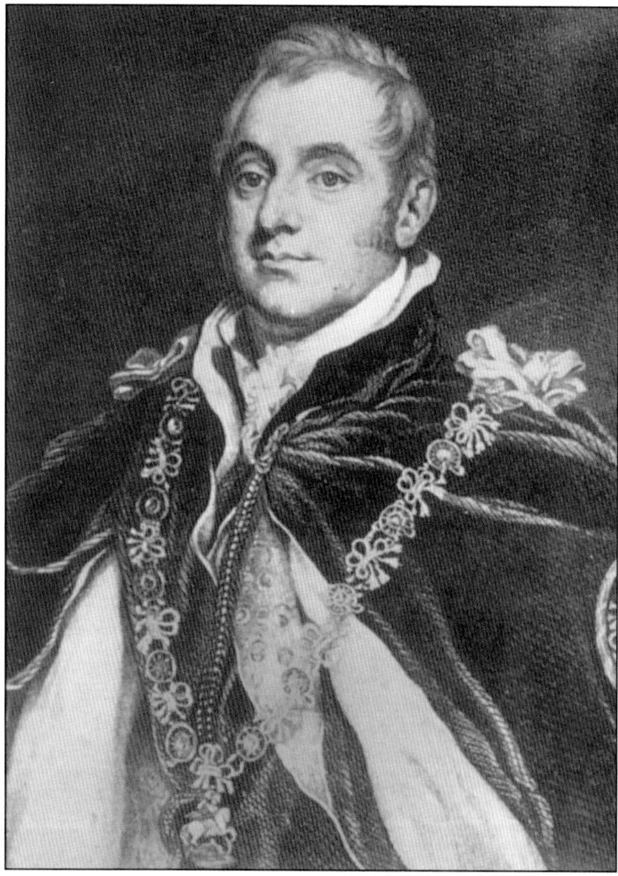

An engraving depicts Lord Henry Somerset, Duke of Beaufort, the Palatine of Carolina in 1712, in whose honor Beaufort County was named. (Courtesy of NC State Department of Archives and History, Raleigh, NC.)

INTRODUCTION

This book is a pictorial documentation of several Beaufort County towns and many of its families, dating from the 1700s and 1800s to the year 2000. Genealogy was supplied by each family represented and is believed to be reliable.

COLONIAL BEAUFORT COUNTY

The first historical reference to the area now called Beaufort County was made in 1584 by Capt. Arthur Barlowe, who raved about the "abundance of waterfowl" along the river, while traveling with Sir Walter Raleigh's first Virginia expedition. In 1696, the "great county of Bath" was formed and named in honor of John Granville, Earl of Bath and Palatine of Carolina. The English called this region Beaufort Precinct in honor of Lord Somerset, the Duke of Beaufort (pictured on page six). Beaufort Precinct became Beaufort County in 1729 and, by 1792, had a population of 5,452 white settlers and 1,622 black slaves.

TWENTIETH-CENTURY BEAUFORT COUNTY

Of North Carolina's 100 counties, Beaufort County is the eighth largest, with one-seventh of its area lying beneath surface water. Many consider the Pamlico River and the numerous creeks that drain into it Beaufort County's most important asset. These waterways not only supply the county's basic living requirements, they also provide a wealth of beauty and enjoyment. The Pamlico River also provided wonderful economic opportunities for commercial fishing, shipping and ship building, lumber mills, and mercantile trade in the late 19th and 20th centuries. Lumber industry expert Louis G. May said, "The lumber manufacturing business was by far Beaufort County's largest industry during the 1890s through the 1950s".

Beaufort County was endowed with hundreds of square miles of virgin timberlands and excellent ports from which lumber and farm products could be shipped. The sale of cut lumber and the production of timber products, such as turpentine and resin, created a substantial source of income for merchants and farmers. Prior to 1900, such products had to be hauled by water. At first great sailing ships were built in Washington and Bath to transport these products. Then in the late 1800s steamships and the railroad created stiff competition for the sailing ships. Unlike sailing ships, the latter ran on schedule in foul or fair weather at lower rates, which contributed to an increase in demand for fresh produce and lumber byproducts. However, during the Great Depression of the 1930s many area lumber mills were forced to close because the demand for pine wood declined in the Northern markets.

By the mid-1950s, the lumber industry had consolidated, which left only a few mills operational. Cotton, soybeans, and corn became ever more important. Tobacco was "king" and yielded higher profits than any other crop. In the Terra Ceia region, farmers raised large herds of steers, oxen, and hogs. In more modern times, the growth and sale of bulbs, perennial plants, and flowers contributed to the local economy. In 1985, the Pamlico River still offered excellent fishing and crabbing. Over 1,000 licensed commercial fishermen and another 500 seafood processing workers earned their living from the waterways. The river also supported pleasure boating and small boat manufacturing.

Towards the end of the 20th century, however, the river water quality had declined and greatly affected commercial fishing. Fortunately the concerted efforts of many organizations resulted in a reversal of that trend. Tourism and the sale and development of land for retirement communities emerged as a new and lucrative source of income. Once more, the combination of peaceful waterways, good hunting, and abundant fertile land attracted many to settle in Beaufort County. Tourists journey from afar to fish, swim, sail, and cruise, or to just sit back and gaze at the wondrous river sunrises and sunsets. The waterways, as always, remain Beaufort County's most valuable natural resource.

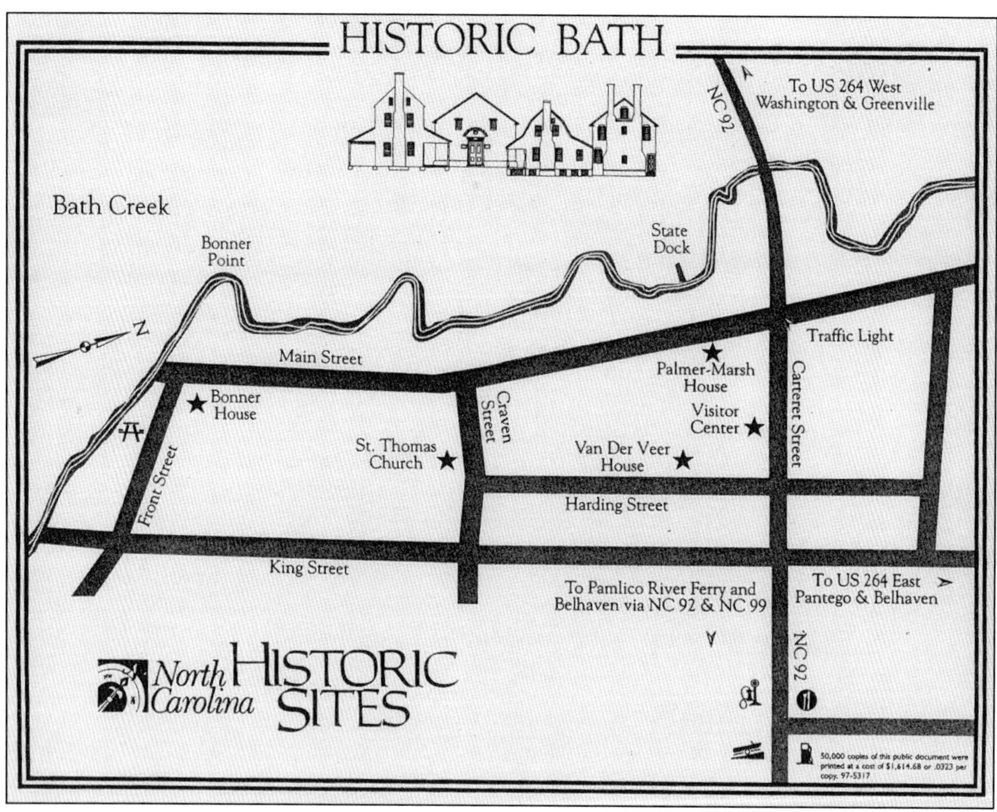

History of Bath

Bath is the oldest town in North Carolina and was built on the location of the Native American village of Pamticough on Old Town Creek (now called Bath Creek). The first white settlers arrived about 1690, and Bath was incorporated in 1705. The town's first commissioners were John Lawson, Joel Martin, and Simon Alderson. Bath was the first colonial capitol of North Carolina, and the North Carolina General Assembly convened here in 1744 and 1752. The first public library was started here in 1700. Bath was a port of entry from 1716 until 1784. St. Thomas Church, built in 1704, is the oldest existing church in North Carolina. Bath was the county seat until it was moved to Washington in 1786 as decreed by the North Carolina General Assembly on December 29, 1785.

One

BATH: 1701–1970

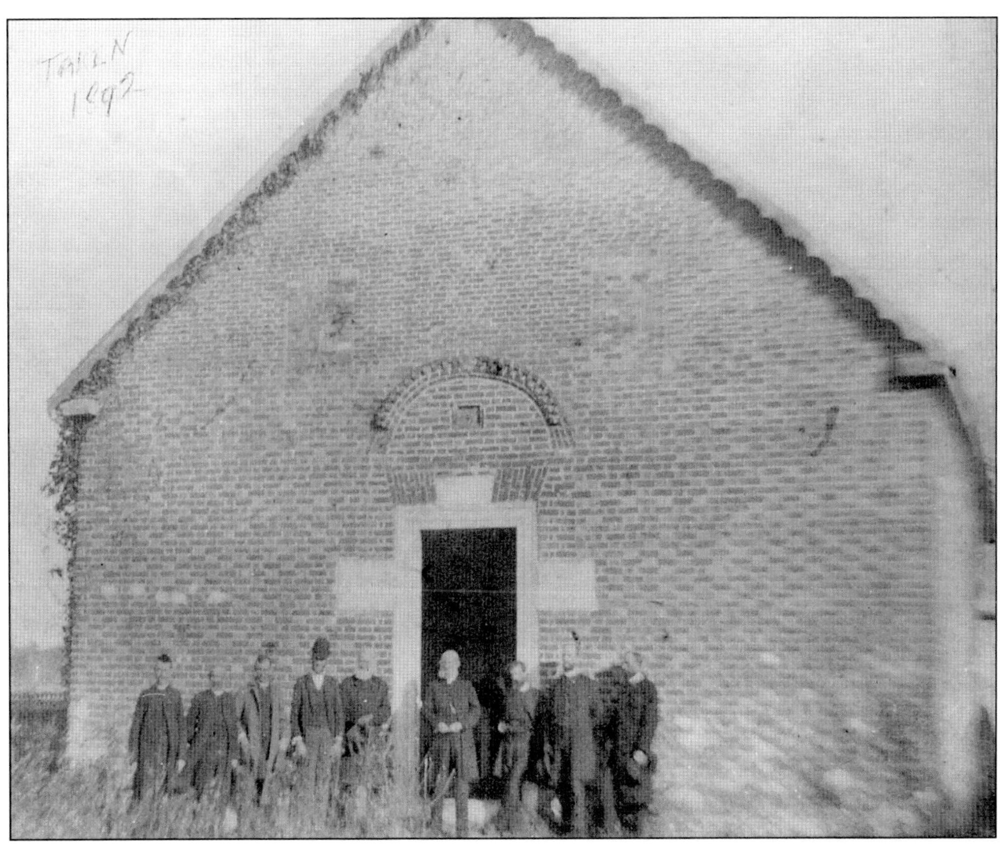

This rare 1892 print shows the vestry of St. Thomas Episcopal Church in Bath. The parish was established by decree of the Church of England in 1701. St. Thomas Church was built in 1734 and is the oldest existing church in North Carolina. (Courtesy of NC Historic Bath.)

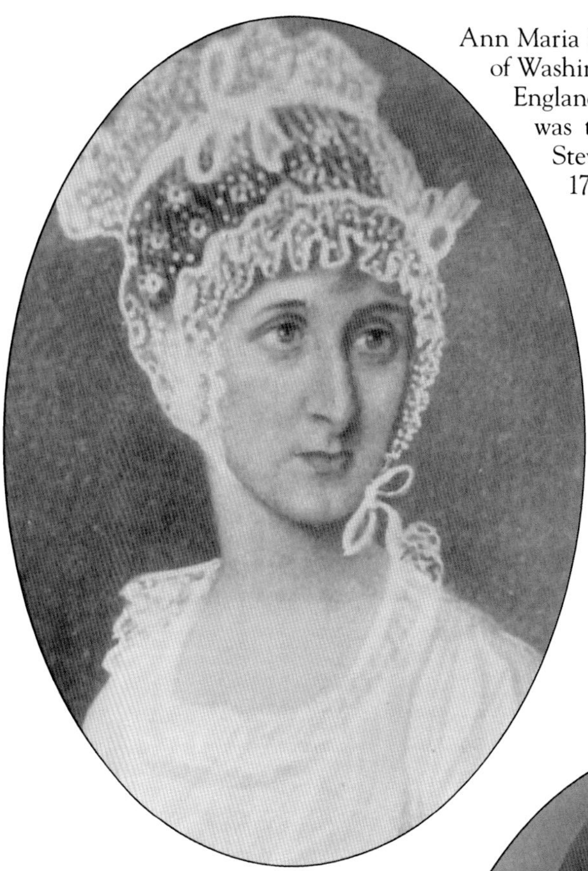

Ann Maria Kewell was the wife of John Gallagher of Washington. She was born in Sussex County, England, on March 22, 1779. Ann Kewell was the granddaughter of Rev. Alexander Stewart who came to St. Thomas Parish in 1753. (Courtesy of L.T. Rodman.)

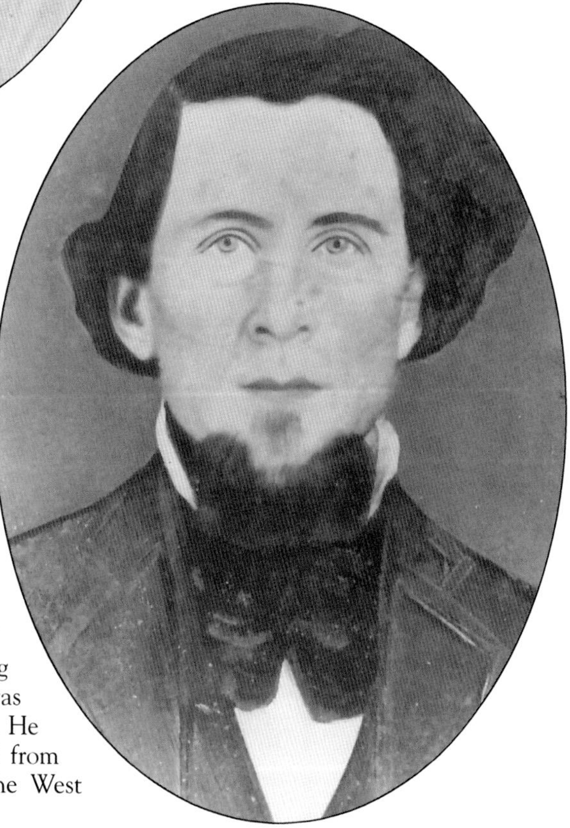

Lewis LeRoy, a Frenchman and a Roman Catholic, was a commission merchant who moved to Washington in 1795. In 1802 he married Helen Palmer, the granddaughter of Col. Robert Palmer; she sold the Palmer House to Jonathan Marsh, who arrived from New England that year. In 1823, Lewis LeRoy donated two of his Washington lots for the building of the first Catholic church, which was constructed in 1829, in North Carolina. He died in 1843 of yellow fever contracted from a shipment of goods delivered from the West Indies. (Courtesy of NC Historic Bath.)

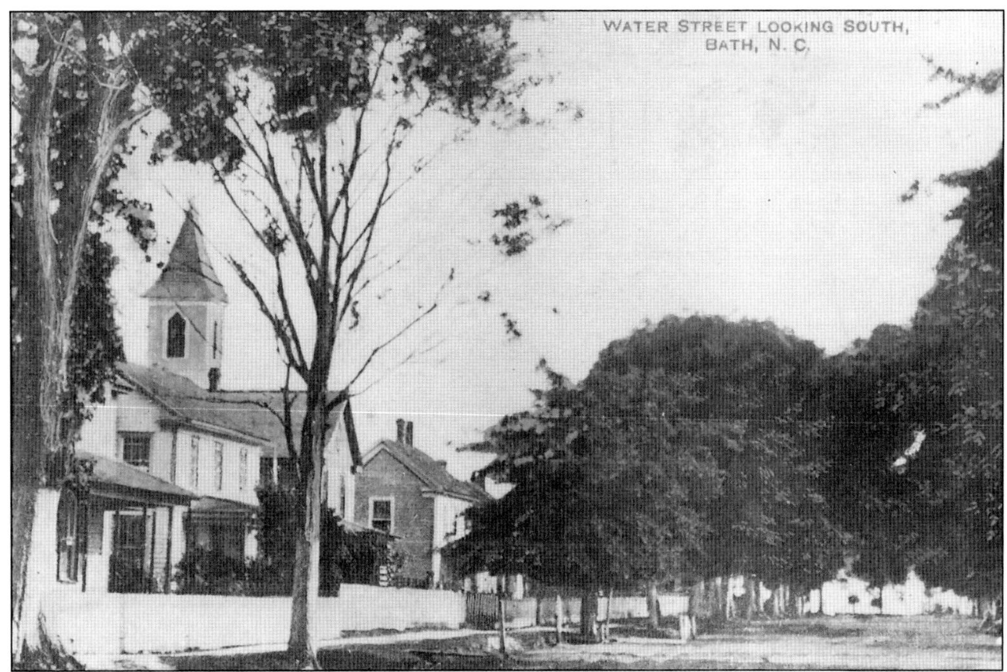

This is Water Street (now Main Street) in Bath, looking south about 1912. Bath Town, was named in honor of John Granville, the Earl of Bath, one of the original Lords Proprietor. The village plat was laid out by John Lawson in 1704 and was incorporated in 1705. Bath Town was the county seat of Beaufort County until 1785. Beaufort County's first courthouse and jail were constructed in Bath Town in 1723 on plat lot number 62. The courthouse and jail were built to serve Beaufort, Hyde, and Craven precincts (now called Beaufort and Hyde Counties). (Postcard courtesy of Oden's Store.)

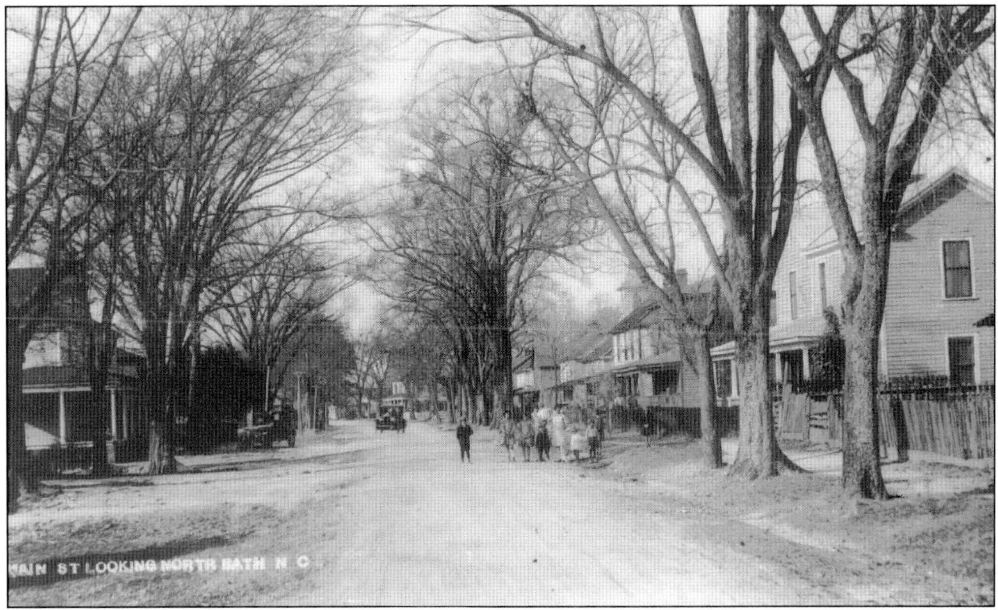

This early 1900s scene of Main Street, looking north from Bonner Point, was photographed by T.R. Draper. (Courtesy of Yvonne Selby.)

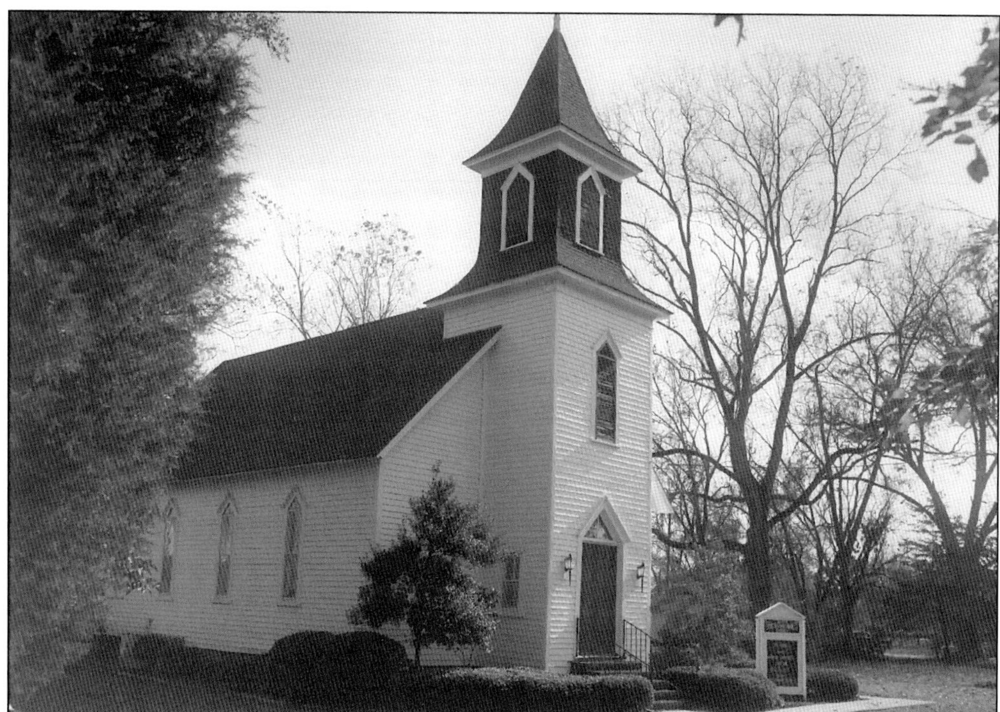

The first Bath United Methodist Church building was a small frame structure erected in 1840 on North Carteret Street. The trustees were James Arant, George N. Gregory, Thomas B. Long, Thomas Windley, Robert W. Eborn, John Tyler, and Joseph Long. The existing church was built in 1892 on Main Street. Currently, in the year 2000, the congregation is under the direction of the Reverend Ronald Estes, pastor. (Photo by Louis Van Camp.)

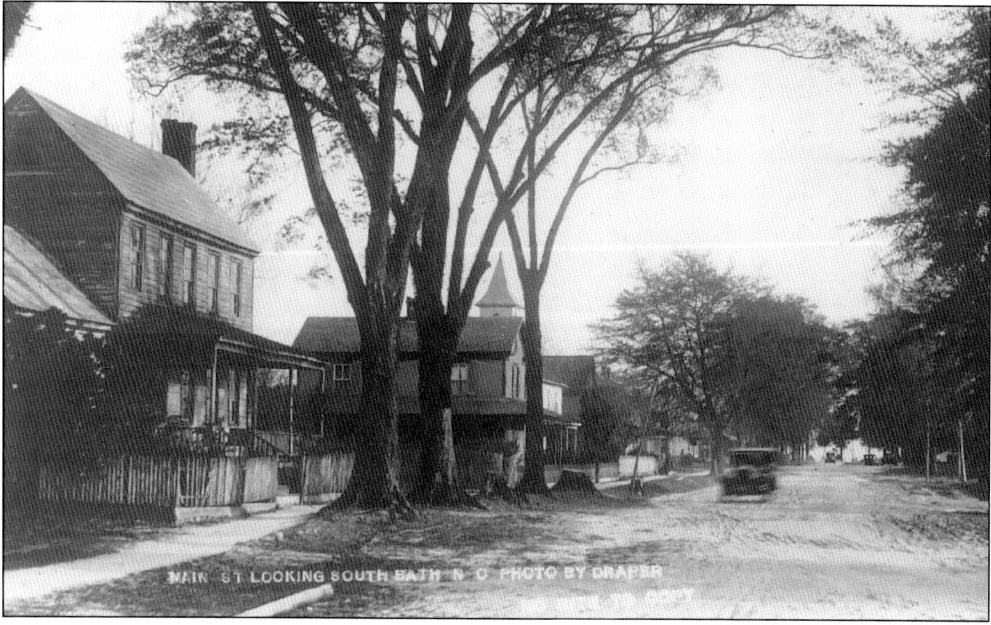

This is Main Street looking south from Craven Street around 1915. Visible in the distance is the bell tower of the United Methodist Church. (Courtesy of Yvonne Selby.)

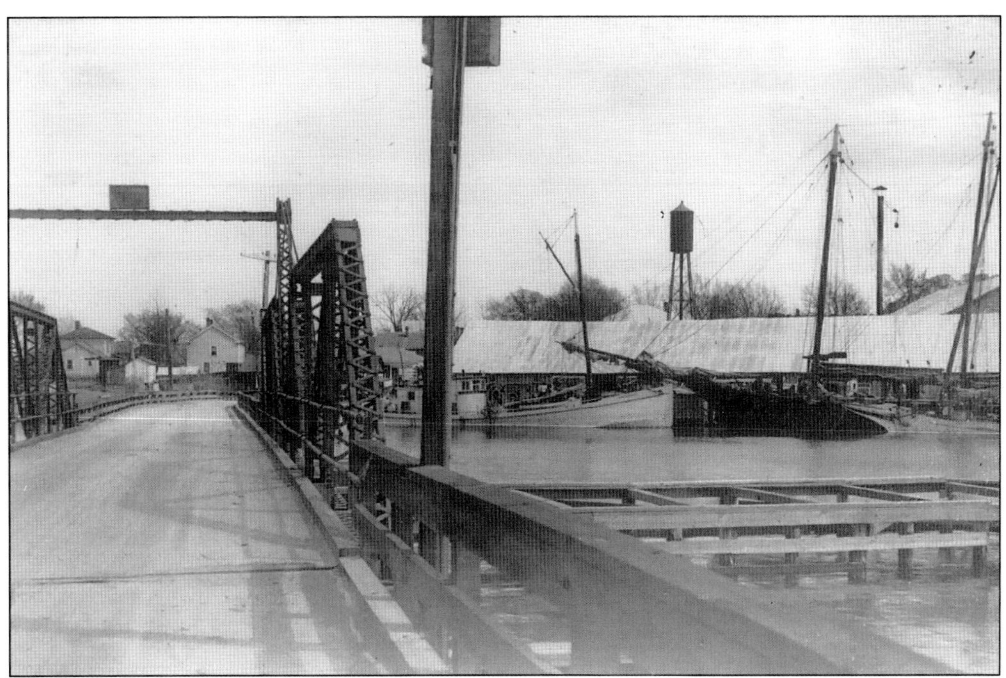

The first bridge across Bath Creek was built around 1887. This 1915 Draper photo shows the swing bridge built in the early 1900s. The T.A. Brooks saw mill and lumber yard are visible behind the schooners. (Courtesy of Yvonne Selby.)

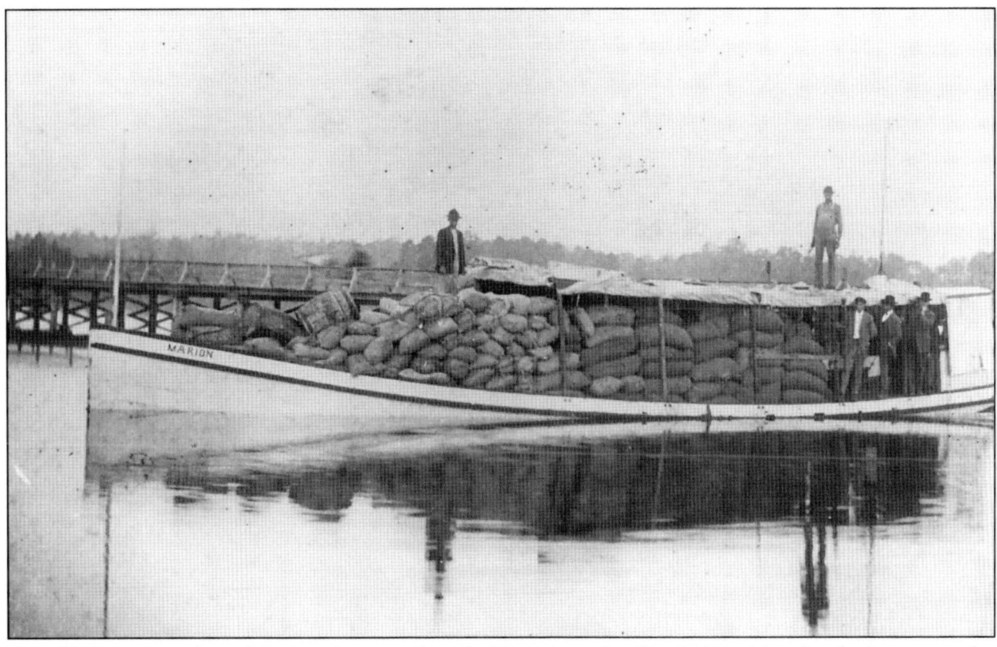

The 50-foot cargo boat *Marion* departs Archbell's Point wharf in 1916 with a load of potatoes for delivery to Washington. The *Marion* was gas powered and her skipper was Capt. Lawrence Tate. Standing on the dock behind the *Marion*, from left to right, are Jessie B. Archbell (1896–1923) and John Edgar "Jack" Cahoon (1896–1989). The *Marion* capsized and sank on June 16, 1916, with the loss of four lives. Jack Cahoon's widow lives in Bayview. (Courtesy of Yvonne Selby.)

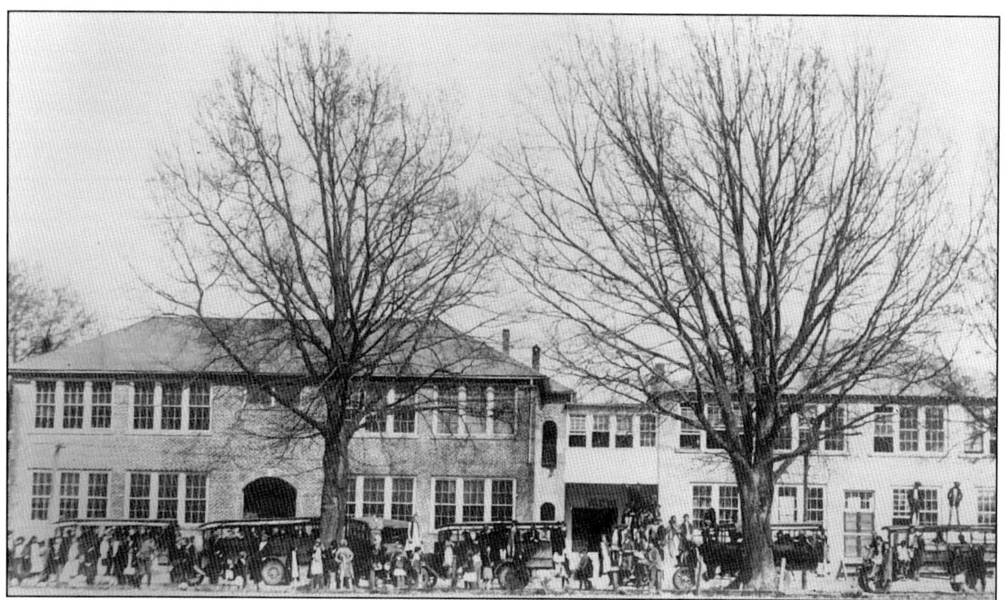

Bath High School was opened in 1923 and closed in 1989. In 1930, Principal Dave Arnold supervised the teaching of kindergarten through senior high. The closed school stands on the corner of Carteret and Harding Streets. (Courtesy of NC Historic Bath.)

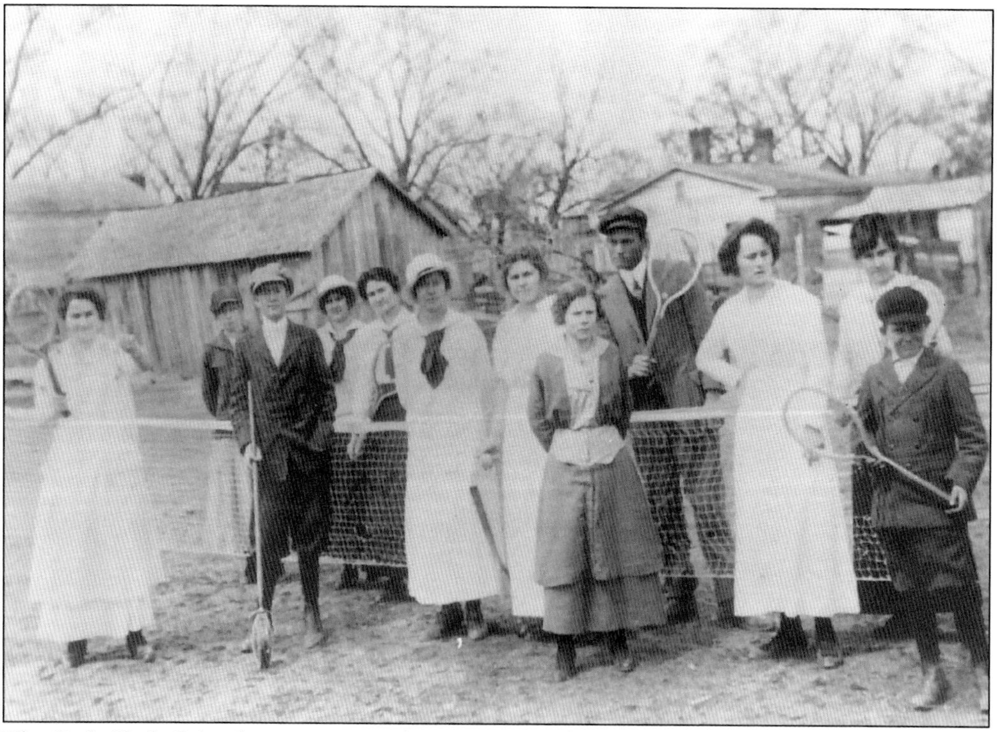

The Bath High School tennis team of 1910–1915 included, from left to right, Audrey Brooks Archbell, Mildred Winfield Payne, Frost Lewis, Hallie Brooks Cox, Ruby Stilley (teacher), Eva Gurganas Wingate, Vonnie Satchwell Marsh, Ethel Wallace Huffman, Charlie Hardison, Katie Curtis, Henry Bonner, and unidentified. (Courtesy of Yvonne Selby.)

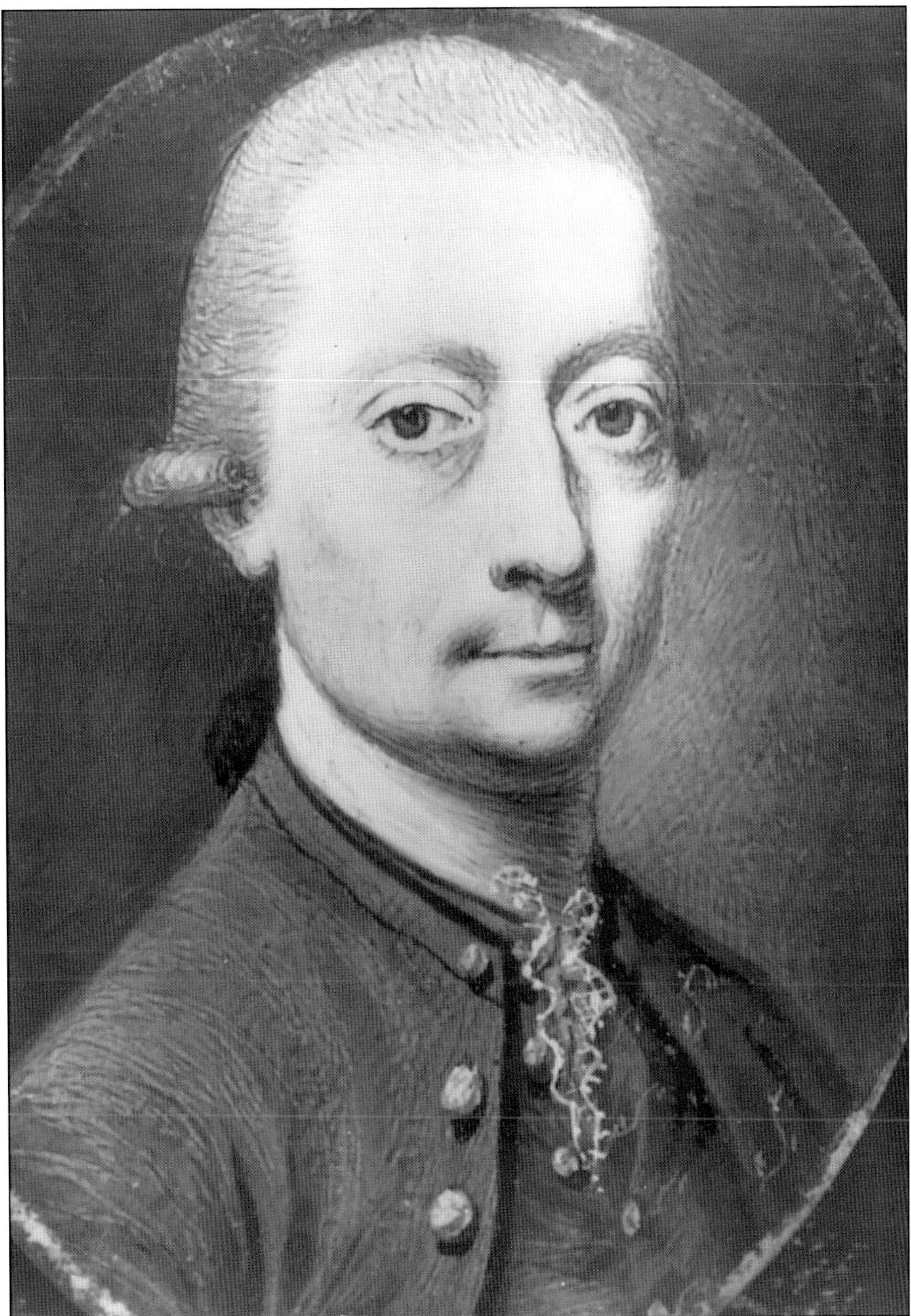

Col. Robert Palmer (1724–1790) was surveyor general of the province and tax collector for the Port of Bath. Palmer acquired the Michael Coutanche house in 1764. There is a tablet in St. Thomas Church in memory of Colonel Palmer, who later became an admiral, and his wife, Lady Margaret. (Courtesy of NC Historic Bath.)

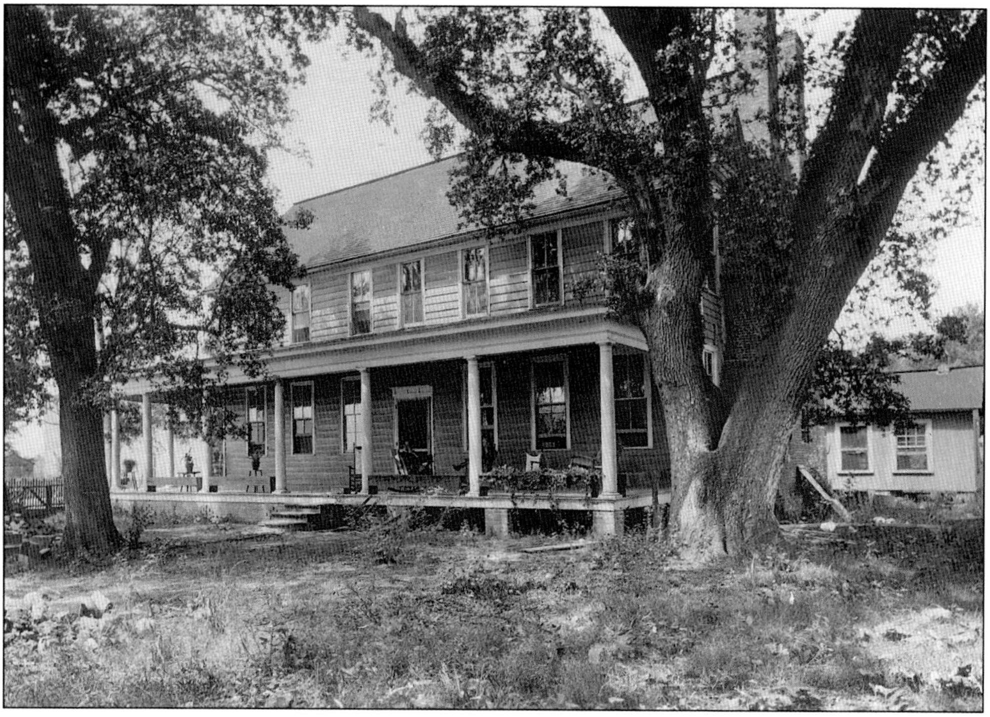

The Palmer-Marsh House was built by Michael Coutanche in 1751. This house is notable for its 54-foot-long center beam and its 17-foot-wide double chimney on the east end. Col. Robert Palmer acquired this house in 1764. In 1802, Jonathan Marsh, a New England merchant and ship builder, married Ann Bonner and purchased what is now called the Palmer-Marsh House. (Courtesy of NC Historic Bath.)

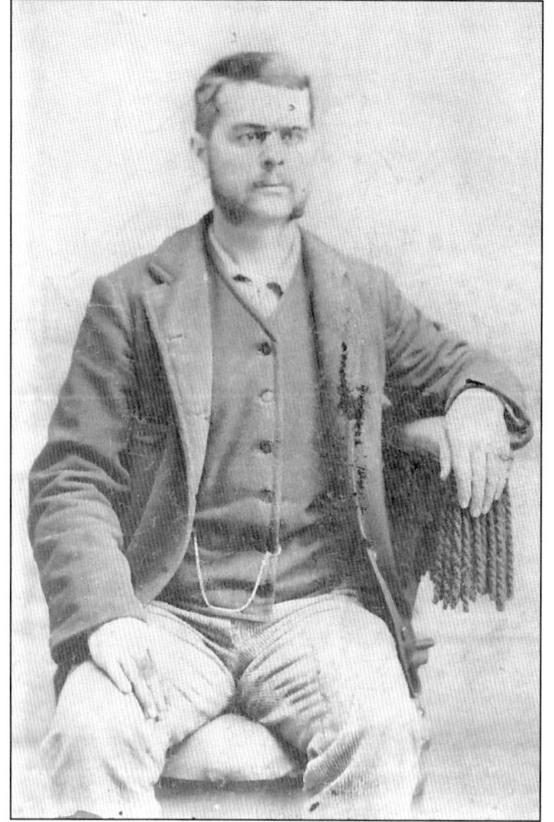

In the 1920s, Henry Ormond, who ran a sawmill on Bath Creek, owned the Palmer-Marsh House and operated it as a boarding house. In the spring of 1925, the famous American playwright Edna Ferber booked a room there for two days while awaiting the arrival of the James Adams Floating Theater. (Courtesy of Wayne Woolard.)

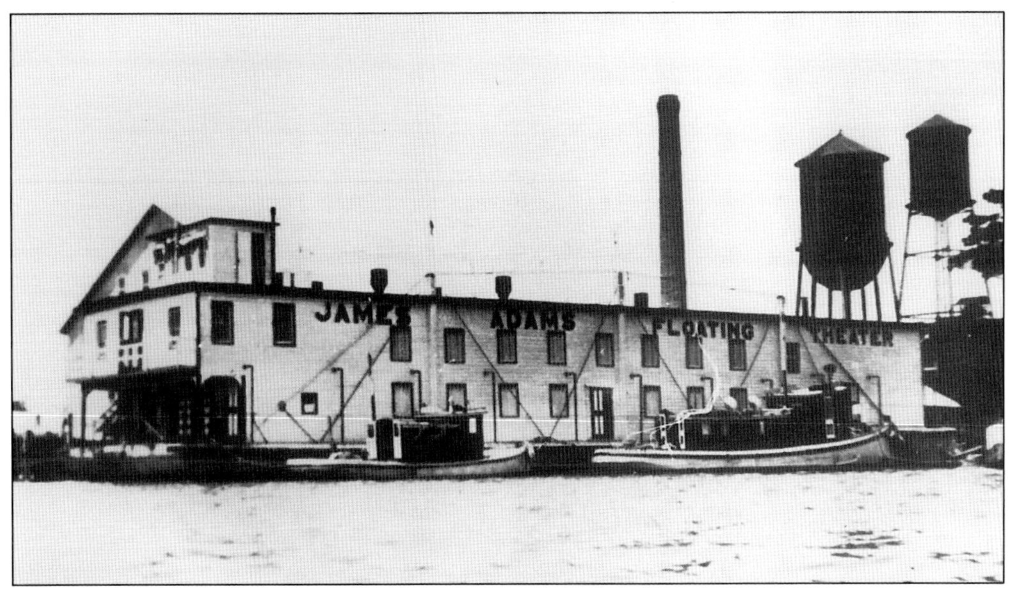

The James Adams Floating Theater entertained thousands of people from 1913 through 1941. This 128-foot-long, 34-foot-wide showboat was hauled by two small gas-powered tug boats. She traveled from one coastal port to another along the waterways of Eastern North Carolina. This was the show boat that author Edna Ferber spent four days on, gathering background material for her novel *Showboat* in 1925. Ferber's acclaimed novel was later turned into a successful Hollywood musical. (Courtesy of NC Historic Edenton.)

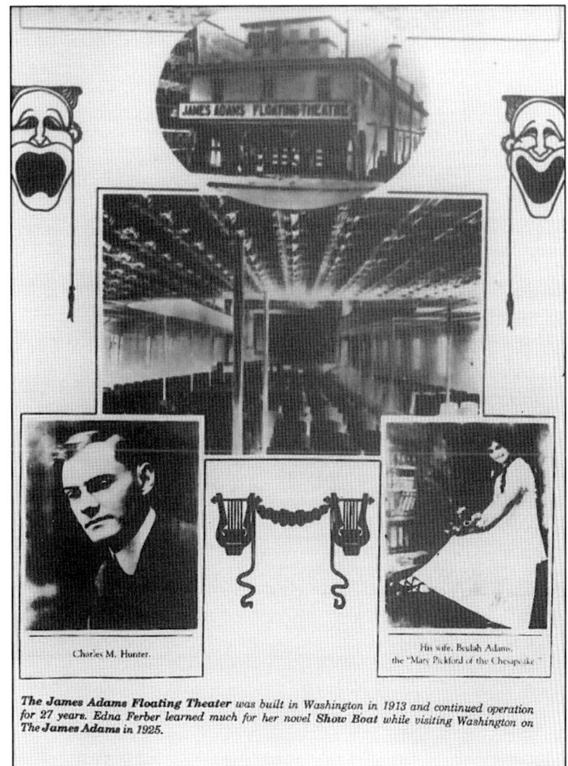

This billboard display shows the front (bow) of the floating theater and the interior with the stage at the far end. Charles M. Hunter was the show manager and Beulah Adams (nicknamed the "Mary Pickford of the Chesapeake") was the female lead actress for all of the shows. (Courtesy of BCM.)

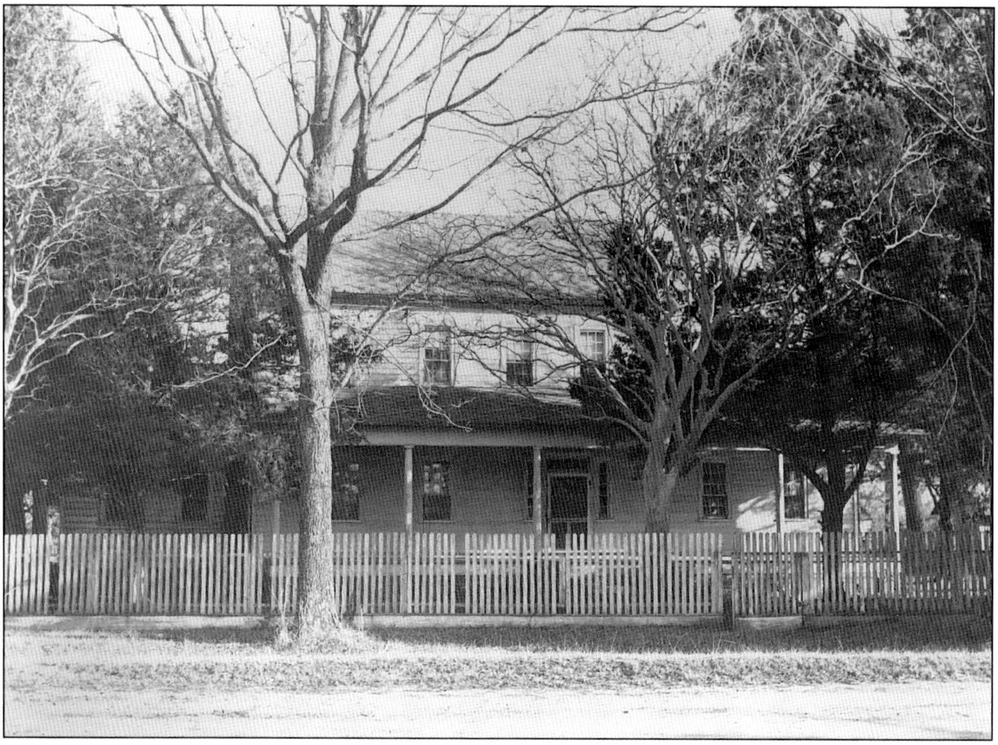

This 1960 photo shows the Bonner House before it was restored and opened to the public in 1962. It is said that the Bonner House was built from the salvage of shipwrecks at Ocracoke and dates back to around 1820. Joseph Bonner built a steam-driven sawmill along Bath creek, and he and Jacob Van Der Veer became partners in this venture. (Courtesy of NC Historic Bath.)

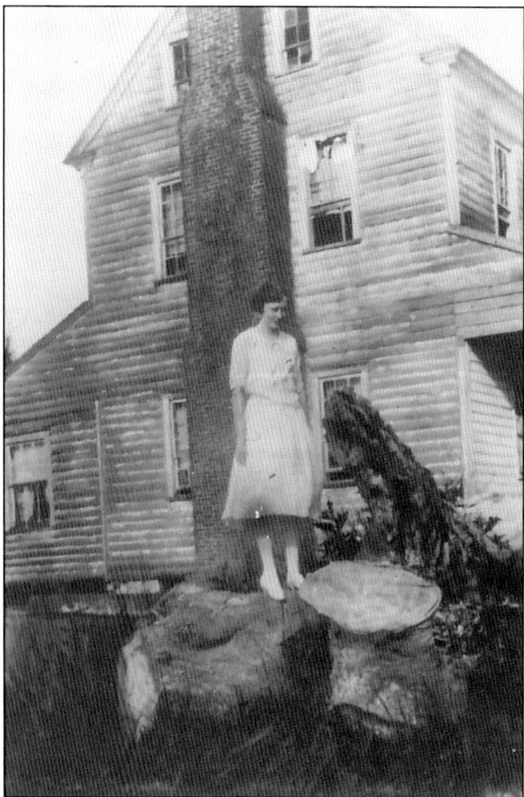

Mary Swindell stands on the stump of a cut tree in front of the Bonner Home at Bonner Point around 1924. (Courtesy of NC Historic Bath.)

Early in 1924, the Works Progress Administration erected a granite monument with a bronze plaque at the junction of Main Street and Carteret Street. This picture shows the ceremony that took place on June 29, 1924 to commemorate the unveiling of the plaque that recorded the history of Bath on its 219th anniversary. The young lady in colonial dress on the left is Mary Arcadia Tankard at about age six and on the right is Helen Waters Brooks at about age seven. (Courtesy of BCM.)

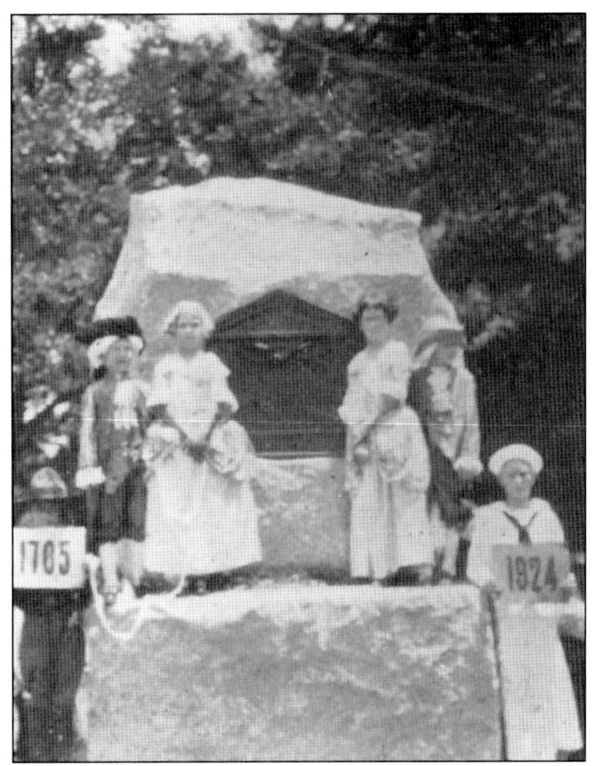

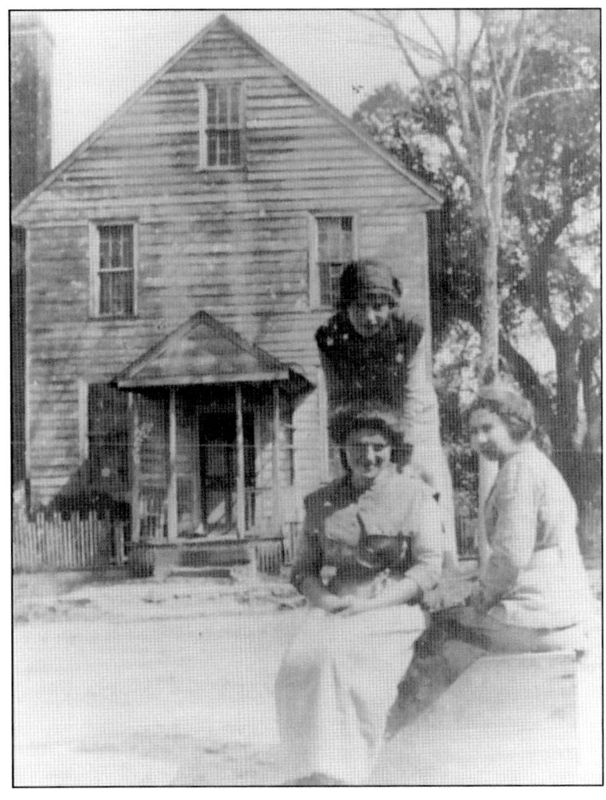

The three Marsh sisters pose in front of their home around 1920. (Courtesy of NC Historic Bath.)

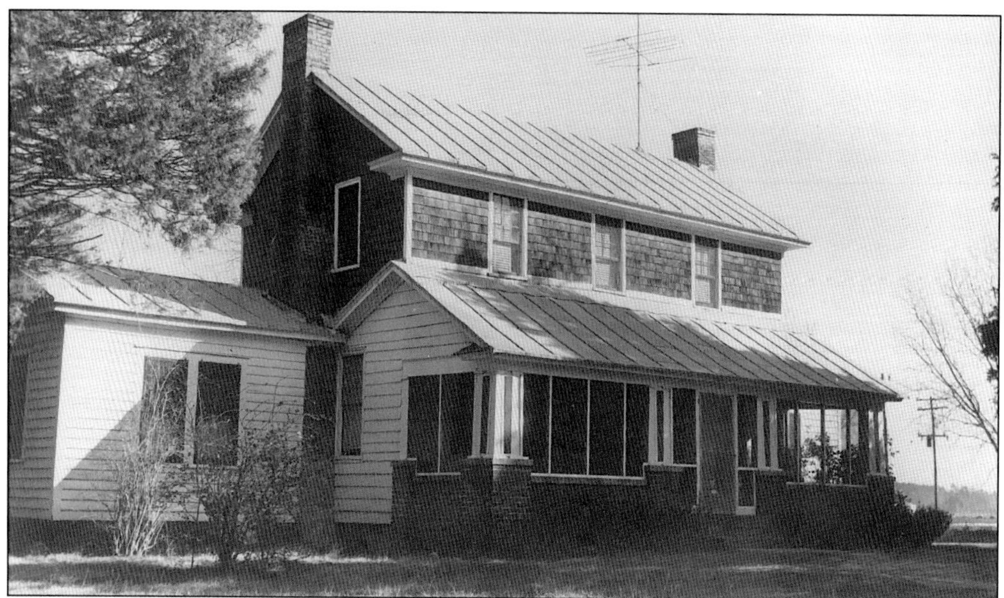

The Van Der Veer House, *c.* 1790, is a Dutch Colonial design with a steeply pitched gambrel roof and quarter-round lights. The exterior was finished with wide horizontal boards and board-and-batten shutters. Jacob Van Der Veer was a merchant and manufactured rope. He was also a partner in Joseph Bonner's steam-driven sawmill company. This 1960 photo shows the home prior to its restoration in 1961–1962. (Courtesy of NC Historic Bath.)

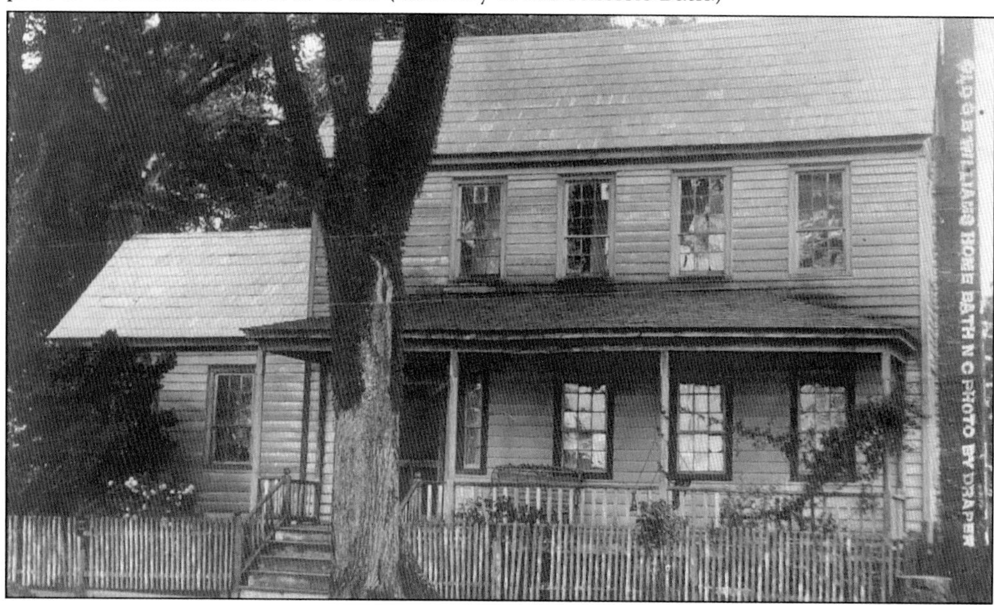

The Williams "Glebe" House was built on Bath town lot number 14 between 1827 and 1832. This house is almost identical in age and architectural features to the Bonner House. It was built by Samuel Lucus, Joseph Bonner's business partner, and sold to the Bonner family in 1847. The Williams family owned it from 1877 to 1937. It became known as the "Glebe" House in 1945 when the Episcopal Diocese of East Carolina acquired it as a rectory for St. Thomas Church. In colonial times, a "glebe" was church land given to a minister for financial support. (Courtesy of Yvonne Selby.)

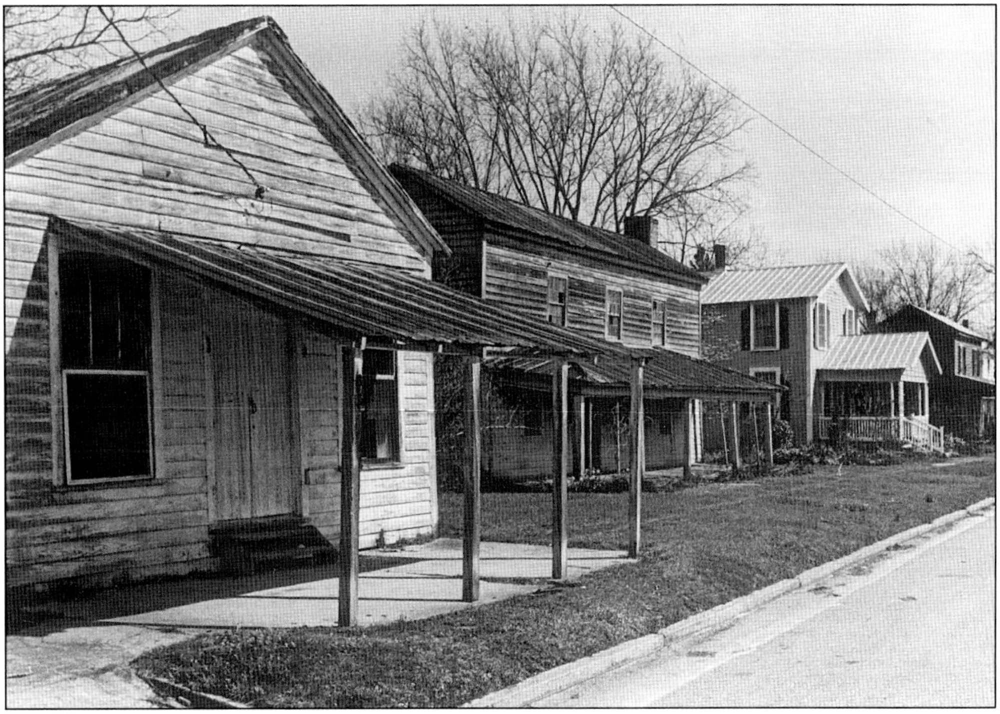

This scene from 1970 shows, from left to right, the Braxton Brooks Store, the old Buzzard Motel, and the Claude Venters House. The Buzzard Motel was demolished in the early 1980s. (Courtesy of Mike Williams.)

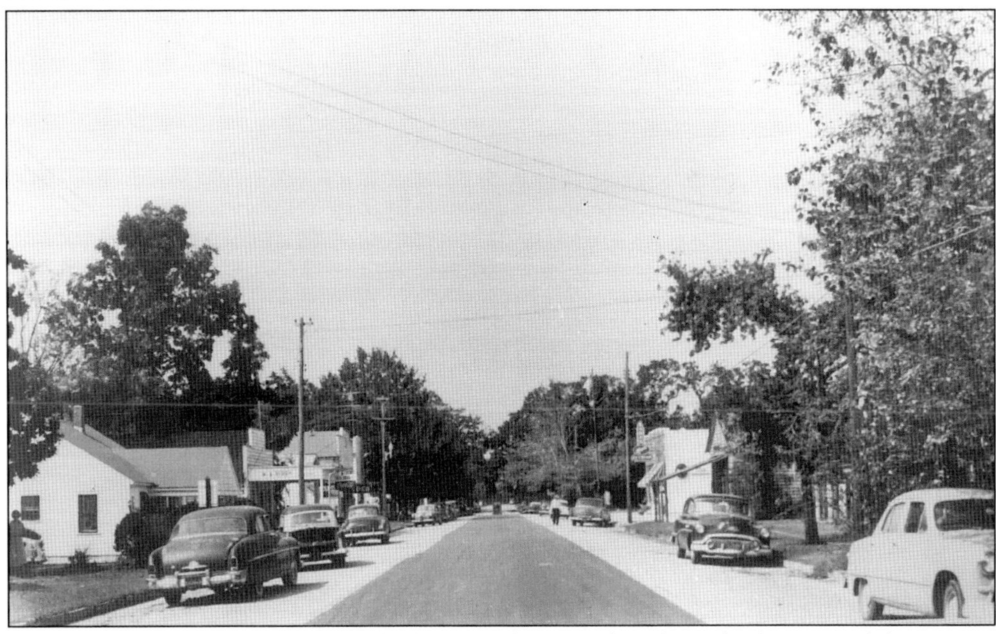

This 1950s picture of Main Street, looking north, was taken from the location of the Venters House. The Orman Berry house is on the left in front of the W.A. Berry store (now demolished). On the right is the old drug store and the post office, which is now Star Realty. (Courtesy of NC Historic Bath.)

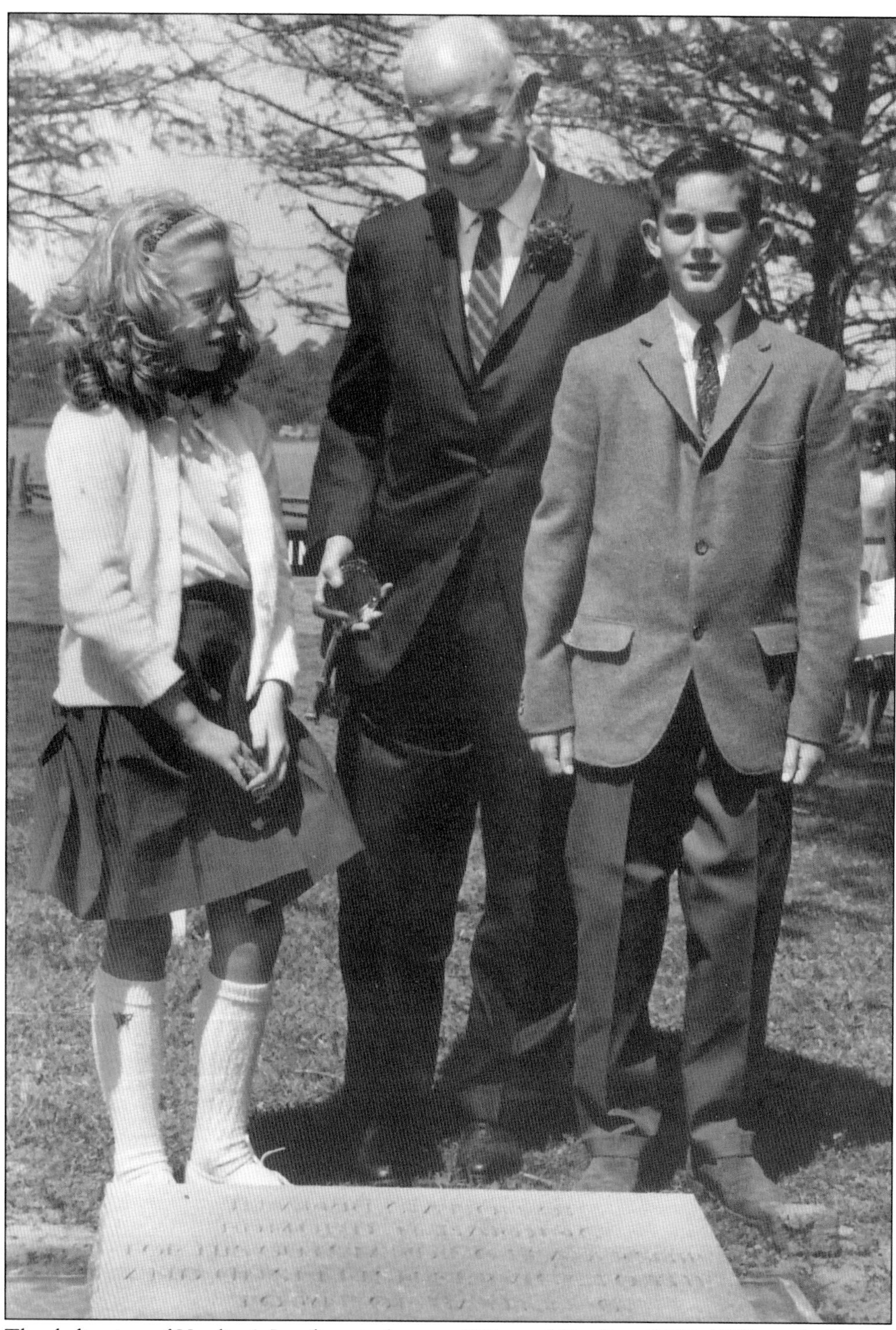

The dedication of Harding's Landing, in honor of Edmund Harding (1890–1970), took place in 1966. From left to right are Theresa Selby, Edmund Harding, and Keith Tankard. (Courtesy of Yvonne Selby.)

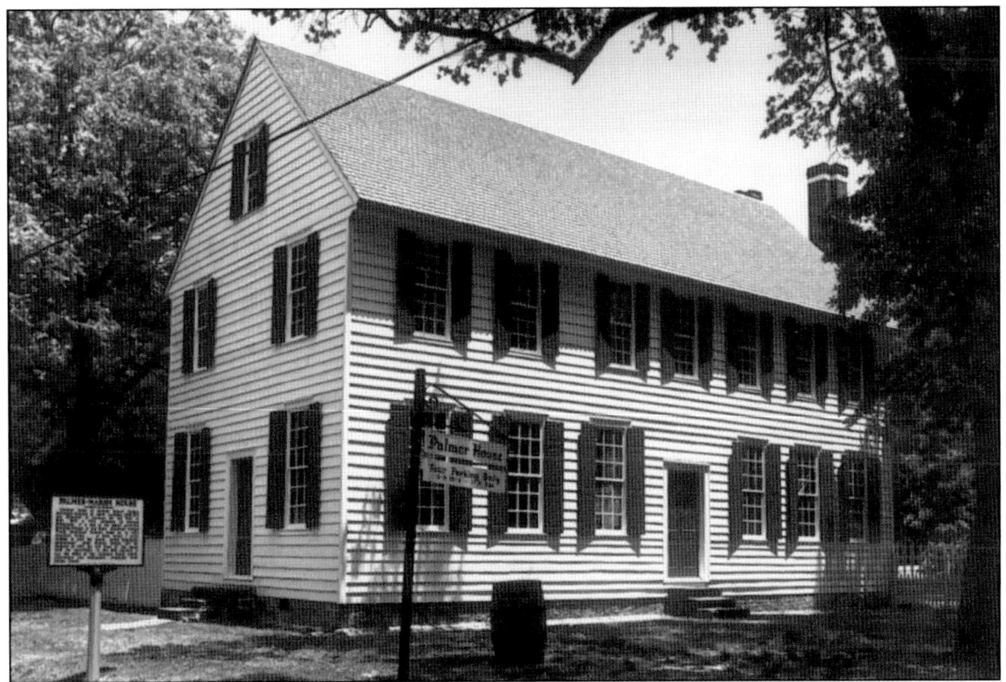

In 1958, the Beaufort County Historical Association, with Edmund Harding as president, took title of the old Palmer-Marsh House and 4 acres of property for the sum of $31,000. Over a period of time, the Palmer-Marsh House was completely restored and outfitted with period furnishings. It is pictured here in 2000. (Courtesy of Louis Van Camp.)

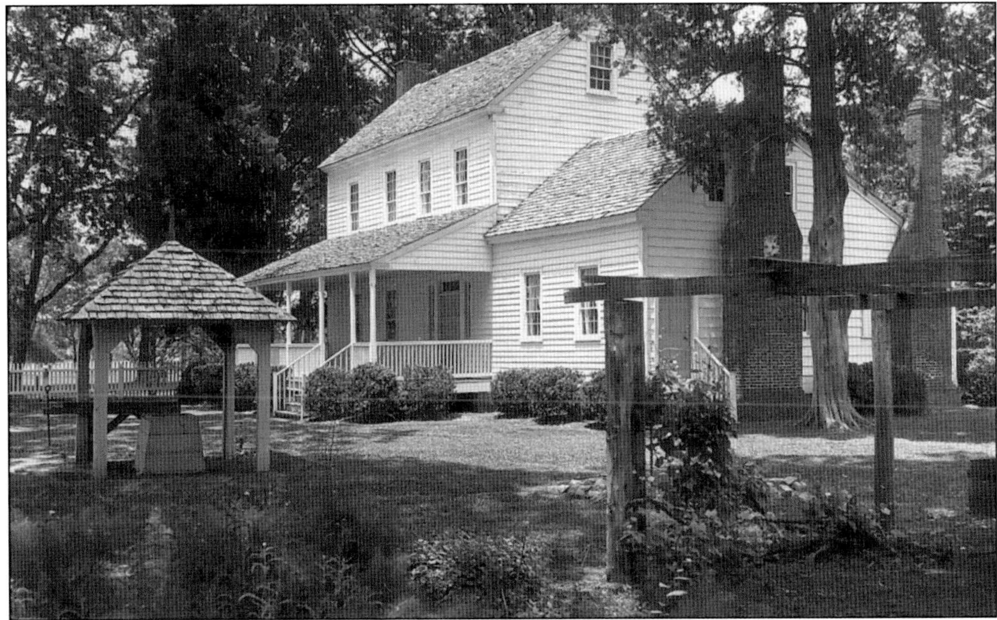

The restoration of the Joseph Bonner House was completed with a grant from the Oscar Smith Family and Memorial Fund of Norfolk, VA, in 1960. The Bonner House is located at Bonner Point at the south end of Main Street and was opened to the public in 1962. (2000 photo by Louis Van Camp.)

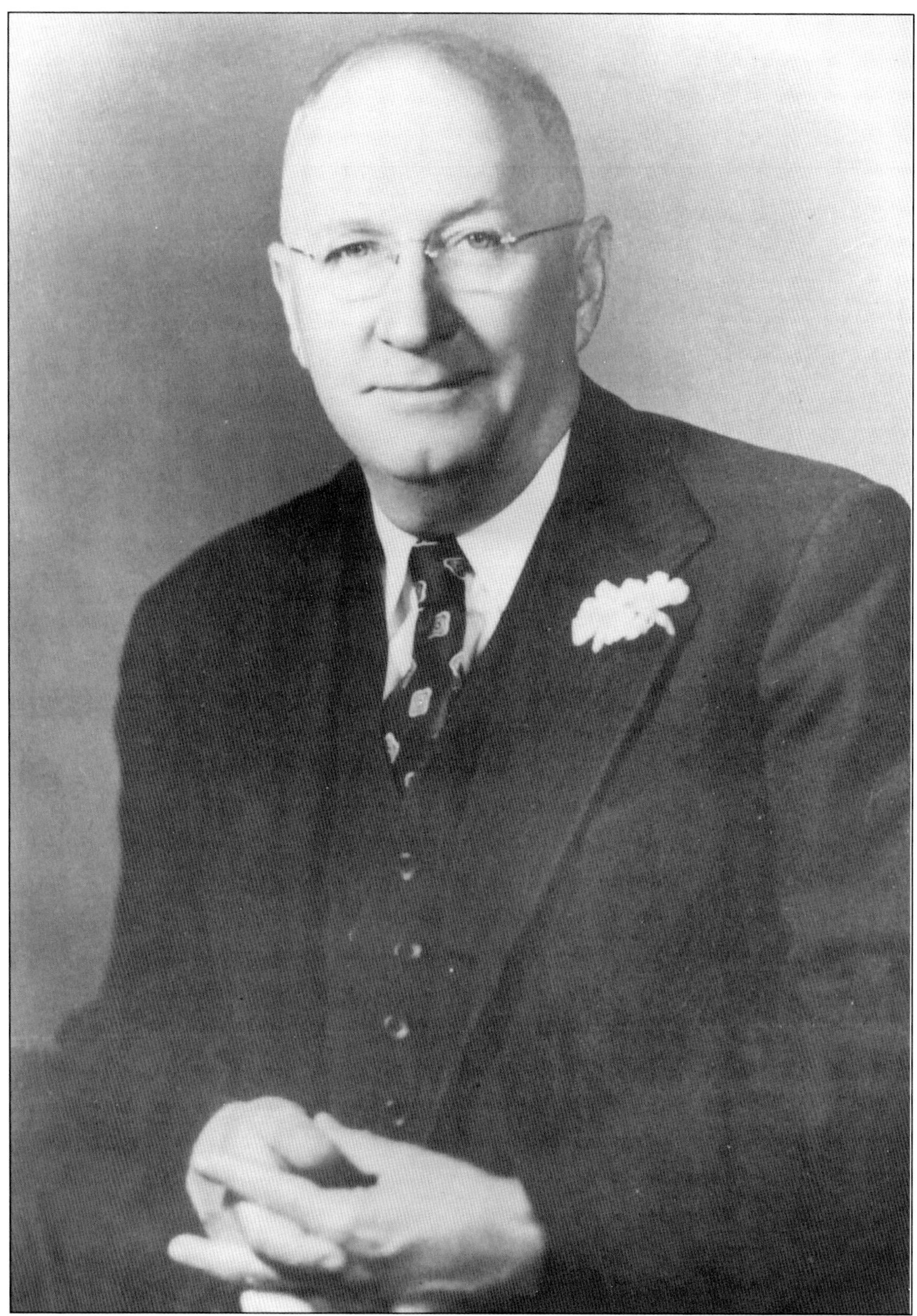

Oscar F. Smith (1891–1970) was born in Bayview. Smith was the founder of the Smith-Douglas Fertilizer Company in Norfolk, VA. In 1960, his family made a bequest from the Oscar Smith Foundation of $75,000 for the restoration of the James Bonner House. (Courtesy of NC Historic Bath.)

Edward Drummond changed his name to "Teach" and became Capt. Edward Teach, the notorious pirate "Blackbeard." Teach arrived in Bath in 1718 and plundered ships; his crew molested planters' wives and daughters. Virginia Governor Spottswood sent two frigates of his Majesty's Royal Navy to Ocracoke to capture him. Teach blundered into their trap and was killed in a skirmish with Lt. Richard Maynard on November 22, 1718.

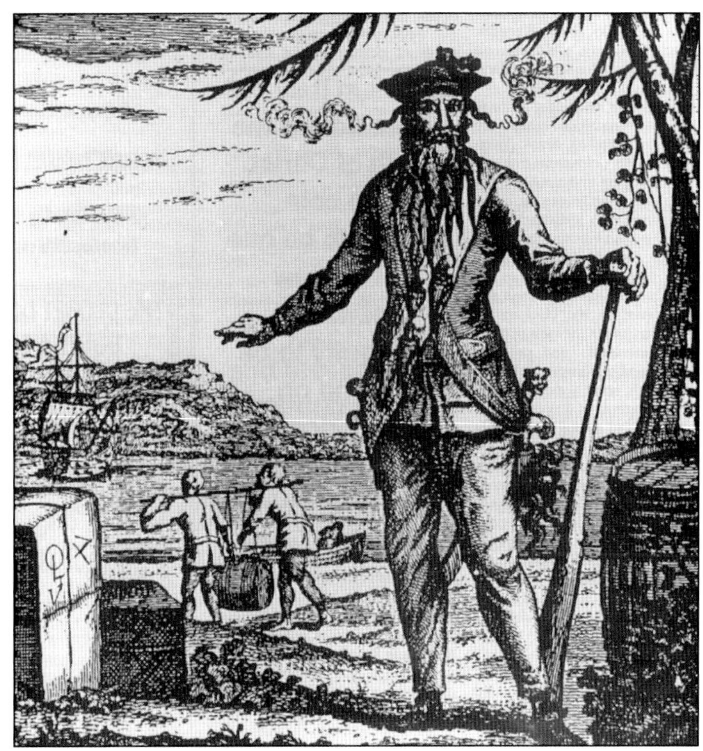

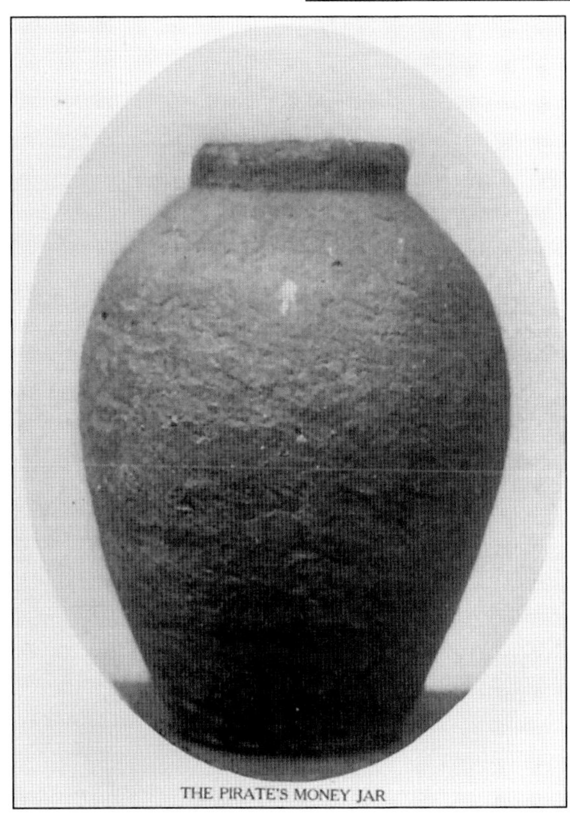

This jar, dug up near Bath around 1900, contained coins thought to have been buried by Blackbeard. Teach was born in Bristol, England, and commanded a 40-gun sloop. He became the terror of the Carolina coast and was killed near Ocracoke at a spot now known as Teach's Hole. (Courtesy of NC Historic Bath.)

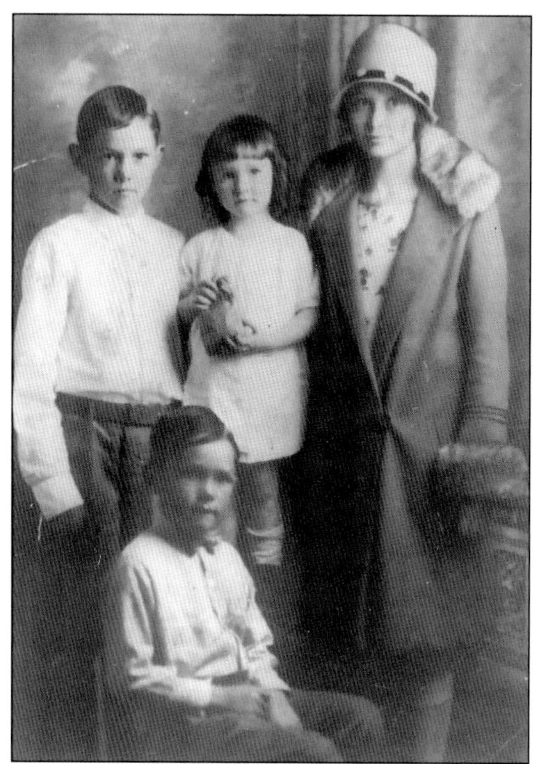

The Everett family lived on Route 1 in Bath. This 1930 picture shows, from left to right, (standing) Robert Thomas Everett Jr. (born 1916), Lalla Ruth Everett (born 1924), and Mildred Inez Everett (born 1914); (seated) David Caldwell Everett (born 1919). (Courtesy of Jean Bowen.)

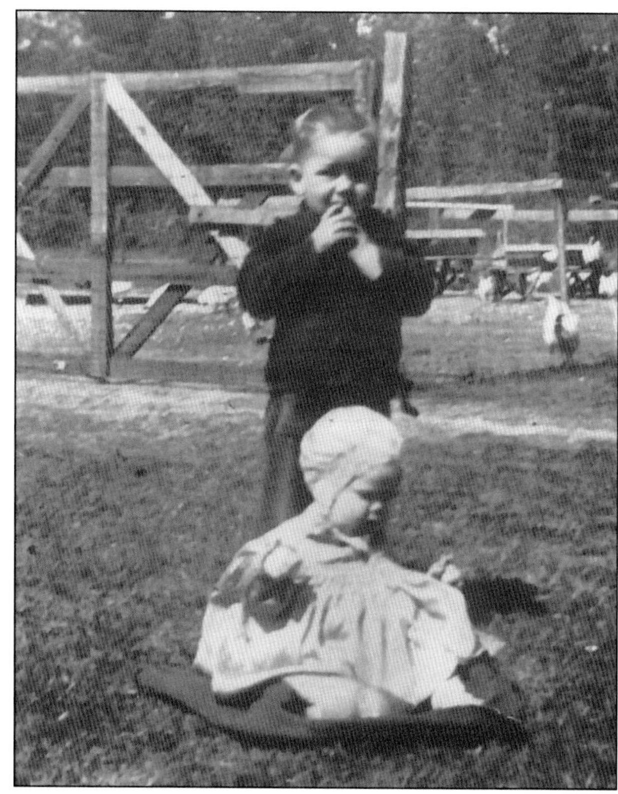

In this photo taken in 1939, Ellis Edward Everett (born 1937) stands guard over his baby sister. Jean Carolyn Everett (born 1939) is now Jean Everett Bowen and lives in Bayview. (Courtesy of Jean Bowen.)

Two

Bayview, Hunter's Bridge, and Ransomville

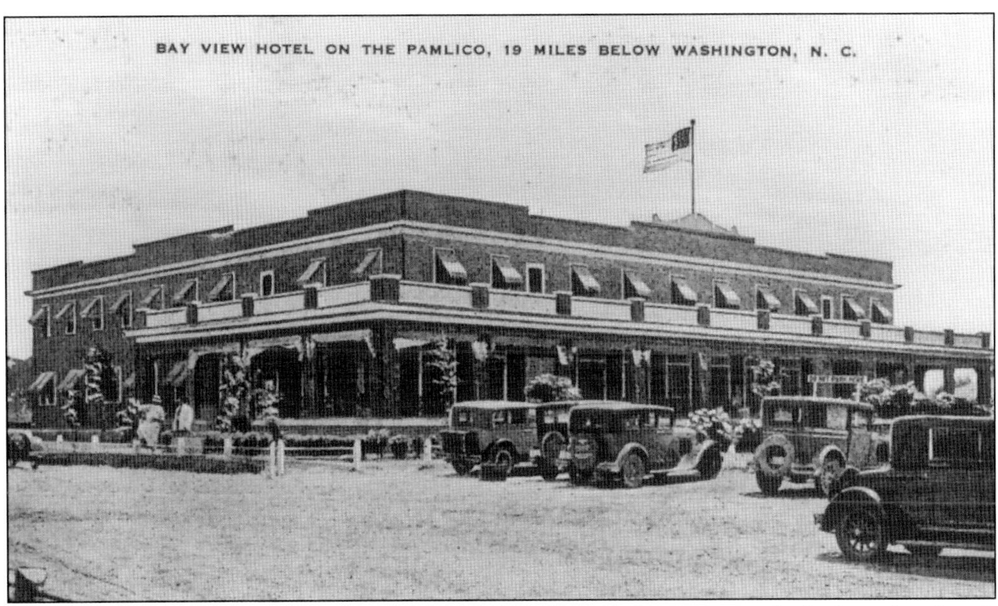

The Bay View Hotel was located east of Bath. This elegant summer resort had a large hotel with a drugstore and a banquet room with sparkling chandeliers. A giant water slide on the beach, a gambling casino, a bowling alley, and a large merry-go-round attracted many visitors. The dance pavilion extended over the Pamlico River and, with its shiny oak floor, was considered to be one of the best along the Pamlico River. Multicolored polka dots reflected around the room from the glass chandelier revolving overhead, adding a dreamy, romantic feeling to slow dances. The Duke University Blue Devils Band played the dance music for two summers. The Bay View Hotel burned down in 1944. (1929 postcard courtesy Oden's Store.)

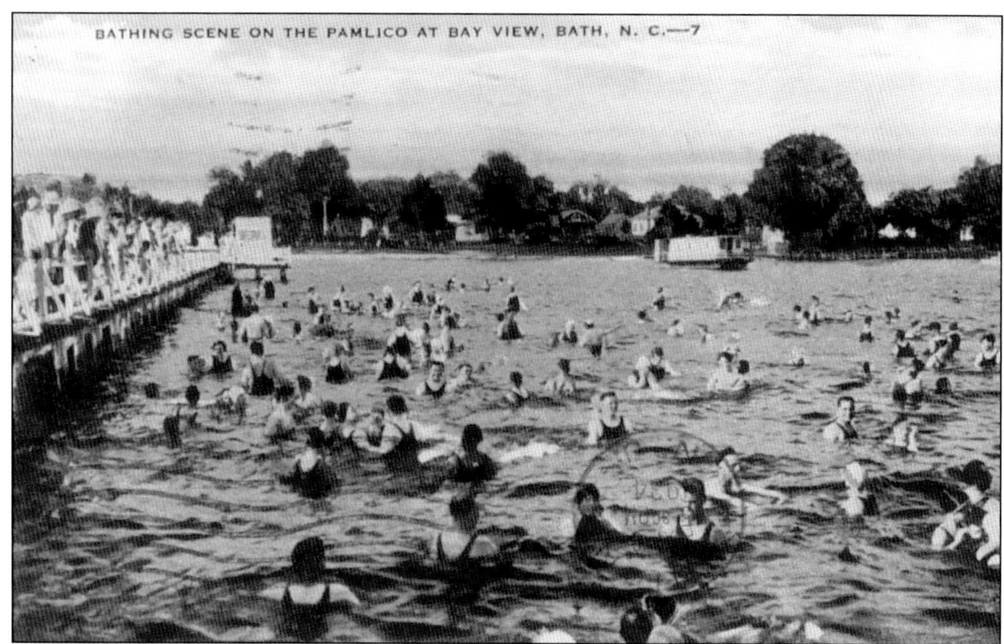

During the day, hundreds of Beaufort County folks had fun in the waters by the Bay View Hotel pier. (1934 postcard courtesy of Oden's Store.)

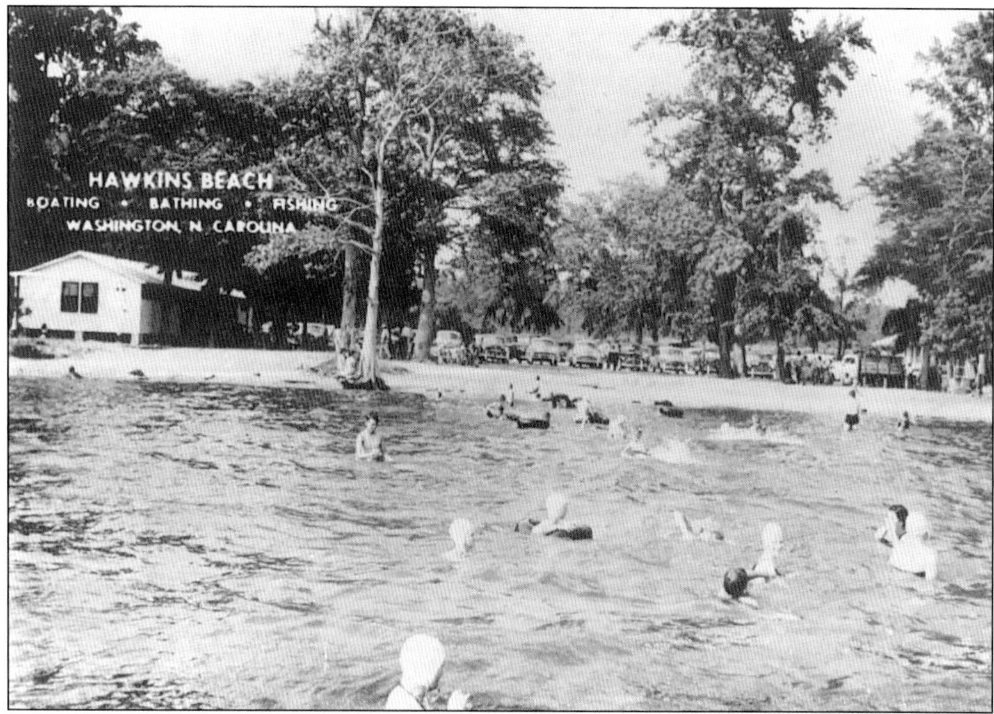

Another fine Pamlico River bathing location was Hawkin's Beach at the end of State Route (SR) 1336, about 2 miles east of Goose Creek State Park. Visiting patrons enjoyed boating, bathing, or fishing. (1940 postcard courtesy of Oden's Store.)

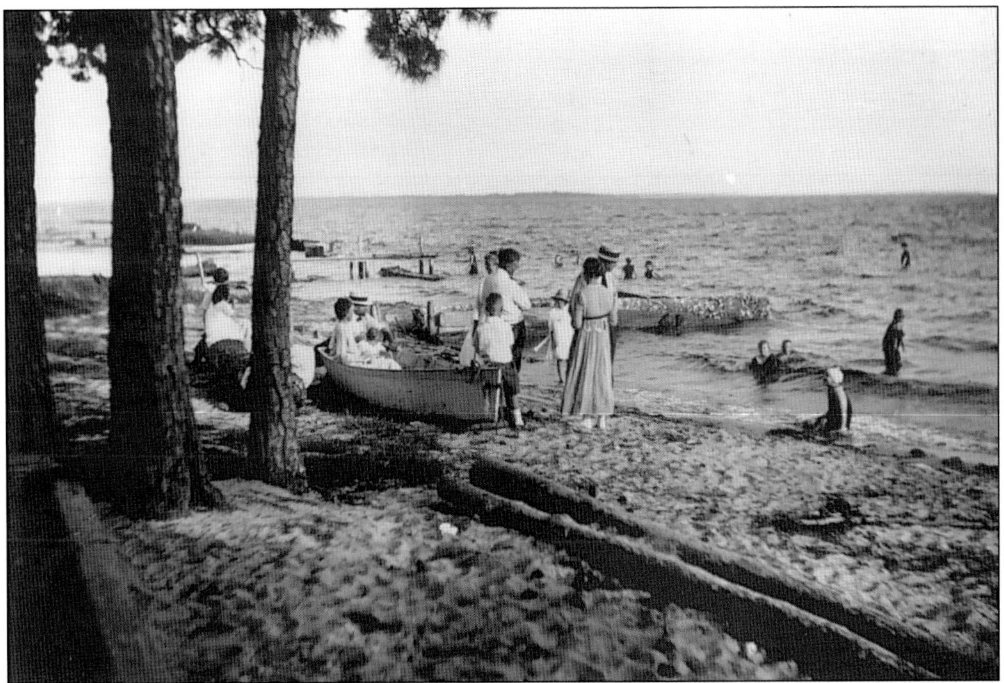

Here is another wonderful Pamlico River beach scene. This 1920s photo was probably taken in the area of Hawkin's Beach. (Courtesy of W. Mayo.)

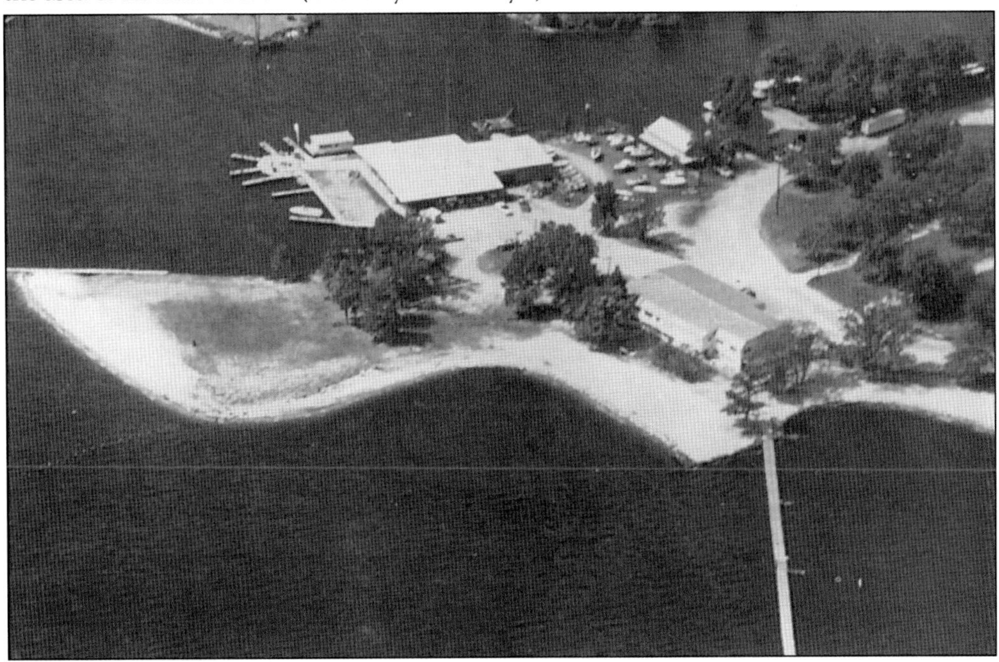

Pamlico Beach Hotel was located at Wade Point, where the Pungo and Pamlico Rivers meet. In the 1930s, this hotel had a dance pavilion built out over the water. It was a popular Saturday night destination for couples from Aurora, Spring Creek, Belhaven, and as far away as Greenville. A violent storm tore away the dance pavilion and badly damaged the hotel in the mid-1940s, and the resort was never rebuilt. (Courtesy of BCM.)

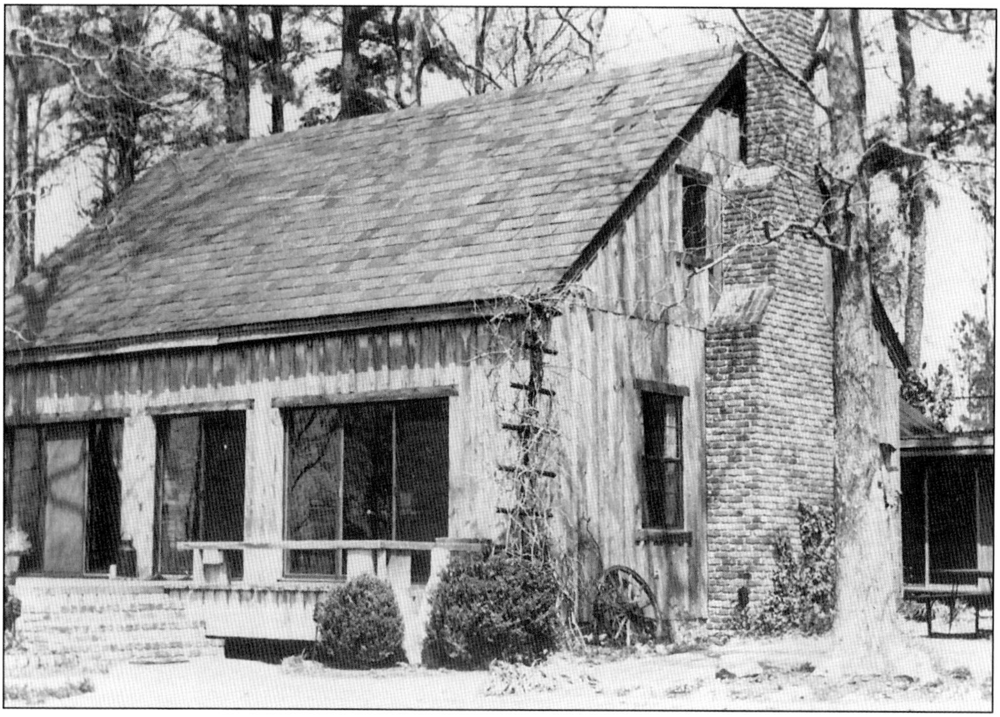

Anne and Leland Flanagan of Greenville began building a year-round home in Bayview around 1975. They built this lovely home with a terraced garden on a high bluff overlooking the breezy Pamlico River. The house was constructed using much lumber salvaged from old homes that Leland demolished in Greenville. (Courtesy of BCM.)

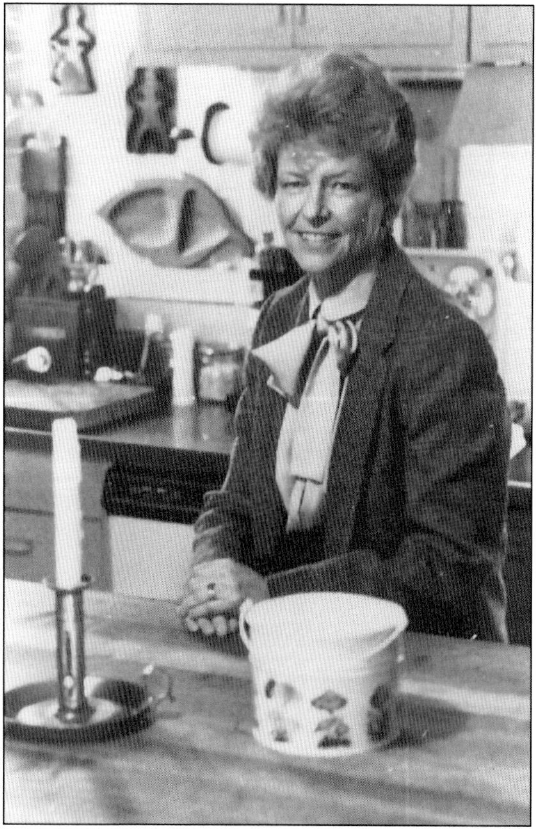

Anne Flanagan recalls being too tired to celebrate the new year of 1979 after spending the last day of 1978 sanding the living room floor. During that time, Anne was also working at the NC Historic Bath Visitor's Center. Here is Anne in 1980 seated at her kitchen's chopping block table. (Courtesy of BCM.)

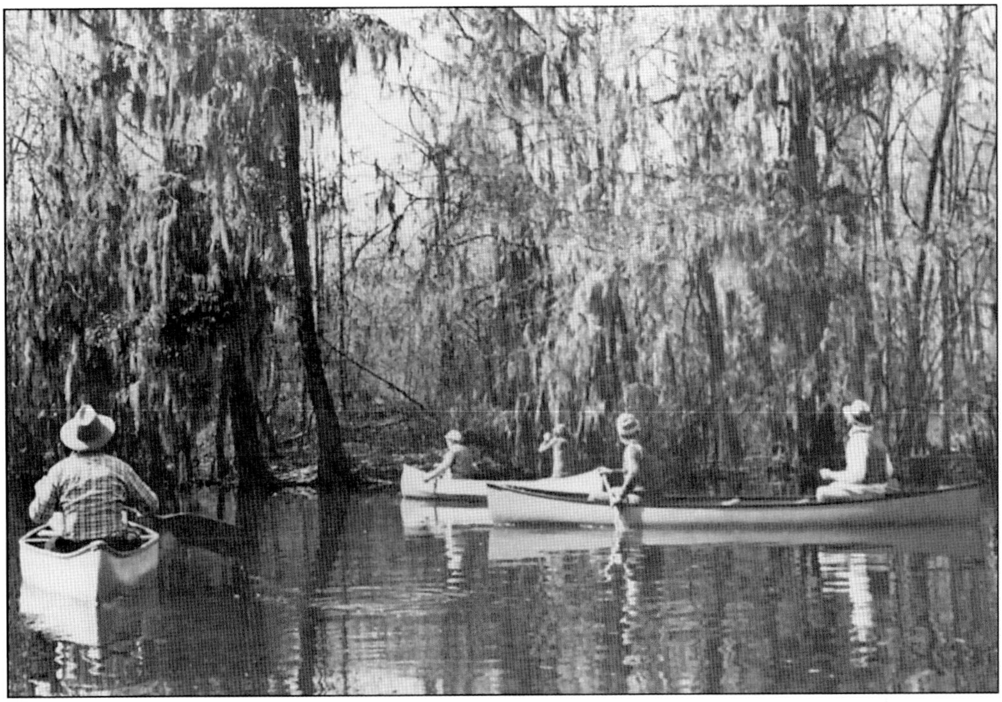

"Our wetlands are the breeding ground of the river and the natural habitat of our wildlife. And they are in danger," said Vincent Bellis, Ph.D., in a wetlands story in the 1986 issue of *Beaufort County* magazine. Paul Nuremberg's fine photo illustrates the sanctity and quiet beauty of the Pamlico-Tar-River wetlands. (Courtesy of BCM.)

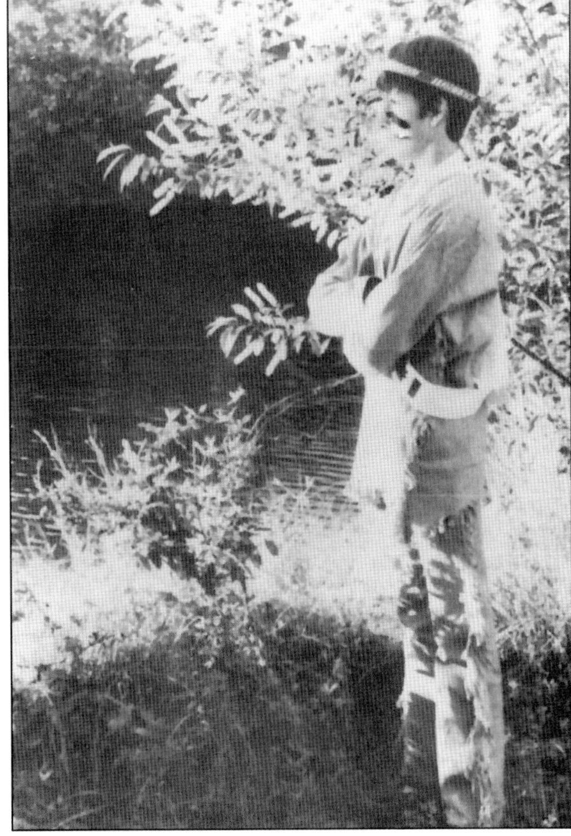

An unidentified Native American enjoys the beauty of the Pamlico wetlands of Goose Creek State Park. (Courtesy of BCM.)

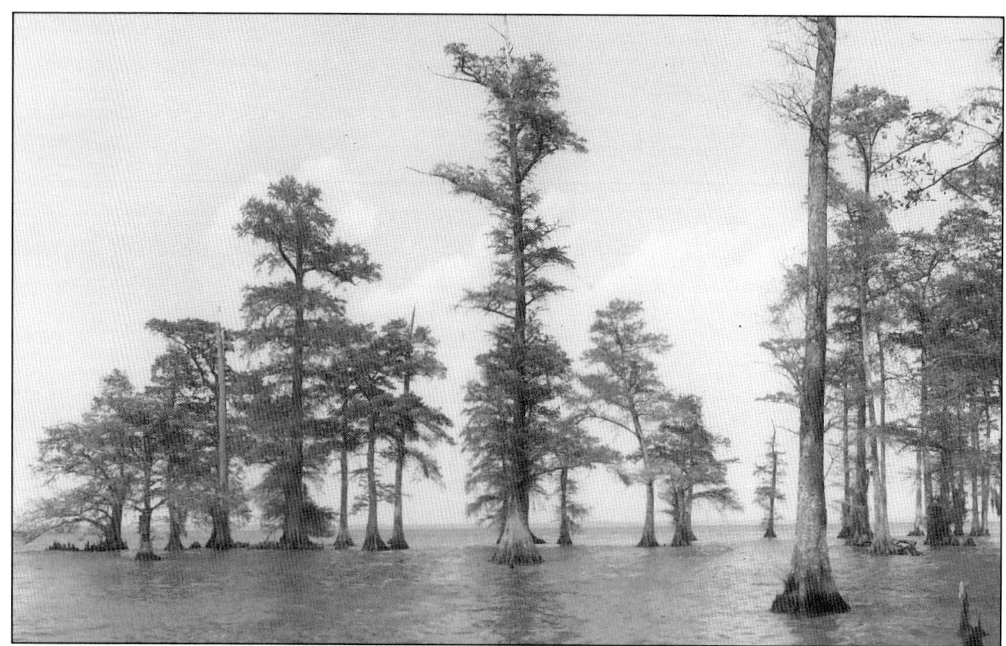

Goose Creek State Park borders Goose Creek and the Pamlico River some 8 miles east of Washington. This serene park has a fine nature museum and features walking trails and canoeing through pocosin wetlands (swampy land) with stands of beautiful cypress trees. (Photo by Louis Van Camp.)

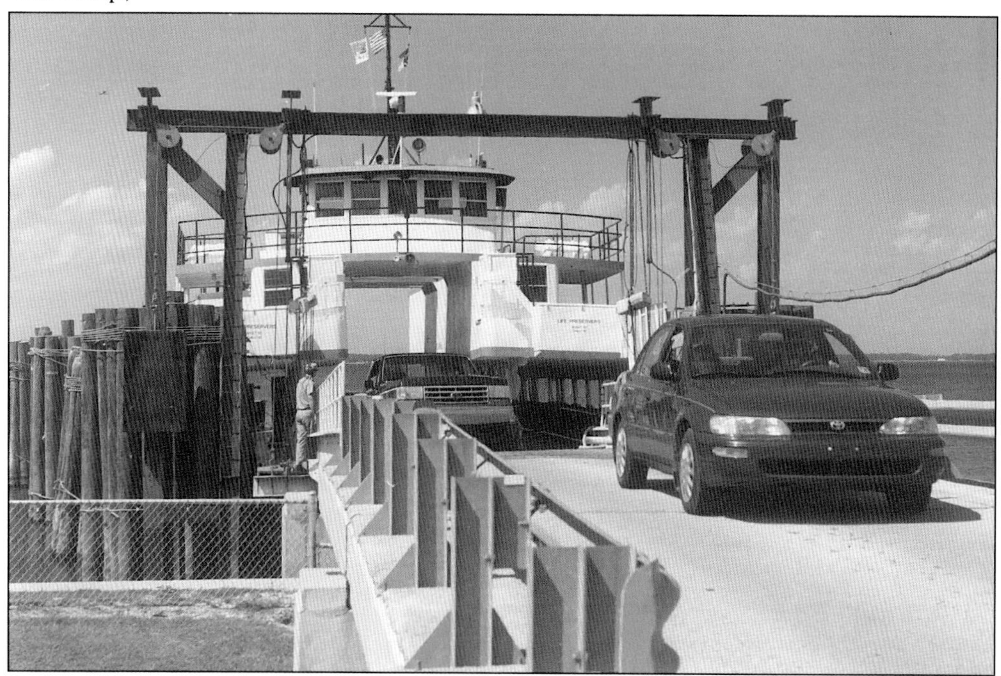

The North Carolina Ferry System runs a free car ferry between Bayview and Aurora on a year-round schedule. From the north shore traveling east take NC 92 to NC 306. Traveling west take NC 264 to NC 99 to NC 306. For departure times call 1-800-293-3779. (Photo by Louis Van Camp.)

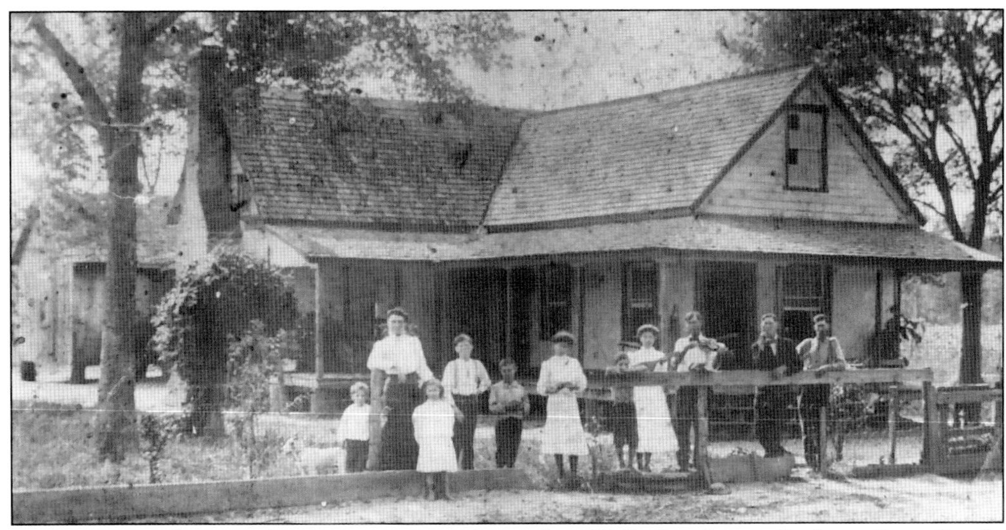

The George Riley Ross home, c. 1911, was located on Kelly Road near Burbage Cross Roads. Notice the kitchen located on the left end of the house. Pictured, from left to right, are members of the Ross family: Roy Benjamin (1905–1995), Mrs. Melissa Elizabeth Ross (1863–1947), Bertha Mae (1903–1994), George Nicholson "Nick" (1897–1927), Blake Ross (1900–1926), Sarah Elizabeth "Bessie" (1897–1986), Robert Bonner (1900–1962), Dennie Matilda (1894–1921), Charlie Edward (1887–1954), Fenner Franklin (1891–1968), and George Riley Ross (1862–1921). (Courtesy of Evelyn Cutler.)

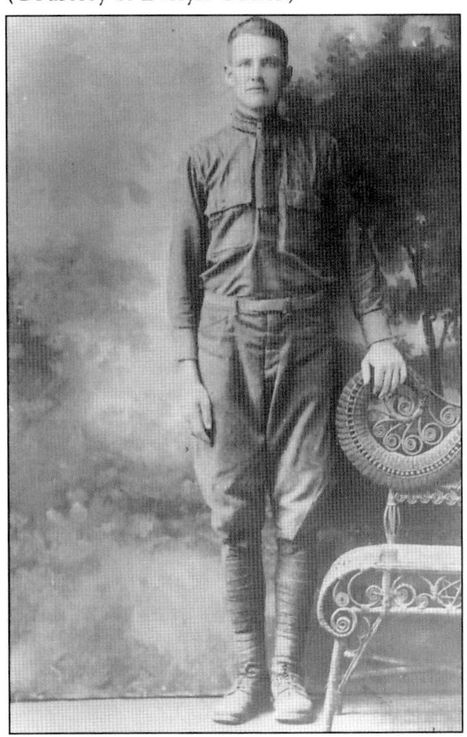

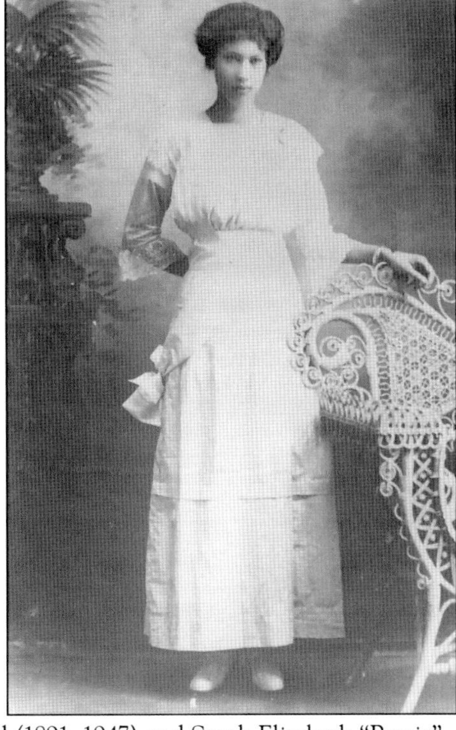

This attractive couple is Charlie Newberry Braswell (1891–1947) and Sarah Elizabeth "Bessie" Ross Braswell (1897–1986). The Braswells were married in 1920 and lived on Kelly Road near Burbage Cross Roads. (Courtesy of Evelyn Cutler.)

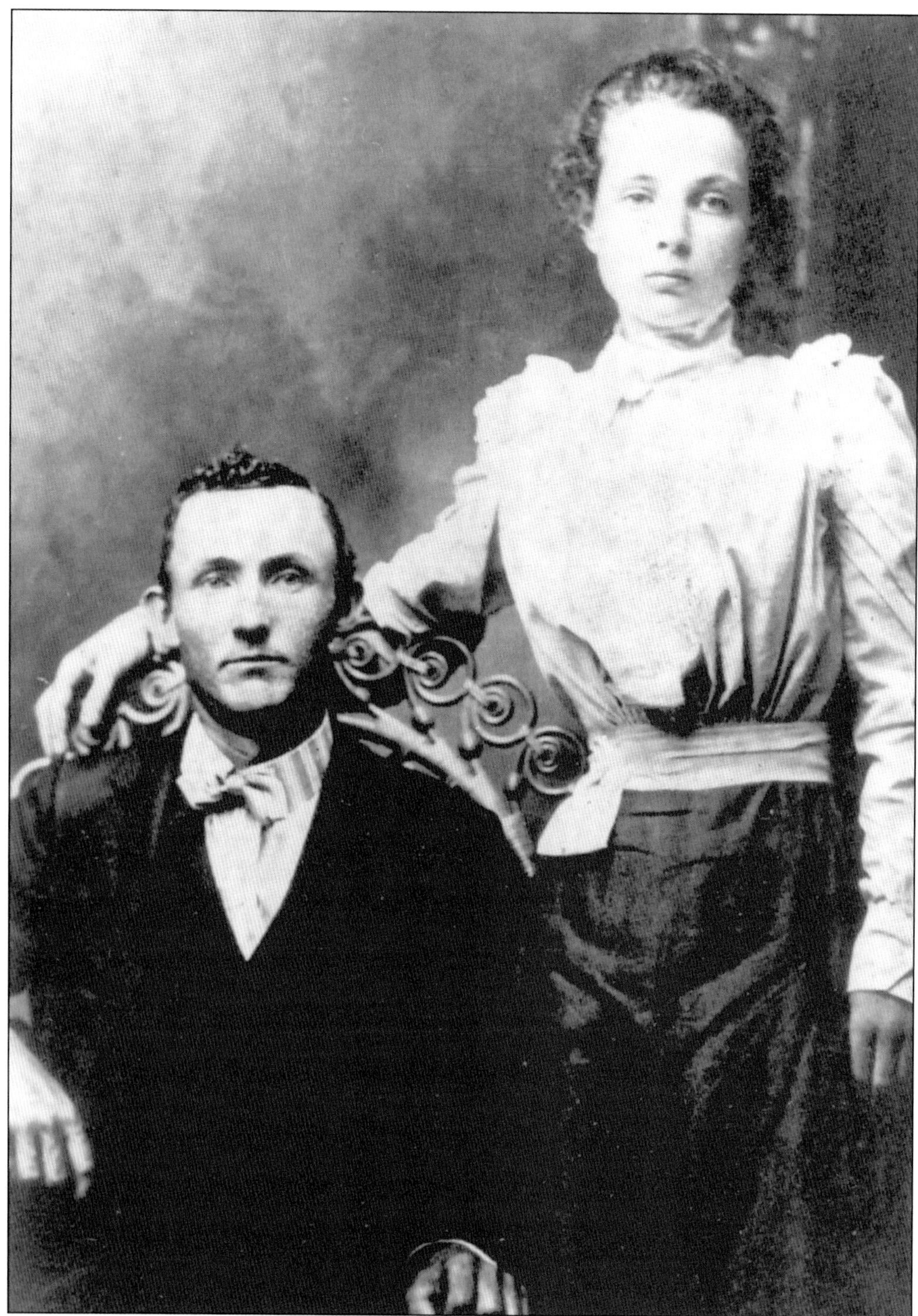

Eddie Frank Cutler (1871–1912) and Hattie Sheppard Cutler Cox (1886–1963) were the parents of Ollie Ola Cutler. This picture was taken around 1899. Eddie Frank was 45 and Hattie Sheppard was 13 when they were married. They lived in the Goose Creek area. (Courtesy of Evelyn Cutler.)

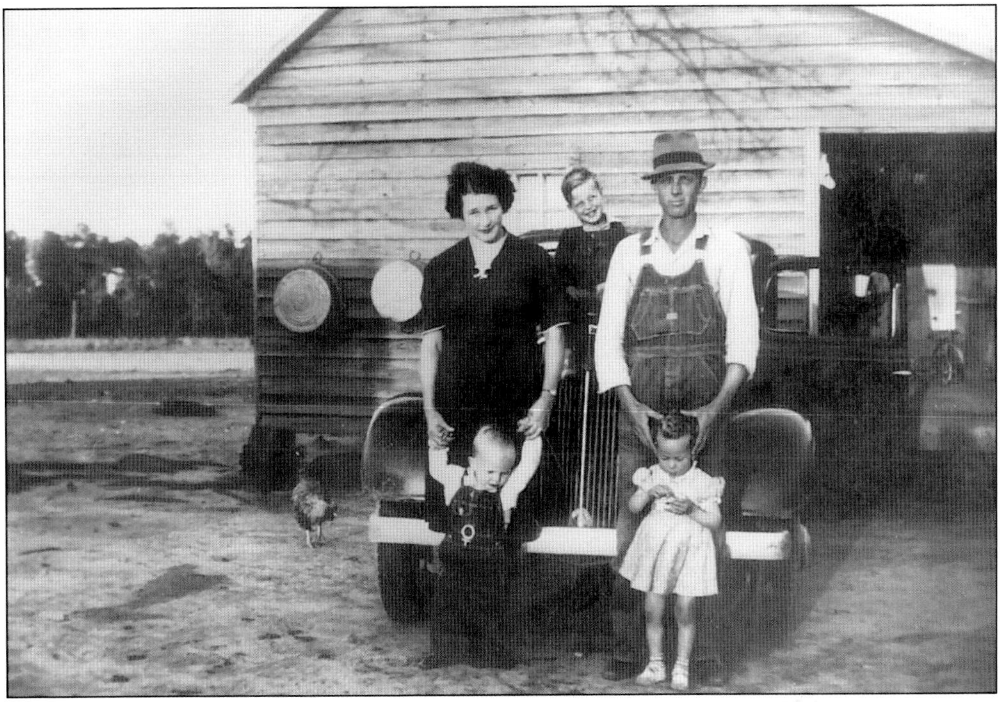

This picture was taken in 1940, when Ollie Ola Cutler was tending farmer at John Cutler's place. The Cutler place was located on Goose Creek Road off NC 264. Shown with their 1934 Chevy, from left to right, are Elsie Jefferson Cutler (1913–1993), Ollie Ray "Buddy" (1935-), and Ollie Ola Cutler (1908–1989). Seen in front are little Larry "Pee Wee" (1938-) and cute Peggy Cutler Main (1937-). (Courtesy of Evelyn Cutler.)

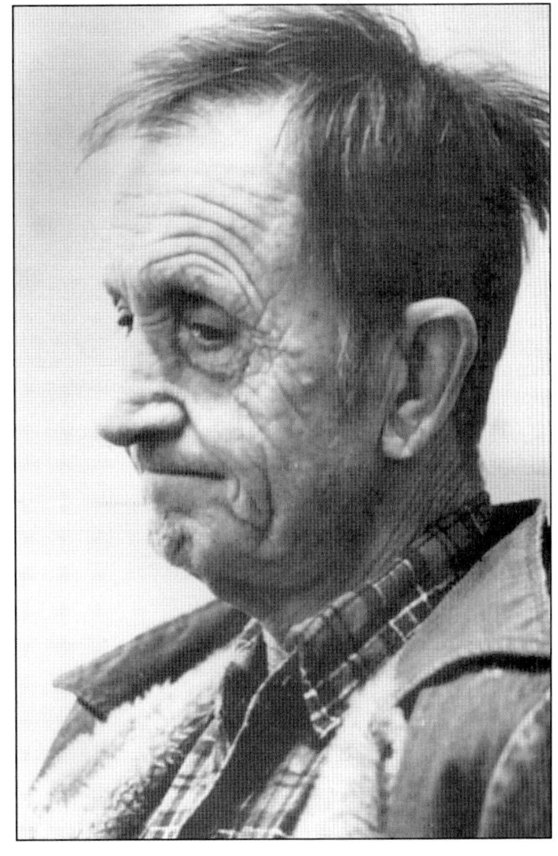

Bill Mayo, pictured here in 1986, has a classic fisherman's face. Mayo operated a "run boat"—a ferry service for the oyster-dredging motorboats on Pamlico Sound. Mayo started his venture after World War II ended in 1945. He would make daily trips to the oystermen and bring their catches to the Hobucken ice house for shucking and packing. (Courtesy of BCM.)

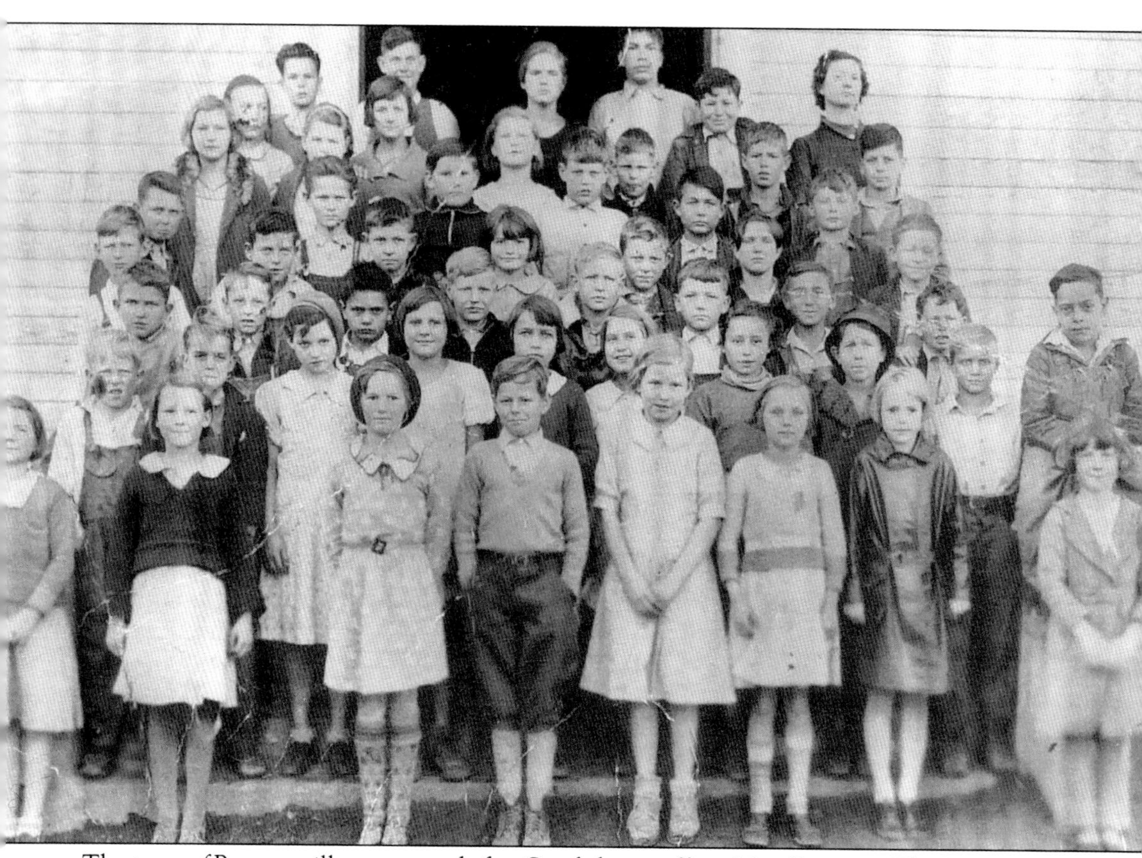

The town of Ransomville was named after Confederate officer Matt Ransom. The Ransomville School was located off NC 92 just east of Burbage Crossroads. The fourth and fifth grade students of 1933, from left to right, are (first row) Vivian Moore, Blanche McGowan, Mildred Linton, Edward Mince, Mollie McGowan, Leona Hudnell, Lillian Paul, and Wilma Gray McGowan; (second row) Ray Paul, Horace White, Marie Clark, Emma W. Cordon, Marie Cordon, Lucy Braswell, Nina Brooks, Ruth Credle, Ernest Cordon, and Alubert Cartwright; (third row) Jack Burbage, Warren Harris, Phillip Burbage, Leroy Smith, Carnie Cordon, G.C. Foreman, J.T. Beacham, and Willis Moore; (fourth row) Ray Ross, Luther Cox, Harry Higson, Patty Ormond, Hyman Ormond, Josephine Ross, and H.J. Clayton; (fifth row) George V. Ross, Otis Gibbs, Harry Lee Polson, John Jack Paul, Raymond Jordon, and Frank Clarke Jr. (sixth row) Frankie Mae Foreman, Marie Warren, Carrie Berry, George Braswell, Louis Paul, and Talmadge Selby; (seventh row) Rosa Lee Foreman, Dorothy Jordan, Thelma Brinn, Ira Daw, and Mary Elizabeth Cartwright (teacher); (eighth row) Wilbur Paul, Mack Woolard, and John Paul Jr. (Courtesy of Josephine Roth.)

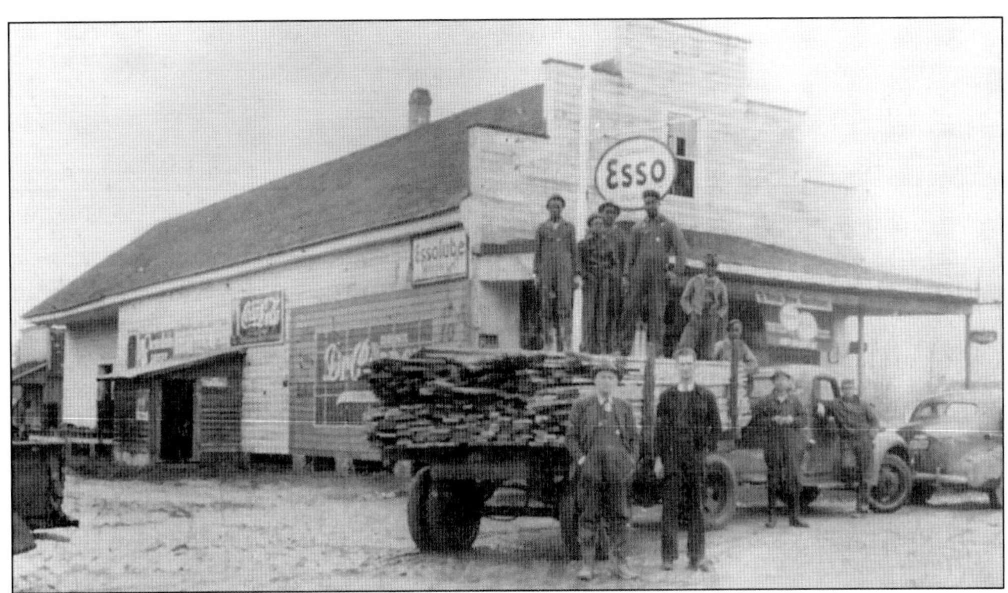

John H. Oden Sr. started a general mercantile store in Hunter's Bridge at the head of Bath Creek in 1904. Oden also owned a sawmill, grist mill, and cotton gin. Pictured standing next to his lumber truck, from left to right, are John H. Oden Sr. (in overalls), John H. Oden Jr., and his foreman Clarence Tetterton. The man behind Tetterton is unknown. One of the black men on top of the lumber truck is Lamb Woolard. The Oden store had a meat market in the rear. The store was rolled on logs to NC 264 from Hunter's Bridge in 1926. Oden's Store was the only building that survived from the original village. Lynda Oden and Sherry Modlin now run it as an antique shop. (Courtesy of Oden's Store.)

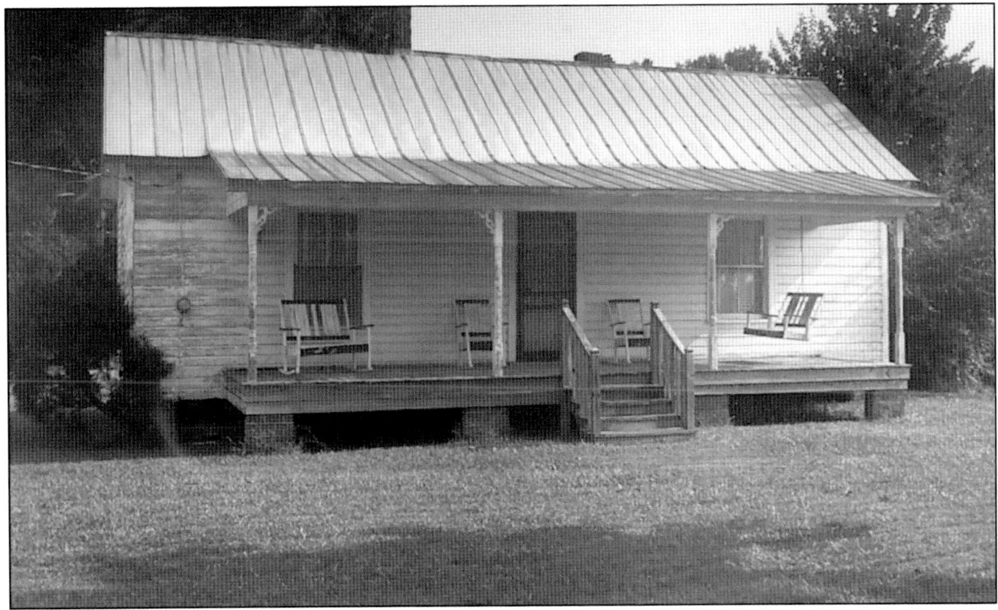

This tenant house was built by John H. Oden in 1930, and was used by his foreman Clarence Tetterton. When Clarence died, Mrs. Ester Tetterton was granted a life estate by the Oden family. Mrs. Tetterton died in 1992 and Hunter's Bridge Church purchased the property. (Photo by Louis Van Camp.)

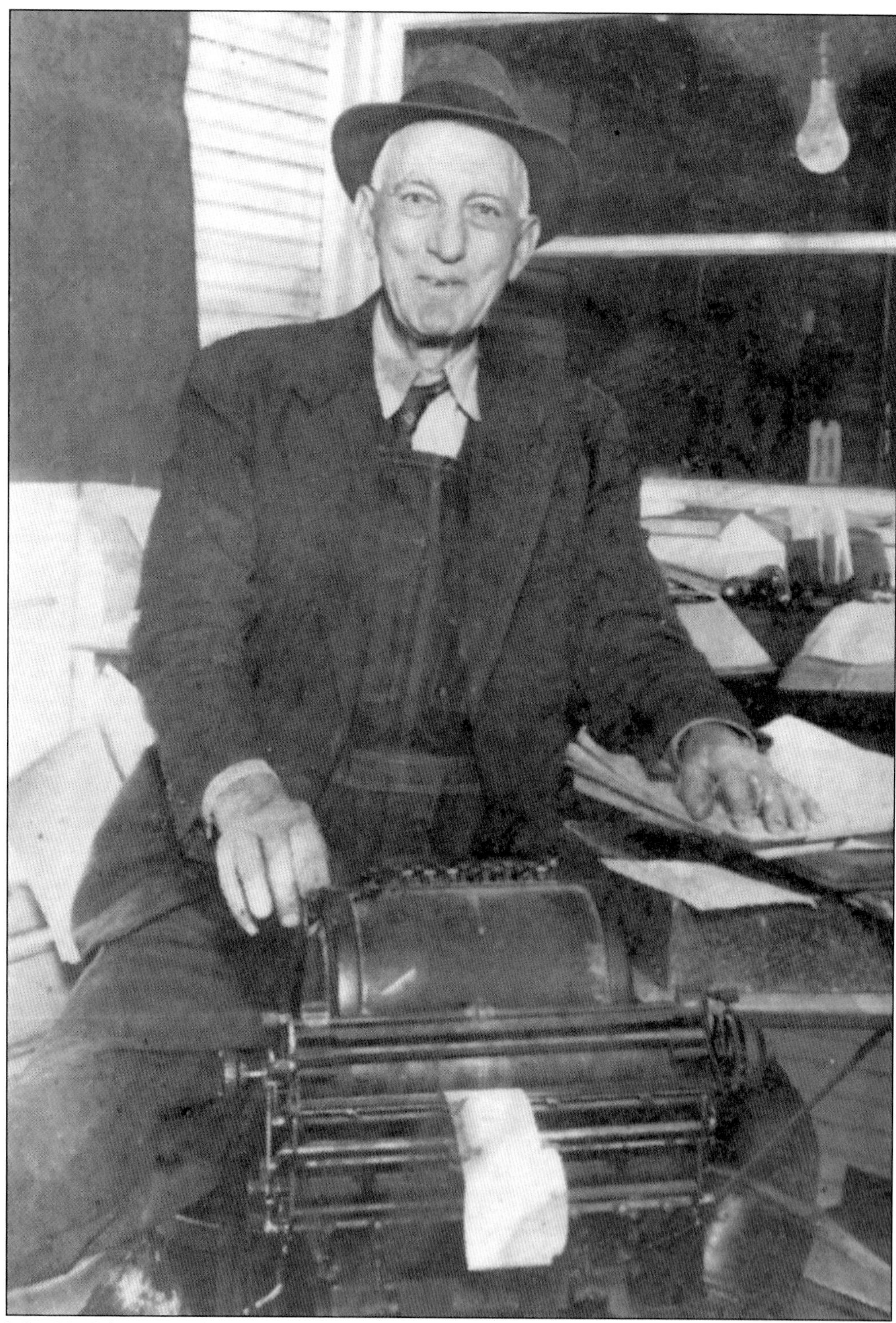

John H. Oden Sr. is shown in his store office in 1934. He died in 1960 at the age of 87, and the Oden family has his old adding machine preserved in a glass case in the store attic. (Courtesy of Oden's Store.)

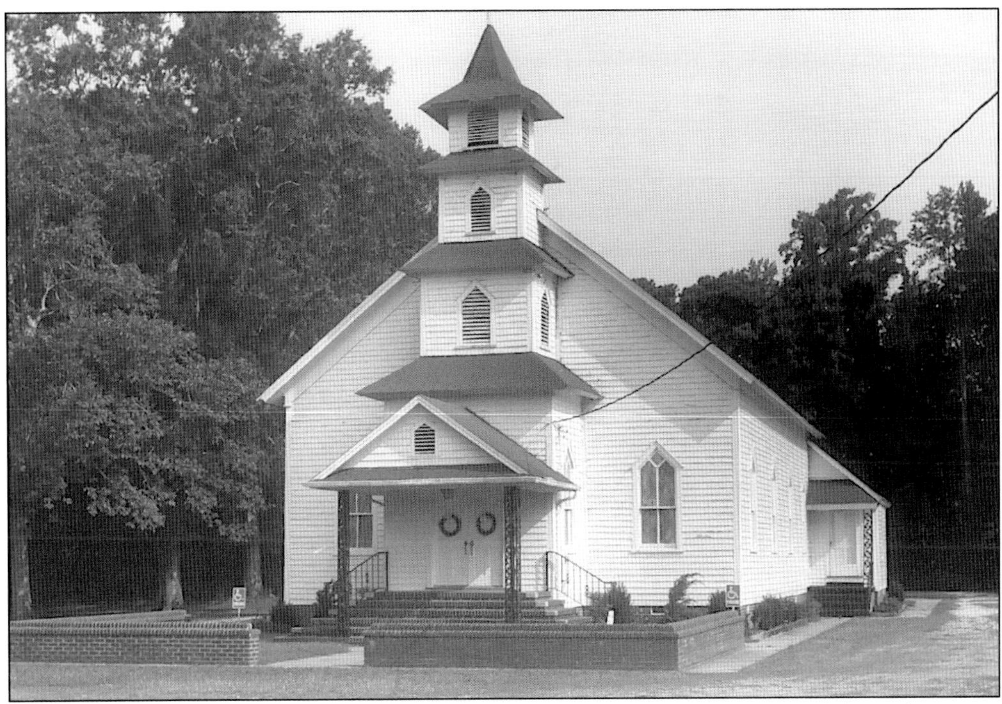

The Hunter's Bridge Church of Christ was built in 1923. It is located behind the Oden Store on the old crossing of the Washington and Leechville Roads off NC 264. "It is supposedly built exactly on the site of the old bar room at Hunter's Bridge," said John Oden. (Photo by Louis Van Camp.)

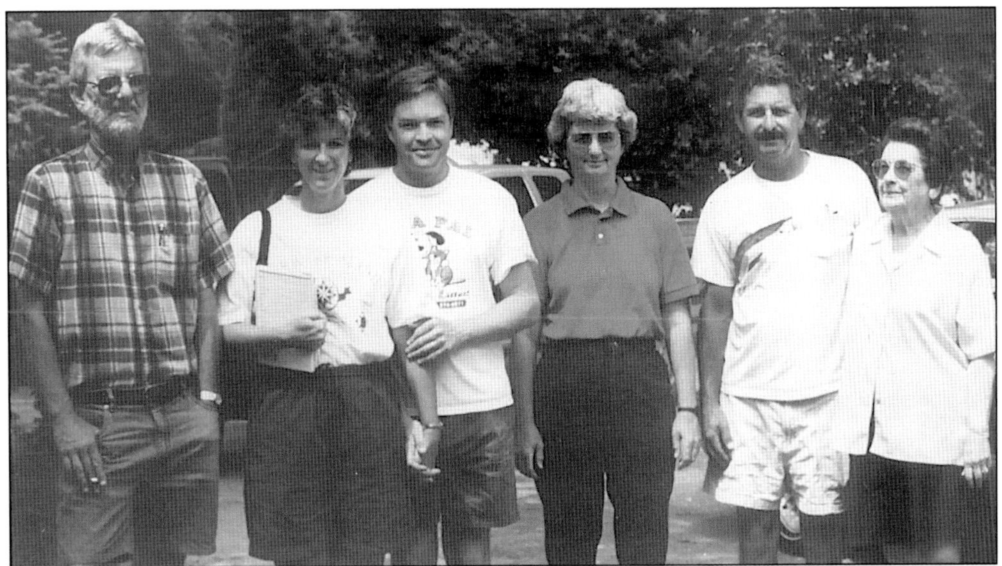

The Oden family is pictured here in 2000. From left to right are John H. Oden, Betsy Oden Boxer, Mark Boxer, Lynda G. Oden, Dale Oden Sr., and Vera G. Oden. (Courtesy of Lynda G. Oden.)

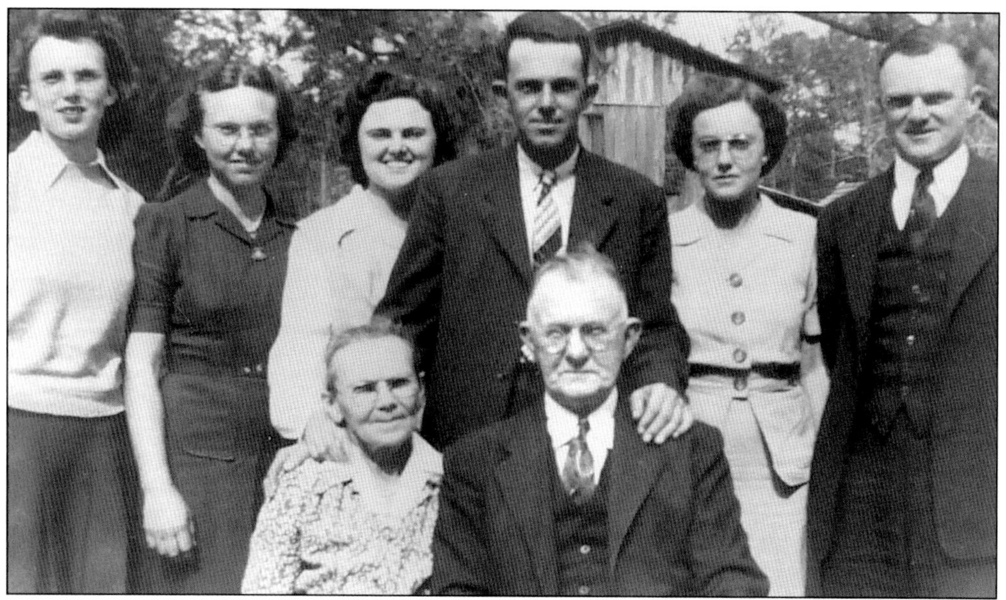

The Boyd family lives in the Everett's Crossroads area off NC 264. This 1946 photo shows, from left to right, (standing) Thelma Boyd Everett (1925–), Lillian Boyd Cox (1922–), Viola Boyd Braddy (1920–), Oscar Boyd (1914–1979), Marcia Boyd Baynor (1910–1994), and Chatman Boyd (1906–). Seated are Edith Iowa Waters Boyd (1879–1954) and James "Jim" Boyd (1878–1950). Iowa and Jim Boyd are the grandparents of Barbara Sullivan Boyd. (Courtesy of Barbara Cox Sullivan.)

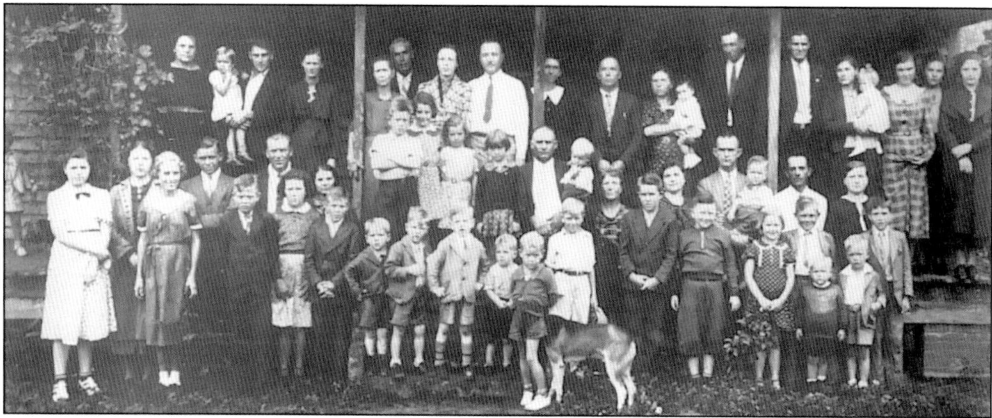

There are 53 Sullivan and Boyd family members shown in this 1937 picture, including Callie Boyd, Francis Boyd, Richard Boyd, Willie Mae Boyd, Mary Francis Stubbs Boyd, Vincent Stubbs, Bertha Boyd, Geneva Boyd, Zachary Boyd, Martha Boyd, Joyce Boyd, John Boyd, Roper Wallace, Rosa Boyd Wallace, Carol Wallace, Lucille Boyd, Hazel Boyd, Louise Boyd, Gerald Boyd, Charlotte Boyd, Francis Boyd, Macy Boyd, Ben Ratcliff, Robert Ratcliff, Jane Boyd Ratcliff, Maggie Elnora Boyd Curling, Fred Wilson Curling, Marvin Haywood Curling, Joseph Moye Sullivan Sr., Joseph Moye Sullivan Jr., Sarah Adelaide Boyd Sullivan, Dorethy Boyd, Eunice Boyd, Salathiel Ratcliff Windley, Garland Ratcliff, George Boyd, Cephus Boyd, Arlease Stubbs, Lethia Boyd, Joseph Boyd, Hugh Norton Boyd, James Wallace, Dallas Boyd, Roy Boyd, James Stubbs, James Ratcliff, Carl Boyd, Fred Boyd Curling, Marion Gray Curling Cullins, Elmo Lee Sullivan, Cecil Ray Sullivan, and Lewis Henry Sullivan (Courtesy of Barbara Cox Sullivan.)

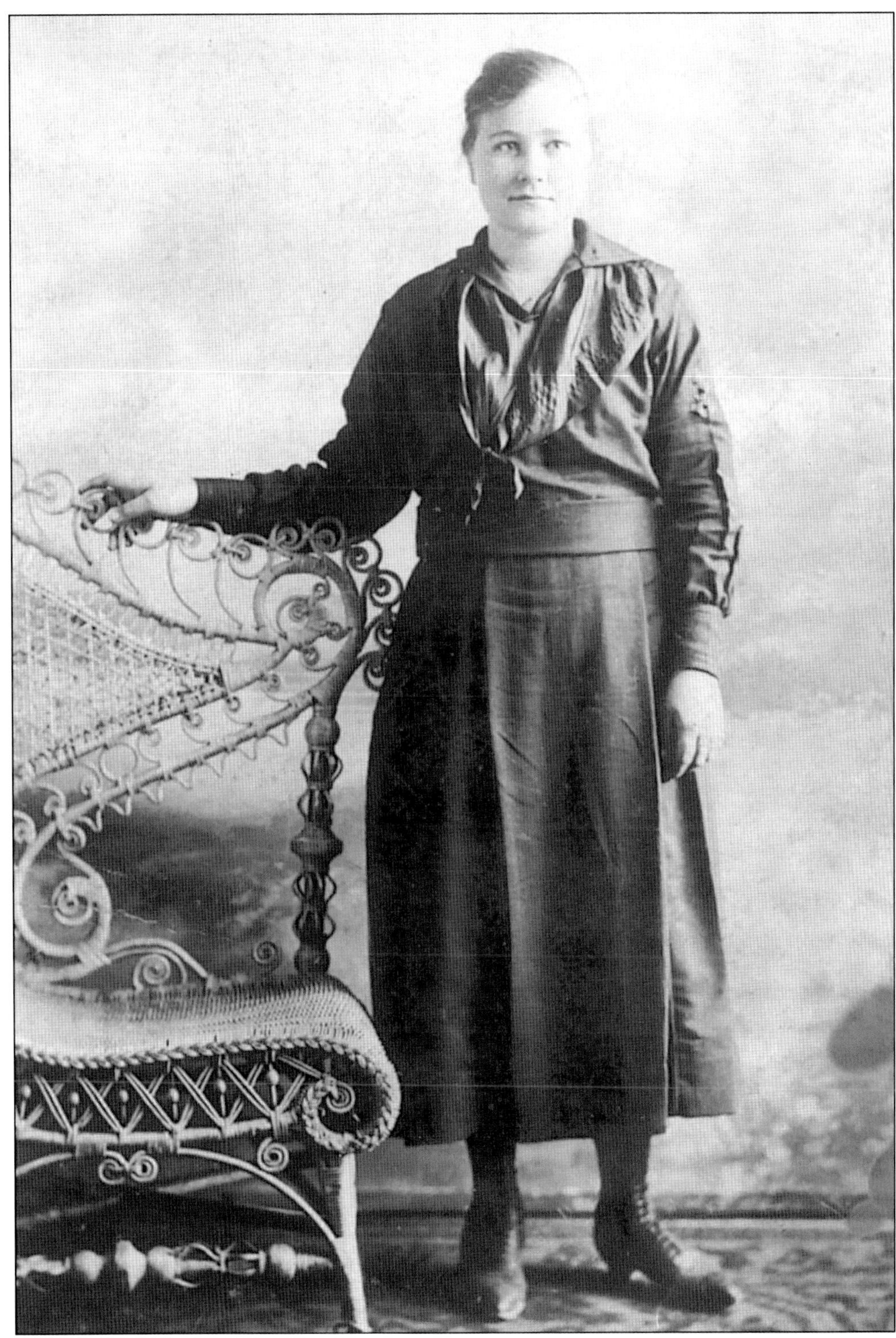

Lovely Sarah Adelaide Boyd Sullivan (1905–1989) and her husband, Moye, owned a farm on Creek Road adjoining the Sullivan farm. (Courtesy of Barbara Cox Sullivan.)

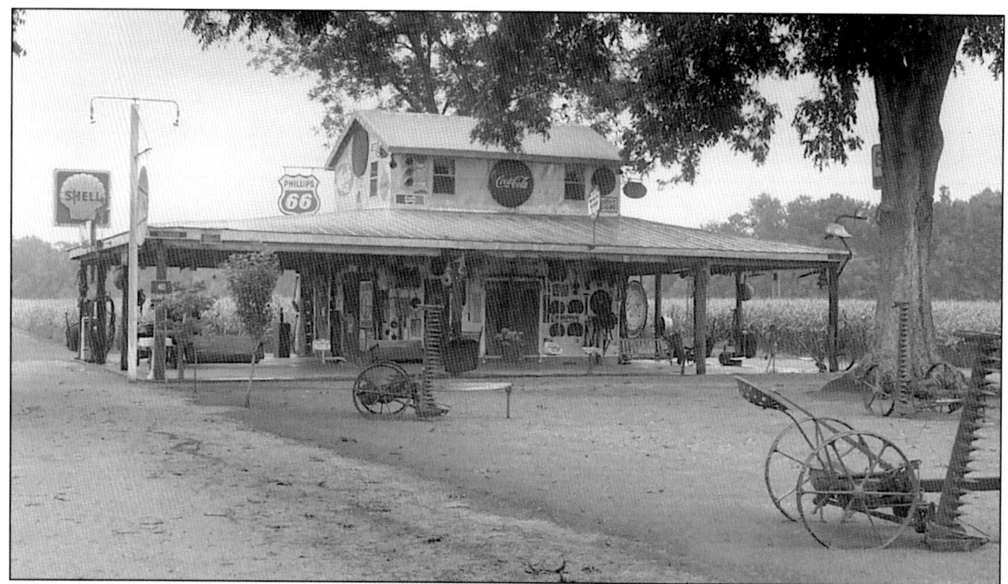

This is not a country store but an old tobacco barn that can almost pass for a 1920s county store. This unusual sight is located on Creek Road near Hunters Bridge. The original barn was part of the Moye (1901–1967) and Sarah (1905–1989) Sullivan farm, inherited by their son Gary Sullivan. Gary rebuilt the barn around 1990, decorated it with store signs from the early 1900s, and named it after his father's old house, which the family called "Yesteryear." Gary has a workshop on the first floor and an apartment upstairs, which his family will make more use of when he retires in a few years. The Sullivan and neighboring Boyd families hold a family reunion here every year. (Photo by Louis Van Camp.)

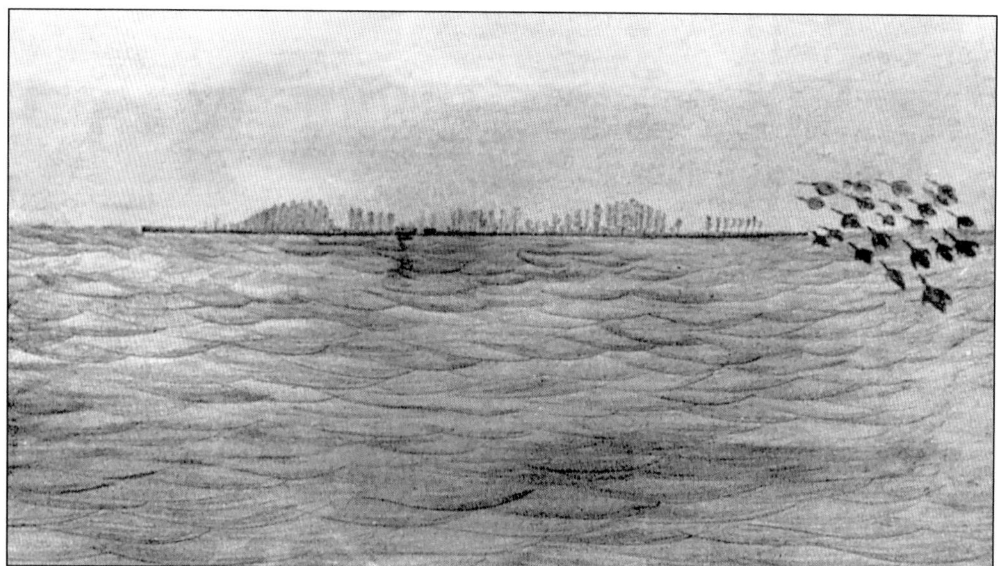

Indian Island is located at the mouth of Spring Creek near Aurora. This island is where the Tuscarora Indians held their tribal gathering on the eve of the Indian War. The Indians attacked unsuspecting colonists on both sides of the Pamlico River on September 22, 1711. They set fire to homes and murdered 130 settlers. Eighty women and children were captured and carried away. (Courtesy of Jean Bowen.)

Three

Belhaven and Pantego

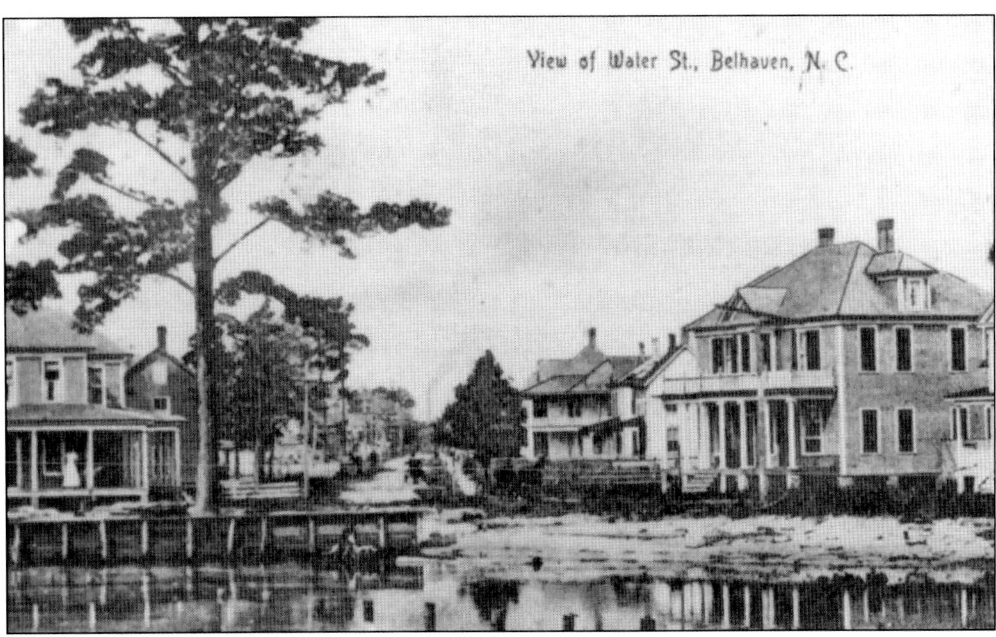

Water Street in Belhaven is pictured in 1910. The original town name was "Bell Haven," and was condensed to "Belhaven" when the town was incorporated by the General Assembly of North Carolina on March 7, 1899. Belhaven was built on the site where the Indian village of Aquascogok was located in 1585. On the right is the home of Dr. Napoleon Bonapart Mariner, his wife, Cora, and children, Douglas and Elizabeth. On the left is the home of James Cox. (Postcard courtesy of Oden's Store.)

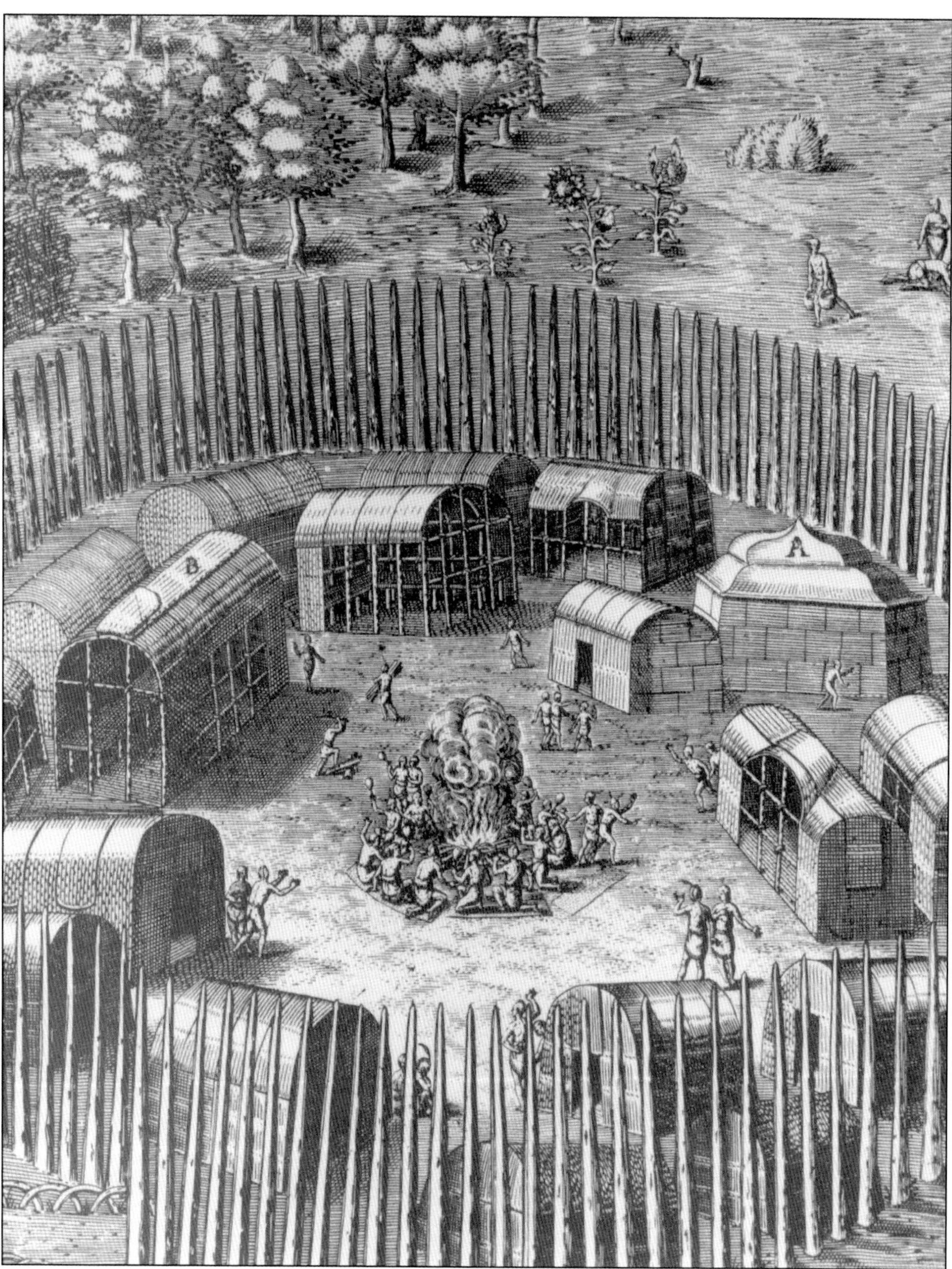

This drawing of the Matcapungo Indian village of Acquascogoc on the Pungo River was made by artist and cartographer John White, who was with the Sir Richard Grenville expedition in 1585. This village was once located approximately where Belhaven is located today. Acquascogoc was destroyed by the English sailors of the Grenville expedition on July 16, 1585. The sailors, angry over the loss of a silver cup, " . . . burnt and spoyled their corne and Towne, all the people being fledde," reported a sailor to Grenville. This ruthless act caused the Matcapungo Indians, who were of Algonqian blood, to spread the word to other tribes that the new settlers were not to be trusted.

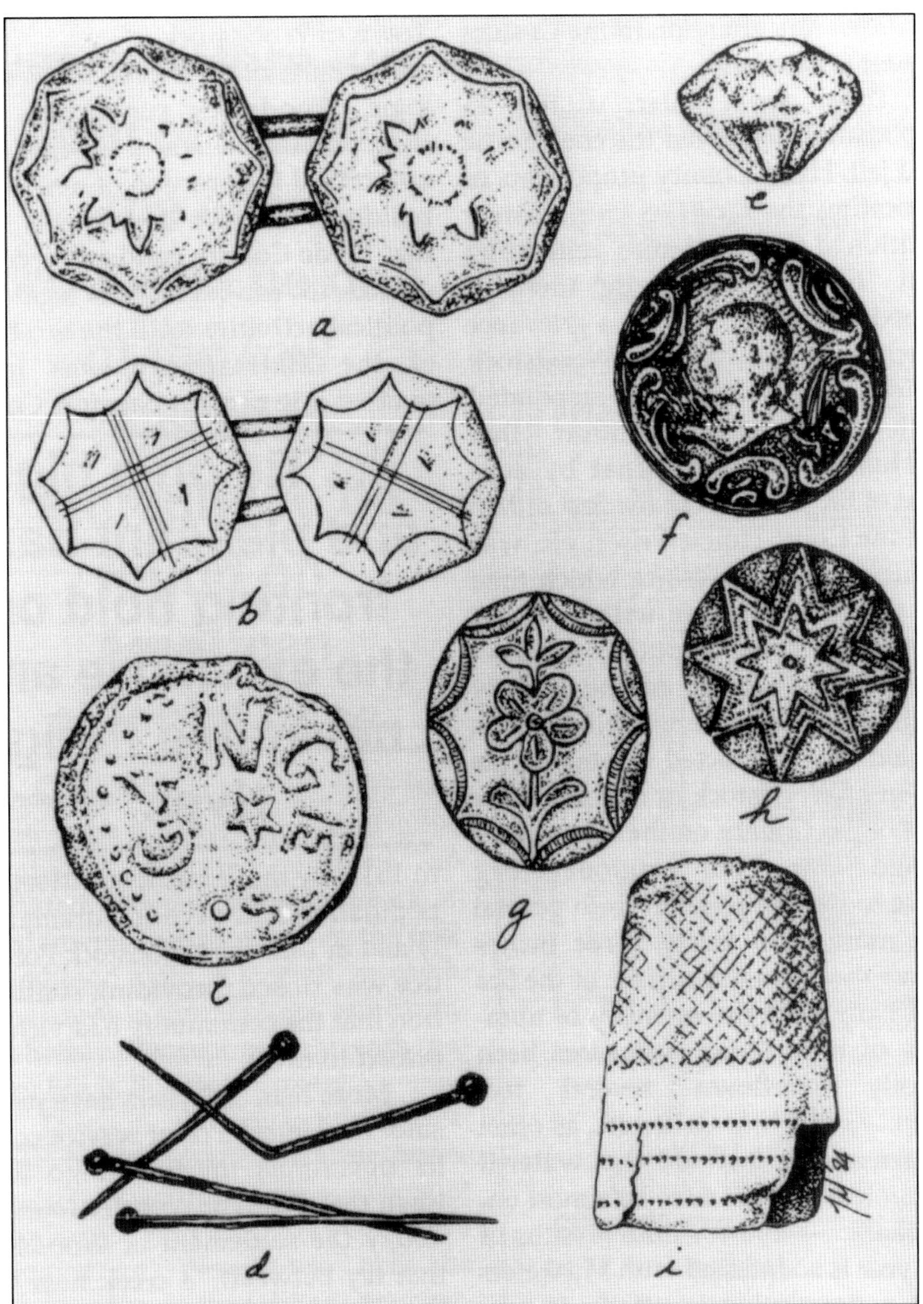

William Webster established the town of Woodstock on the Pungo River near Belhaven around 1729. Woodstock was built on ground some 33 inches above sea level. A number of merchants, planters, and artisans took up residence around 1750. Woodstock now lies submerged beneath the Pungo River. Pictured here are drawings from the Guildhall Museum in London, showing cuff links (a and b), a merchant's bale seal embossed "GANGES" (c), brass straight pins (d), a glass stone from costume jewelry setting (e), buttons (f, g, and h), and a brass thimble (i). All of these artifacts are thought to be from the Woodstock tailor shop of haberdasher William Wooten.

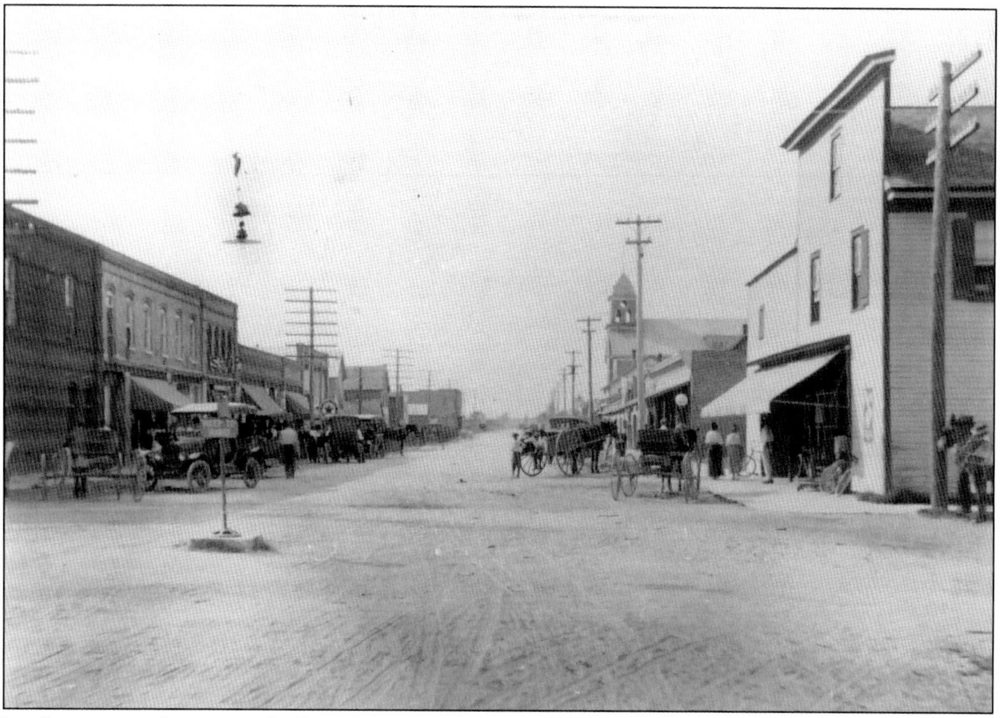

In this scene, the viewer looks west on Main Street from Pamlico Street in 1923. At the time the horse and buggy was a more common sight on Main Street than the Model T Ford. The old 1910 town hall can be seen on the right in the distance. (Courtesy of W. Mayo.)

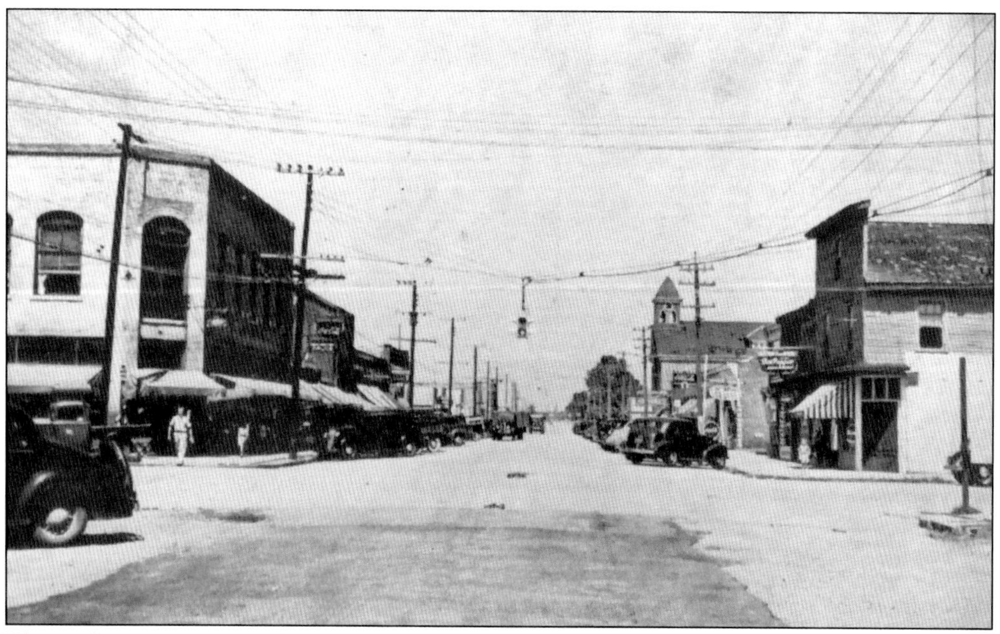

This is the same scene as above, but taken in 1941. By then the horse-drawn buggies and Model T Fords had been replaced by stylish Chevys, Packards, and other brands of cars and trucks. (Postcard courtesy of Oden's Store.)

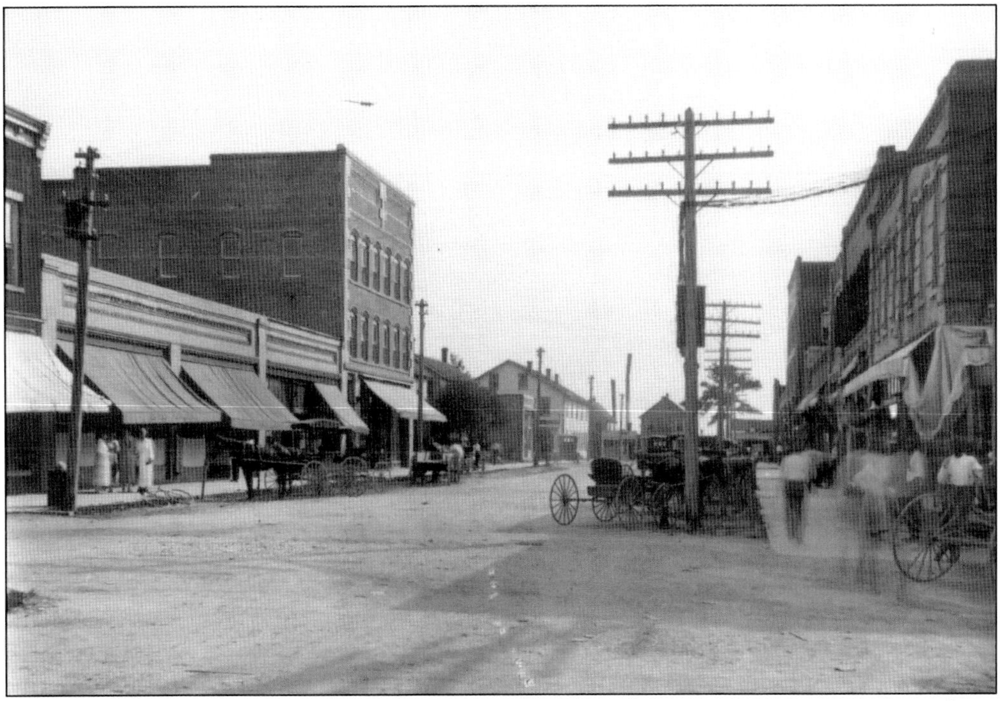

This photo was taken from the northwest corner of Main and Pamlico Streets in 1923 and was probably taken on the same day as the photo on the opposite page. The three-story building on the left was the Cameo Theater, where in the 1920s and 1930s adults could view a movie for 40¢ and children for 12¢. Adults could also attend a home talent minstrel show on the second floor. (Courtesy of W. Mayo.)

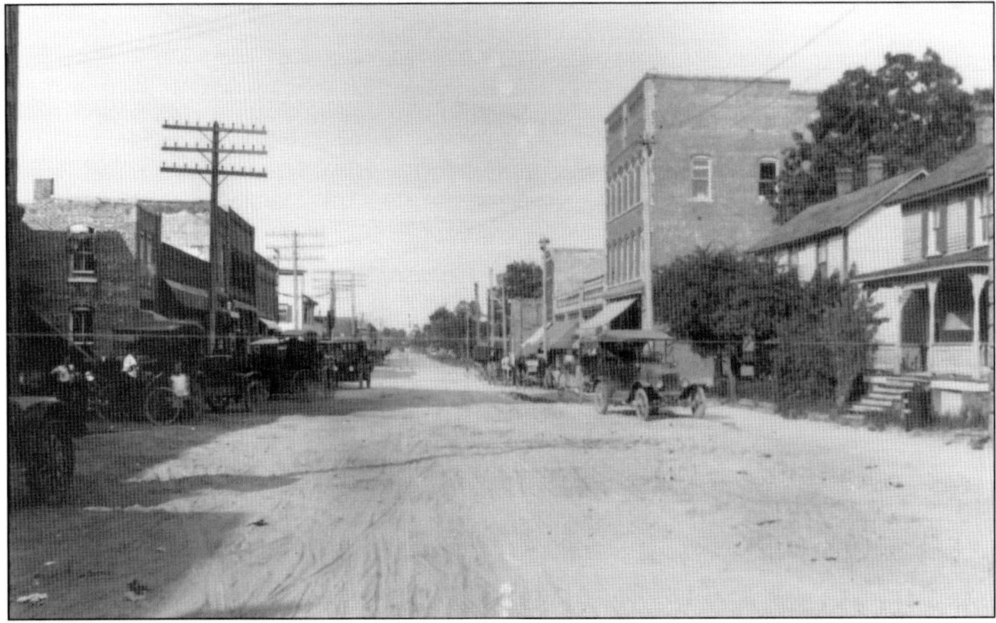

This is Pamlico Street looking north in 1923. The Cameo Theater building is seen on the right. (Courtesy of W. Mayo.)

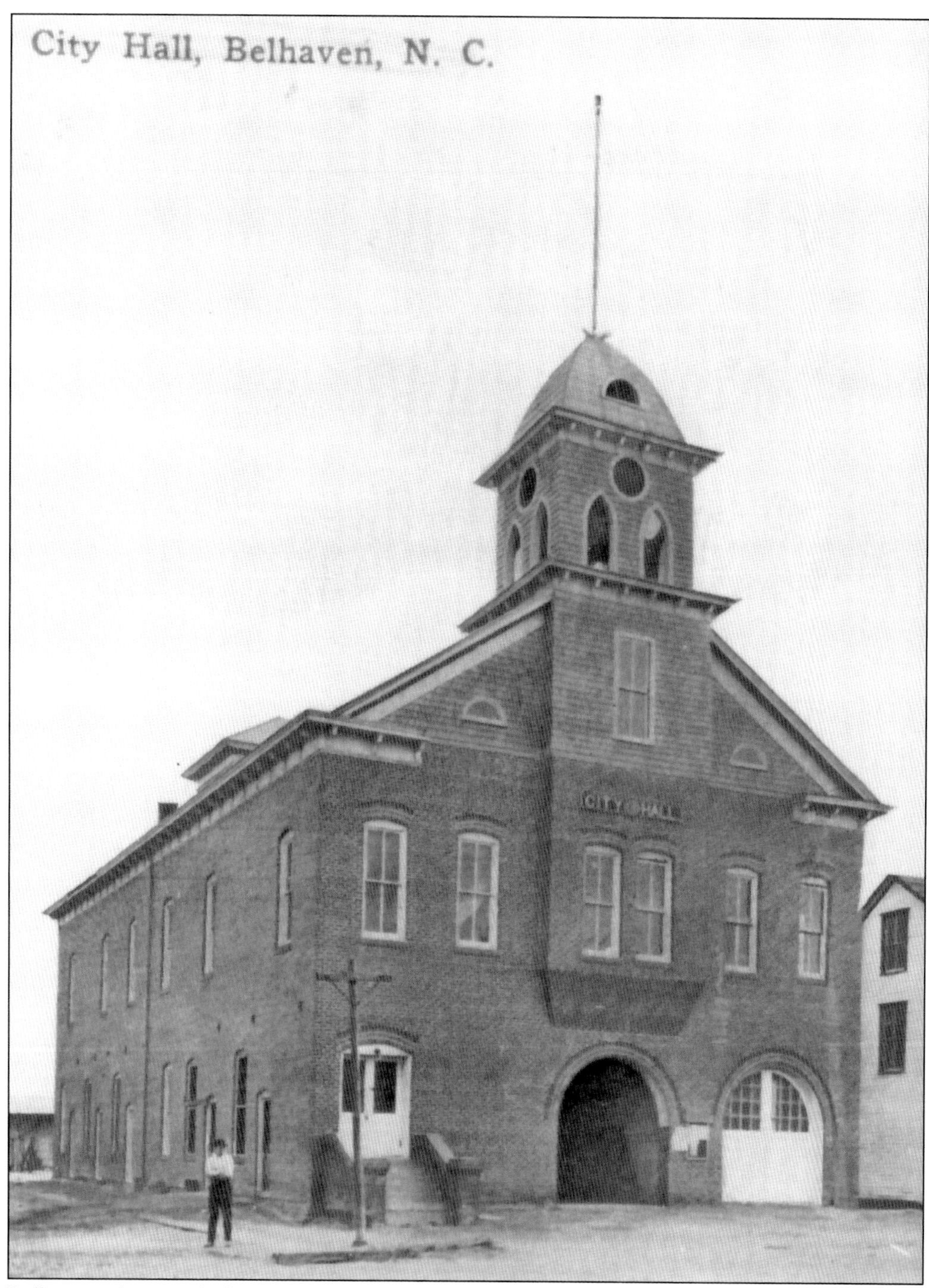

Belhaven's first city hall was built in 1910 in front of the town dock. The steeple housed the fire alarm bell. The second floor was an auditorium, which was used for school ceremonies and local talent plays and by traveling entertainers and local lodges. Capt. Will T. Kirk was the architect and C.F. Doughty was the builder. The structure was also used as the office of the city manager and as the home of the police department and the fire station. This building now serves as the Belhaven Museum. (1911 postcard courtesy of Oden's Store.)

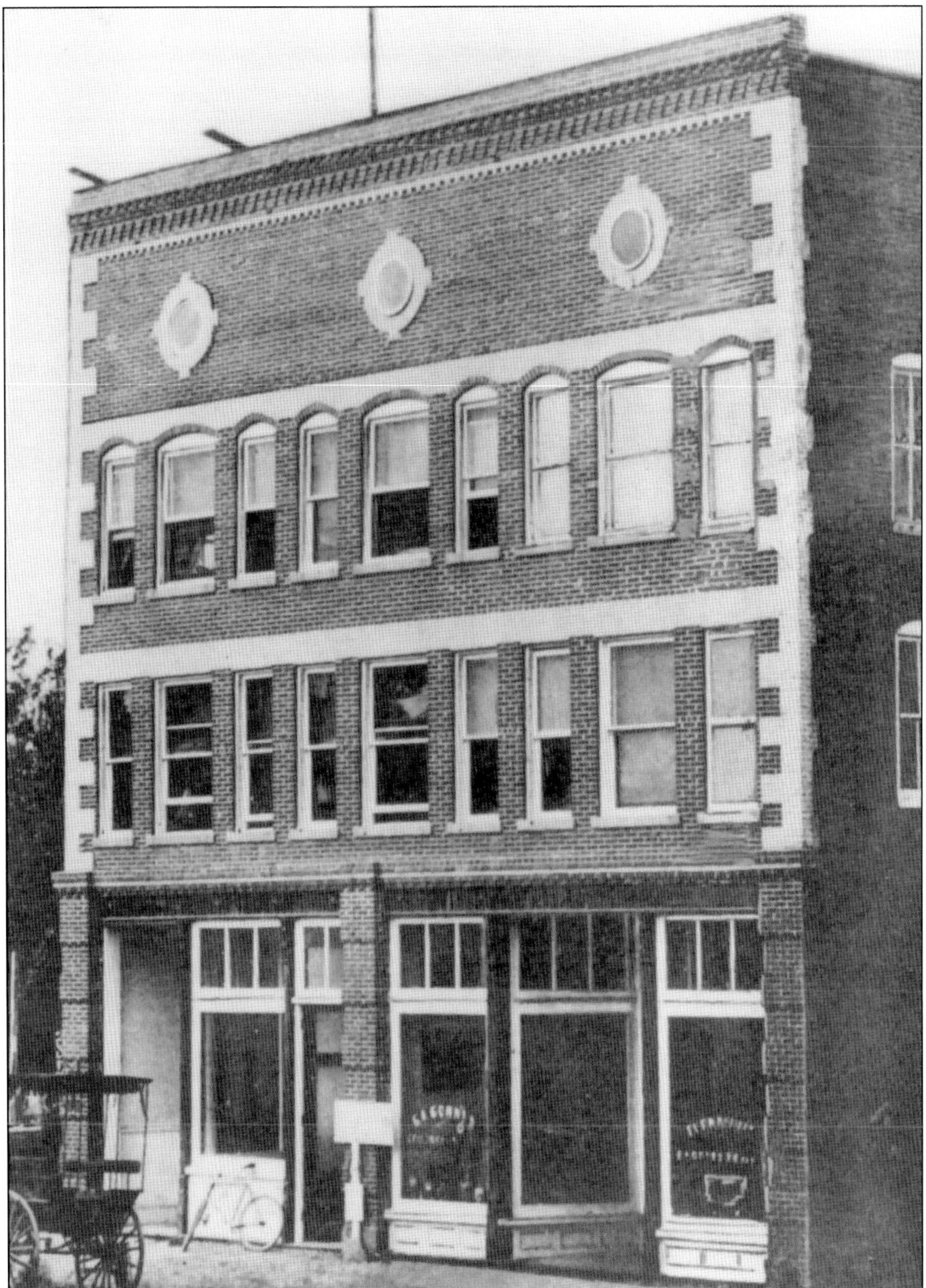

The Hotel Carolina was built in 1901 by W.E. Stubbs, W.L. Oden, and Frank Snyder. The Carolina was located on South Pamlico Street, and its first manager was S.J. Peele. The hotel closed in 1935 and became the home of the first Roses Department Store in Belhaven. The building was demolished in 1966 and replaced by the present-day Roses store. (1915 postcard courtesy of Oden's Store.)

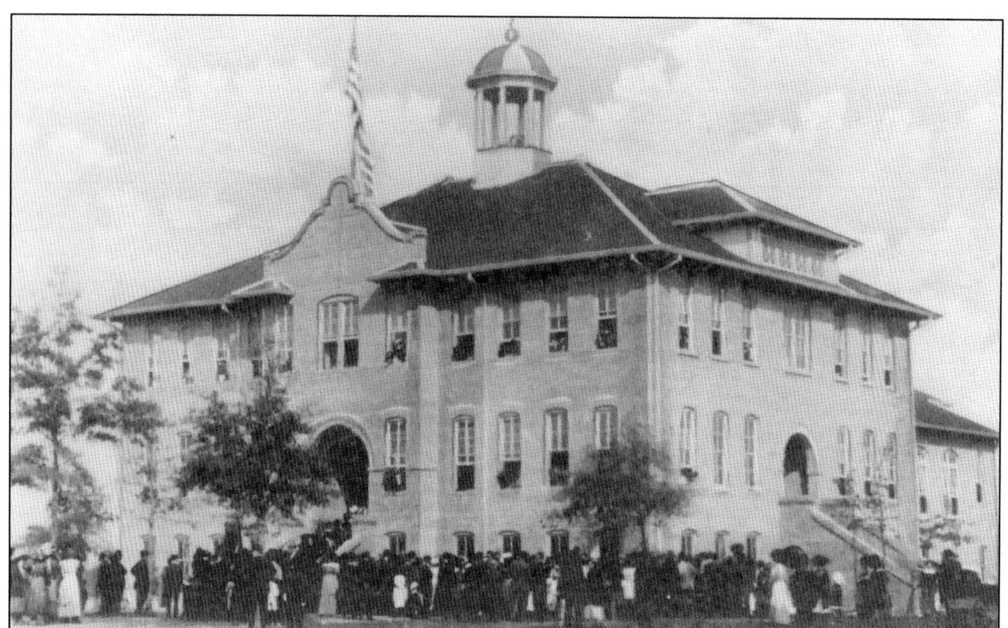

The Belhaven Grade School was constructed in 1905. This dramatic looking two- and three-story structure was built using 13- and 17-inch brick. The partitions were wood lath and plaster, and the gable roof was metal covered. A handsome bell cupola was added prior to 1933. (1915 postcard courtesy of Oden's Store.)

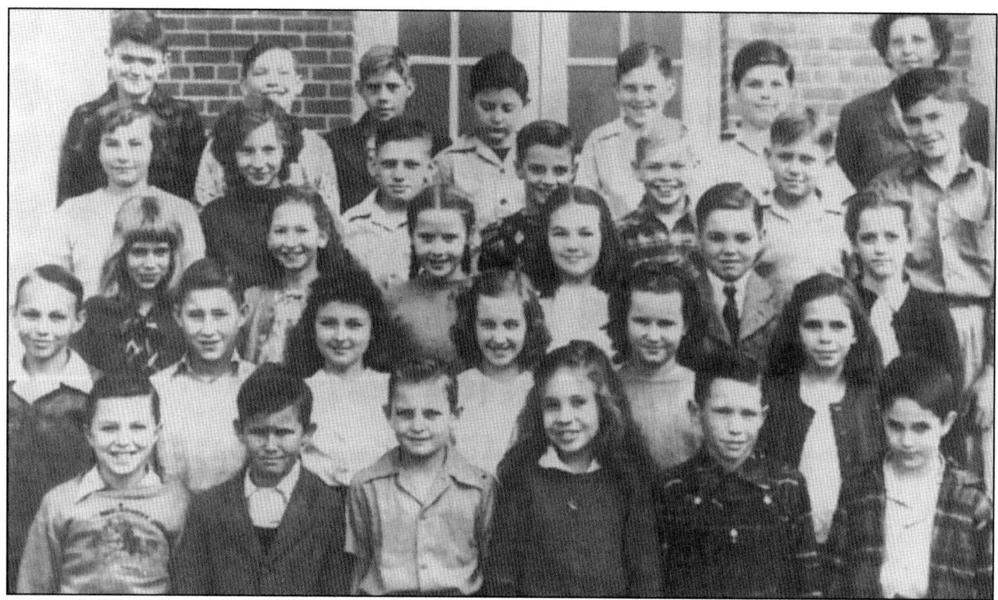

Attending the 45th reunion of the Pantego High School Class of 1955 on August 12, 2000, were Linwood and Carol Keech, Bill and Cleata Roach, Frank and Jenny Hollowell, Bobby and Nell Harris, Leo Berl Keech, James and Nancy Waters, Vicki Paul, Ted Harrison, Bonnie and Ada Waters, Eugene and Naomi Jackson, Billy and Martha Baynor, L.P. and Margaret Harris, Betty McAfee, Ben and Jean Henderson, Russell and Shirley Williams, Pinkie and Patsy Harris, Kenneth Kelly and Kelly Cox, school principal Joe Windly, and teacher Myrtle Carowan. (Courtesy of WDN.)

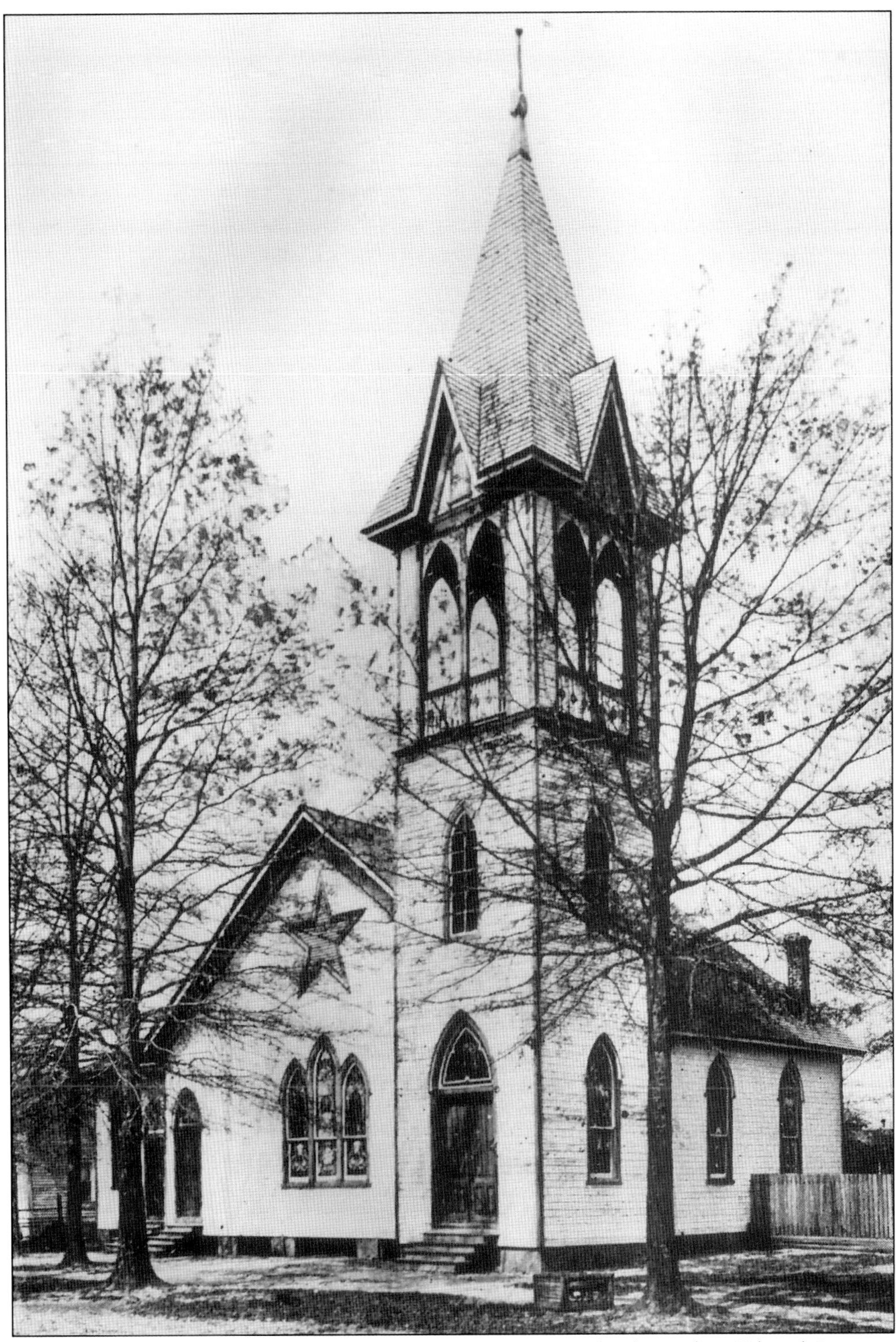

This elegant Missionary Baptist Church was built in 1900 and is located on Edward Street in Belhaven. The present-day pastor is Tony D. Warren. (1915 postcard courtesy of Oden's Store.)

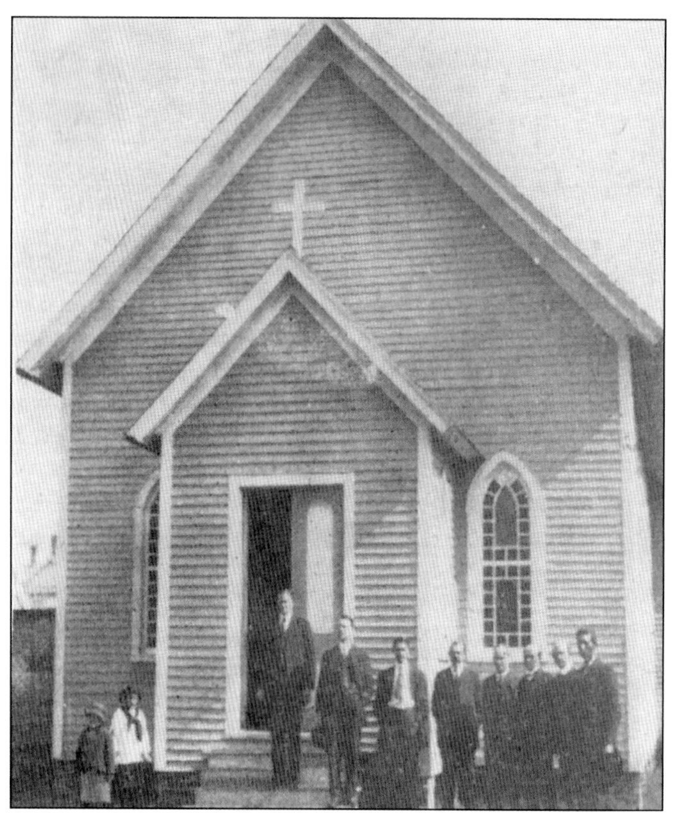

This was the vestry of St. James Episcopal Church in 1917. The men in this picture are G.L. Swindell, senior warden; J.W. Smith, junior warden; T.H. Blount; Tom Marsh; Dr. C.O. Windley; Harry Swindell; and George Old. The Reverend Lucian Malone was ordained deacon in 1910 and served as the church minister. Malone was ordained a priest in 1921. (Courtesy of A.L. "Gus" Gaylord.)

The picture below appeared in the *Match Pungo* yearbook from the Belhaven Elementary Grade School in 1954. Miss Helene Toland was the teacher of this second and third grade class. (Courtesy of Seth Latham.)

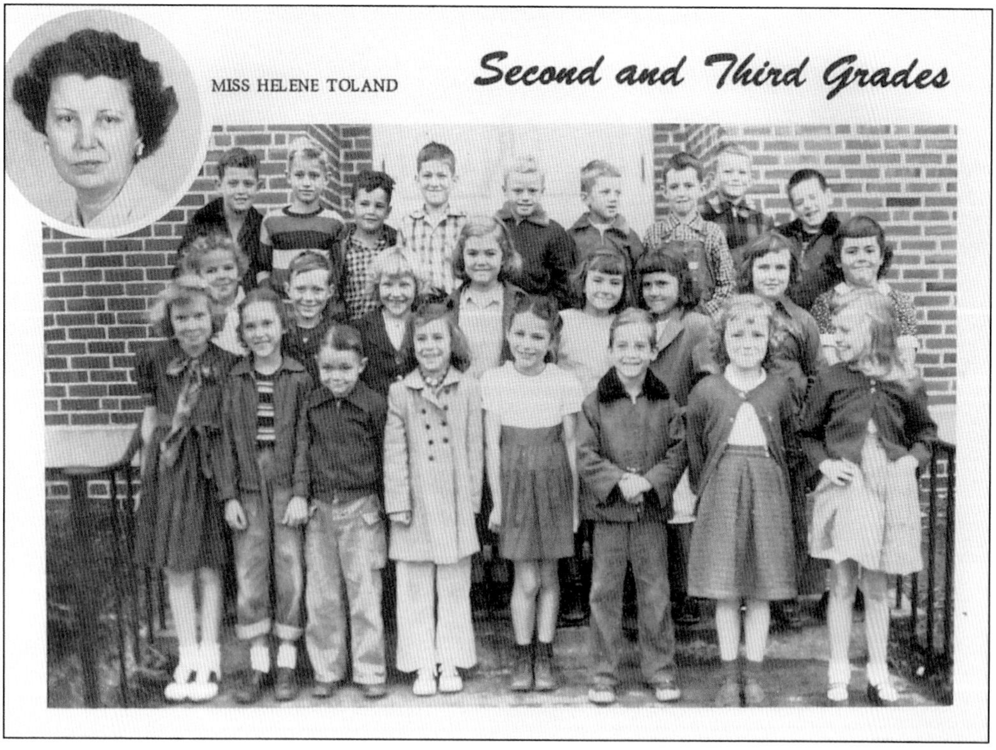

MISS HELENE TOLAND

Second and Third Grades

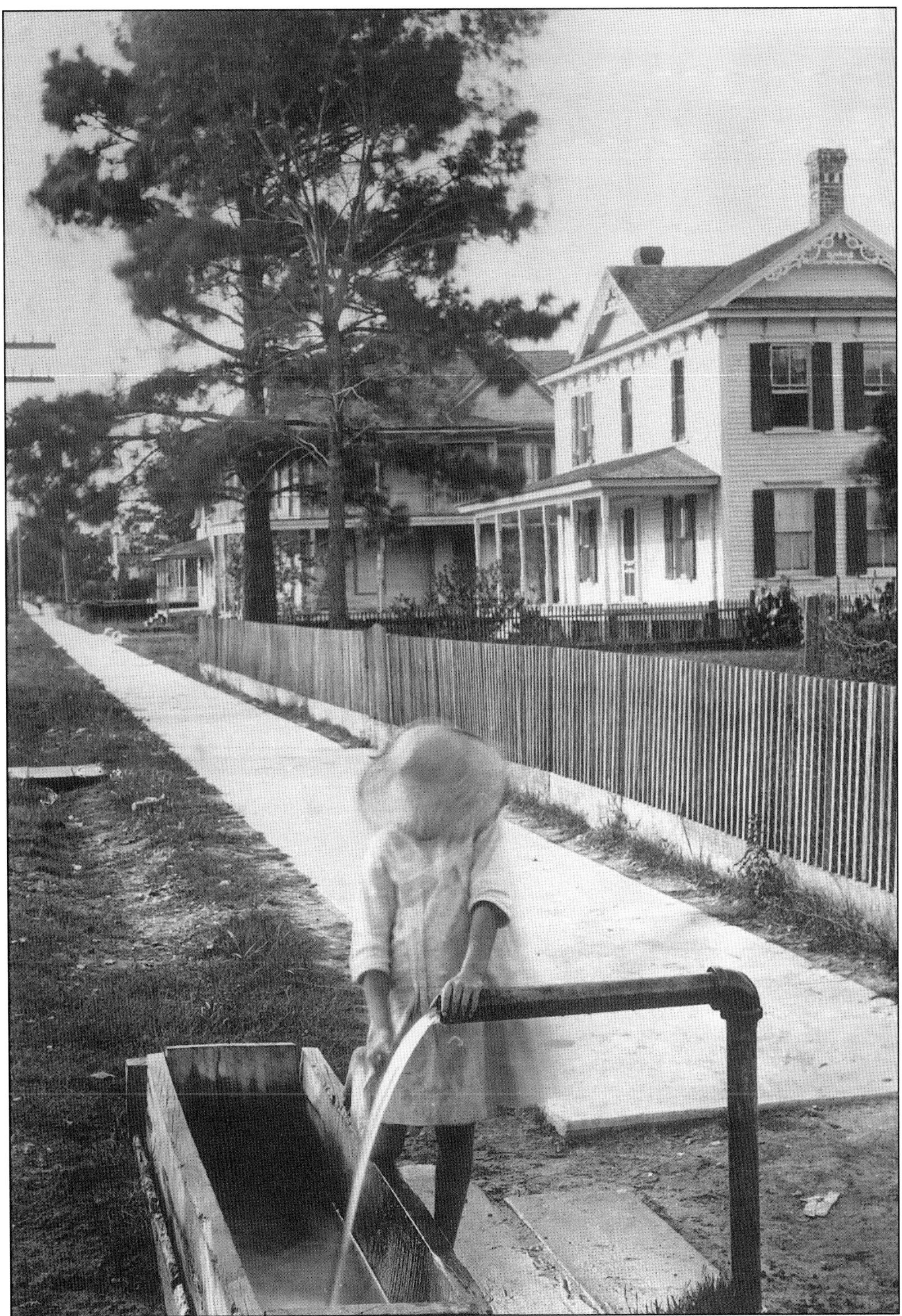

The Riddick house (background) and the Kilpatrick home (foreground) are seen here in the 1920s. In the foreground, on the corner of Water and Magnolia Streets, is an artesian well. (Courtesy of W. Mayo.)

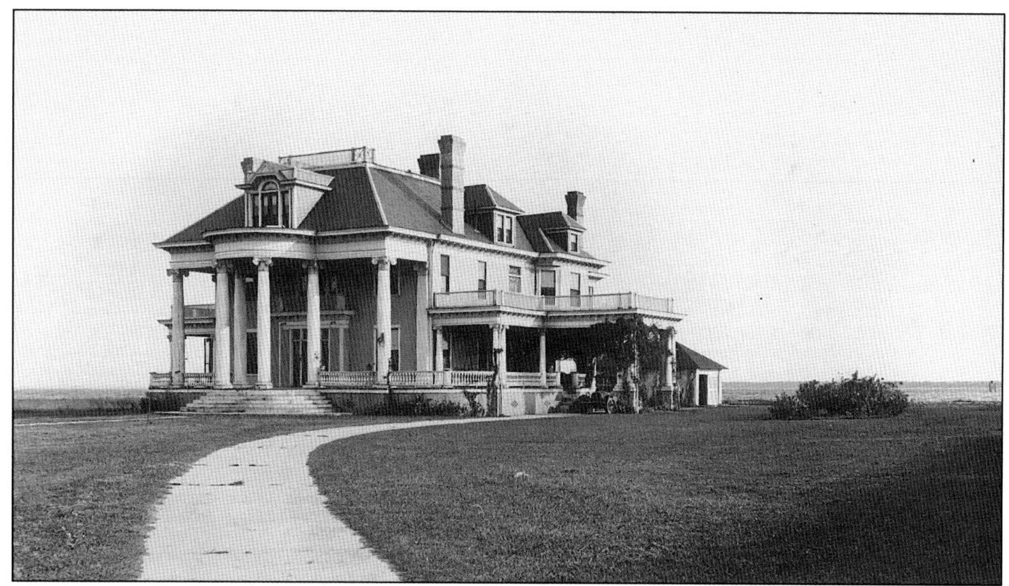

In 1899, John Aaron Wilkerson began building the Victorian mansion now known as River Forest Manor. Italian craftsmen were employed to carve the ornate ceilings. By 1904, the mansion was complete. It had carved oak mantels on each of 11 fireplaces, crystal chandeliers, and two large baths with oversized tubs for two. It has now become a world famous restaurant, hotel, and marina and shipyard. It has been owned by Mrs. Axson Smith, Axson Smith Jr., and Mark Smith since 1947. (Courtesy of W. Mayo.)

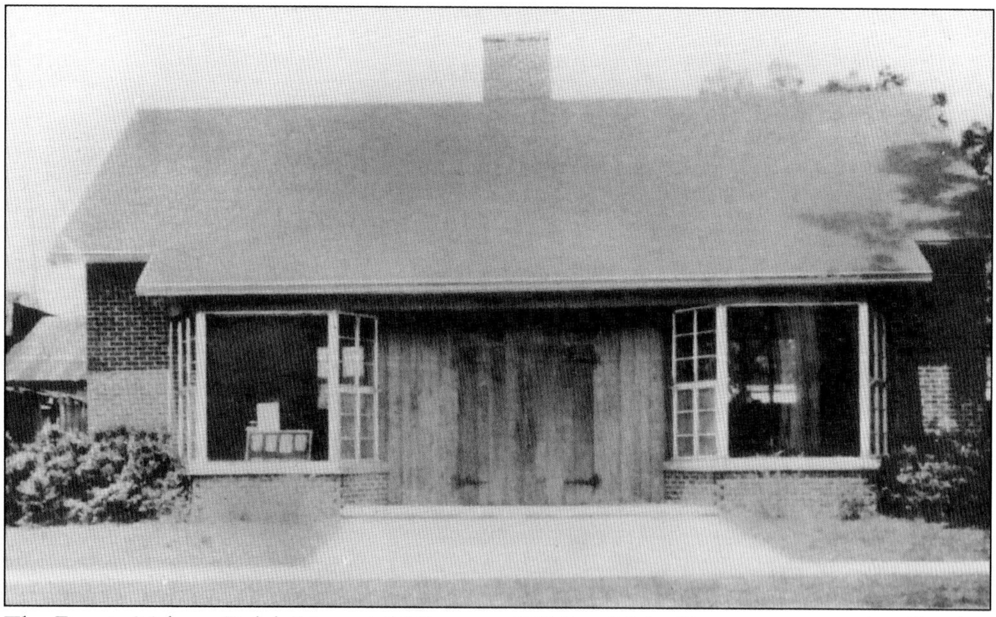

The Fannie Mebane Ralph Memorial Library at 305 East Main Street was opened in October 1952. It was built with a bequest of $5,000 from Dr. W.T. Ralph. After 48 years of community service as a branch of the BHM Library system, it will soon be torn down and replaced by a new and larger library building. A temporary metal BHM Branch Library building, under the direction of Joan Cahoon, branch manager, has been erected on the NC 264 By-Pass, just north of the intersection of NC 99. (1954 postcard courtesy of Oden's Store.)

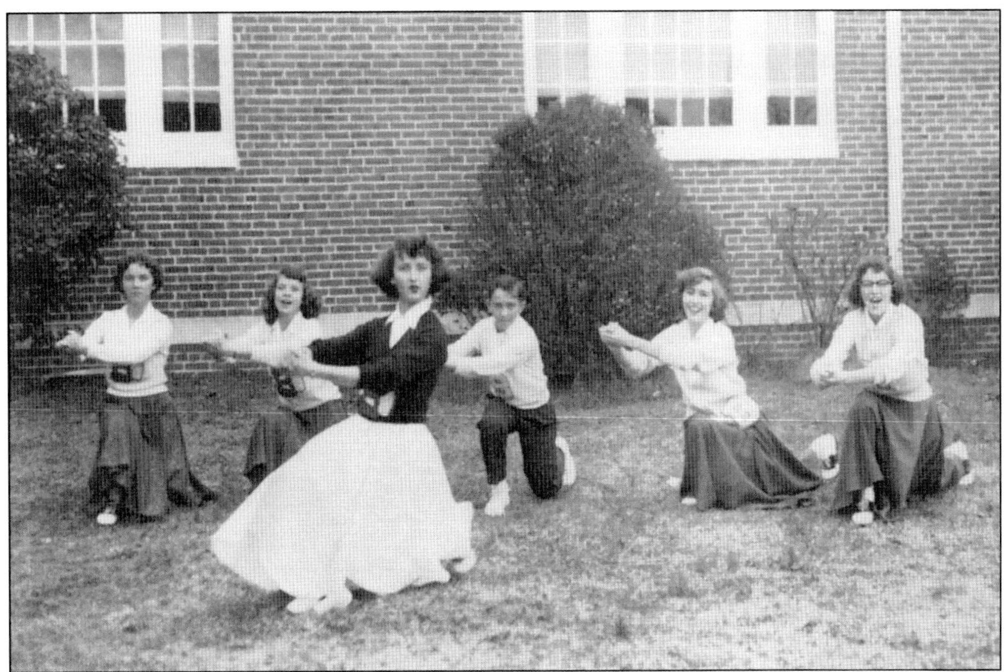

This picture, taken from the 1954 edition of the *Matcha Pungo* yearbook, was labeled "Yea Team." The cheerleaders, from left to right, are Evelyn Paul, Norma McKinney, Essie Cox, Carroll Cox, Carolyn Knickerbocker, and Mary Redditt. (Courtesy of Seth Latham.)

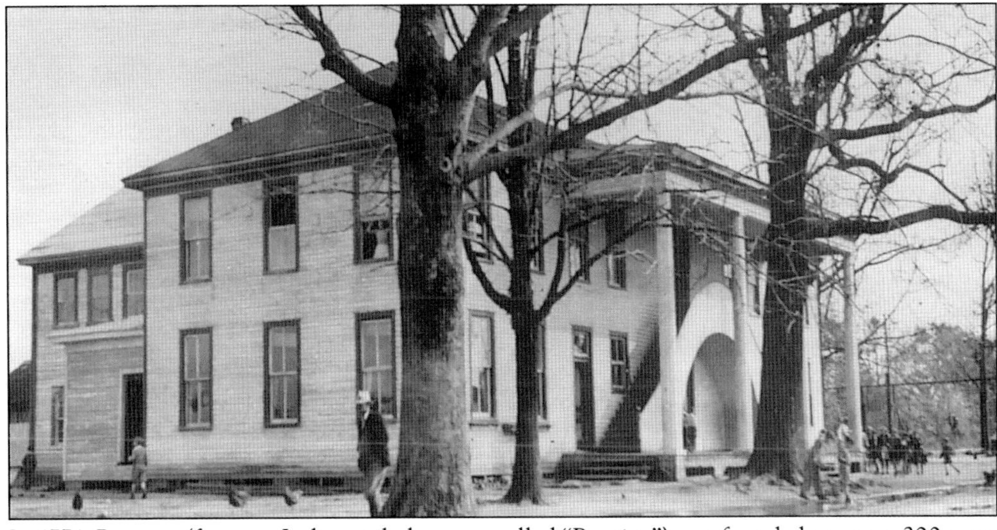

In 1774, Pantego (from an Indian tribal name spelled "Pantigo") was founded on some 300 acres along the north bank of Pantego Creek. The Pantego Educational Academy was a private school started in 1879, and the building shown here was constructed in 1915. The county purchased it and converted it into a public school. A belfry with a 100-pound bell was added sometime after 1933. The structure is unusual in that it has an outside stairway and large white columns in the front. In 1965, an adjoining modern cafeteria was built, and in later years, the building was converted into a library and public recreation center. The last teacher was Miss Betty Judkin, and the school yearbook was called *Ye Olde Academie*. In 1956, Pantego Academy received the Bellamy award of excellence in education. (Courtesy of BCBE.)

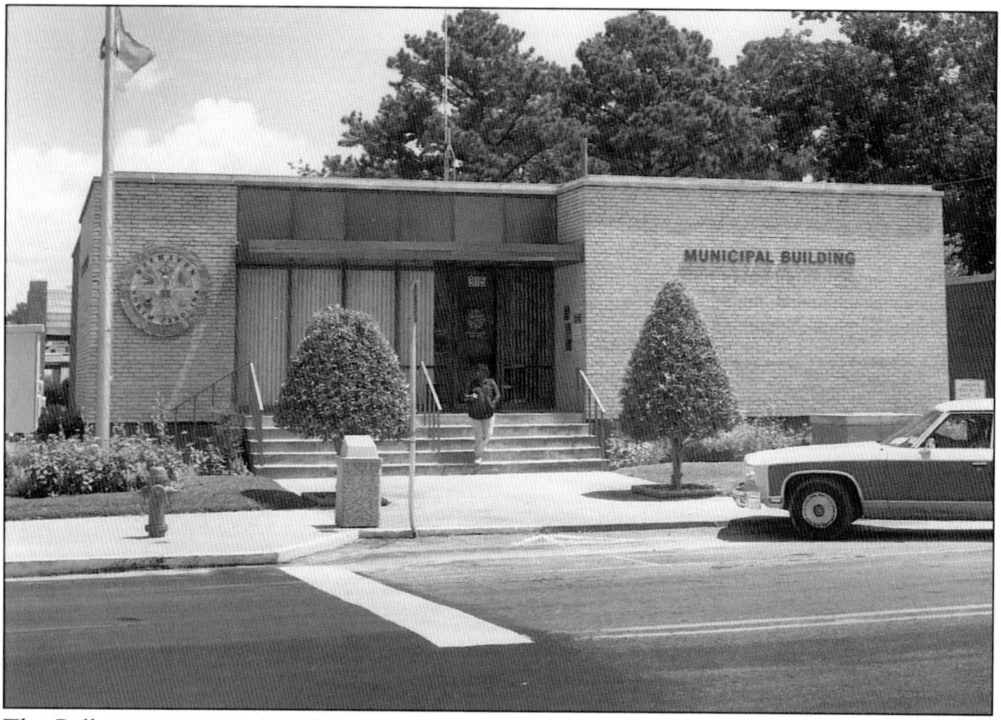

The Belhaven Municipal Building on the corner of Main and Pamlico Streets now serves as Belhaven's town hall. (2000 photo by Louis Van Camp.)

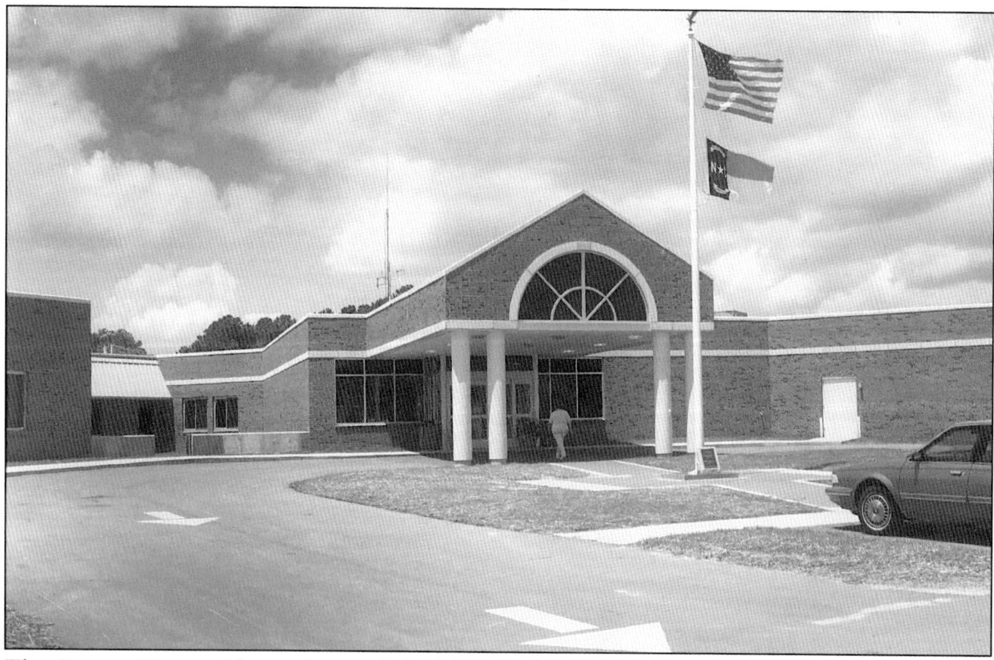

The Pungo District Hospital is a 49-bed hospital located at 202 East Water Street. Pungo Hospital was opened in 1950 and provides general medical and surgical services supported by consulting cardiology, radiology, pathology, and physical therapy. This hospital serves eastern Beaufort County and Hyde County. (2000 photo by Louis Van Camp.)

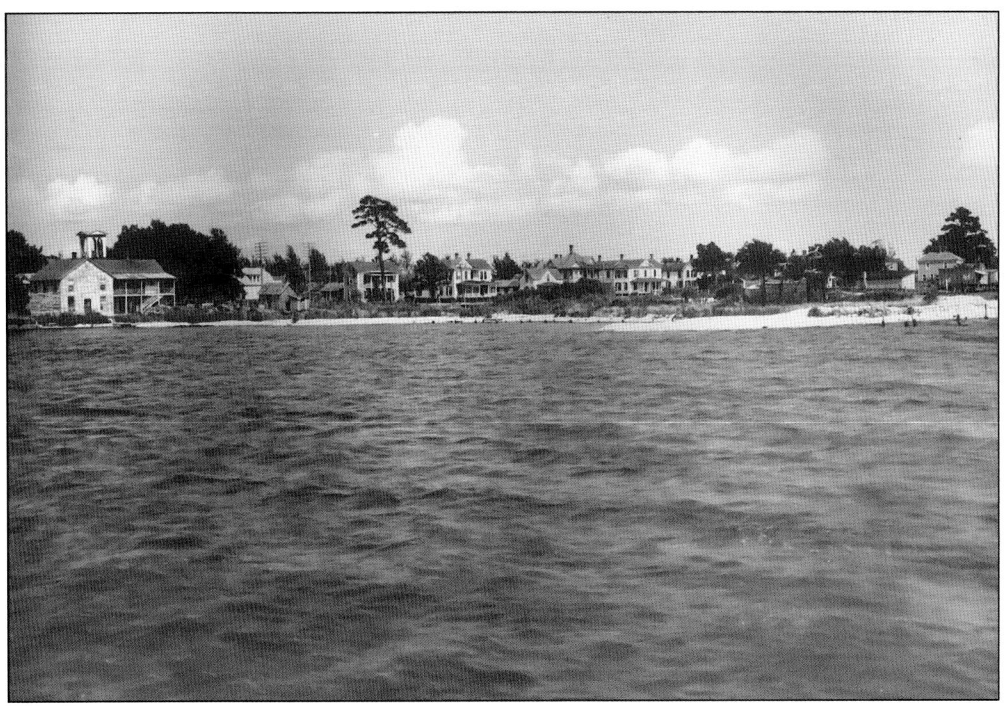

This shoreline view of Belhaven around 1920 shows the Atlantic View Hotel, c. 1910, on the left, and the homes on Water Street. (Courtesy of W. Mayo.)

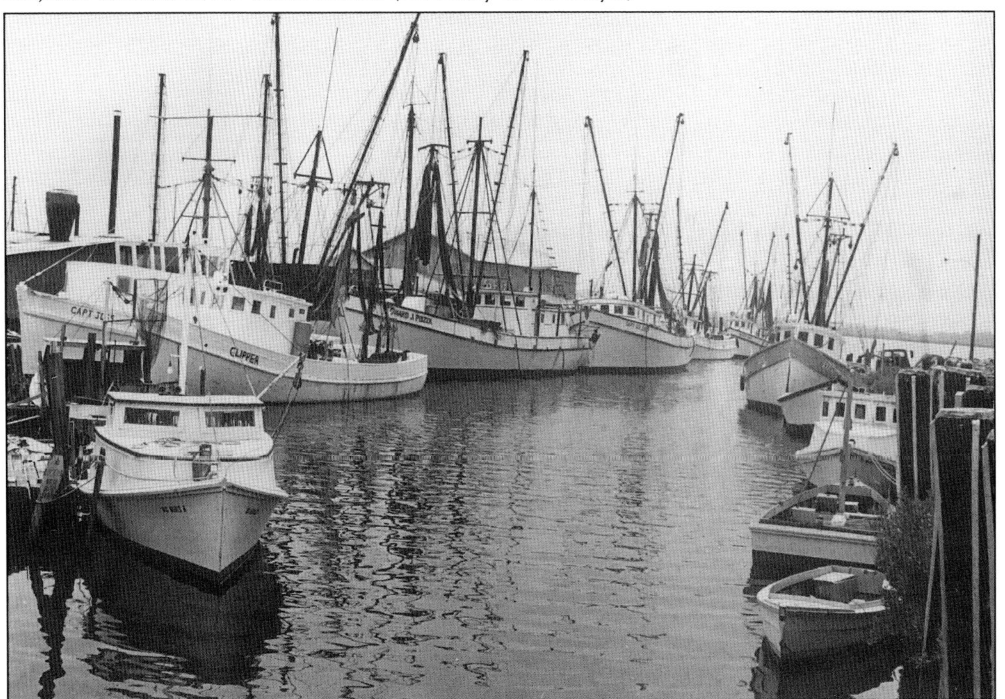

The commercial shrimp boat fleet lay at rest along the Belhaven waterfront on the Pungo River in the early 1960s. Commercial fishing was a major industry in Belhaven until the early 1970s, when it began to decline. (Courtesy of Bill Hamilton.)

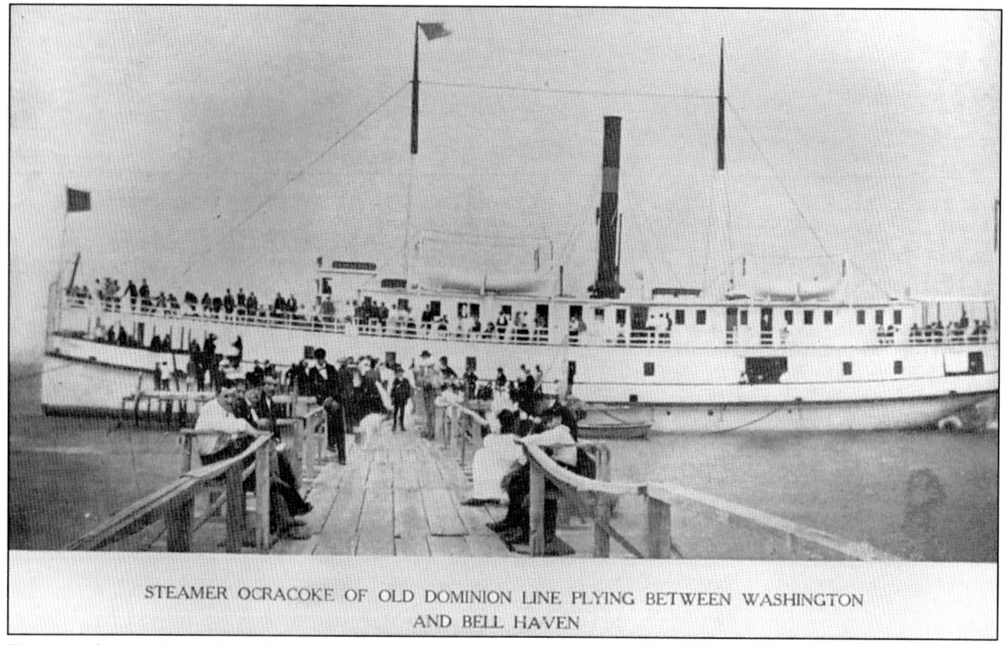

During the 1890s and well into the 1900s, the steamer *Ockracoke* of the Old Dominion Steamship Co. made a regularly scheduled overnight journey to Ockracoke Island from Belhaven (called Bell Haven in 1890). Old Dominion Steamship Co. operated two passenger boats and several freight vessels from their pier at the foot of Haslin Street. (Courtesy of NC Historic Edenton.)

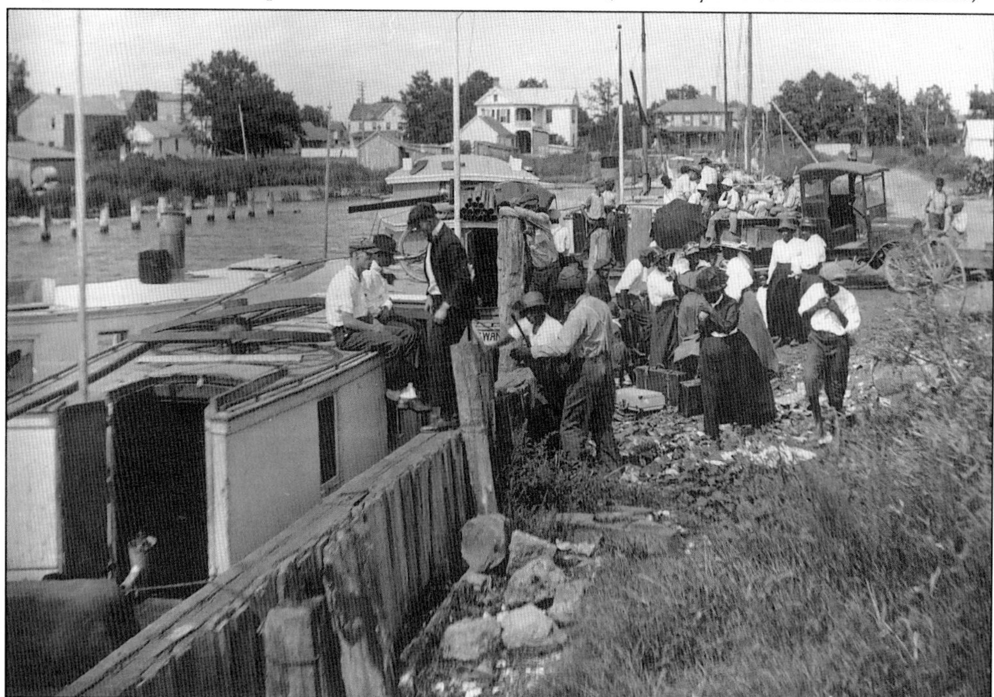

This scene is thought to depict crab or net fishing boats at the Town Dock in the 1920s. The white house in the background was the Keaton home, and to the right was the Jordon home. (Courtesy of W. Mayo.)

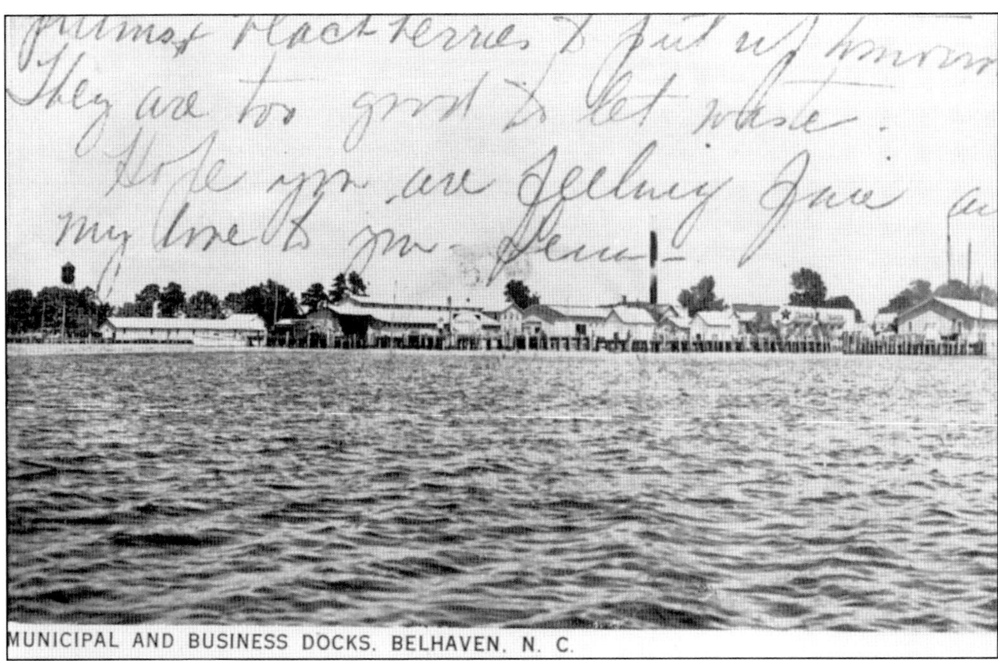

Pictured here are the municipal and business docks in Belhaven around 1941. They are, from left to right, Clyde Porter's Belhaven Fish and Oyster Co., Ruark's Belhaven Fish Processing Co., Standard Oil dock, Texaco dock, and the Town Dock. (Postcard courtesy of Oden's Store.)

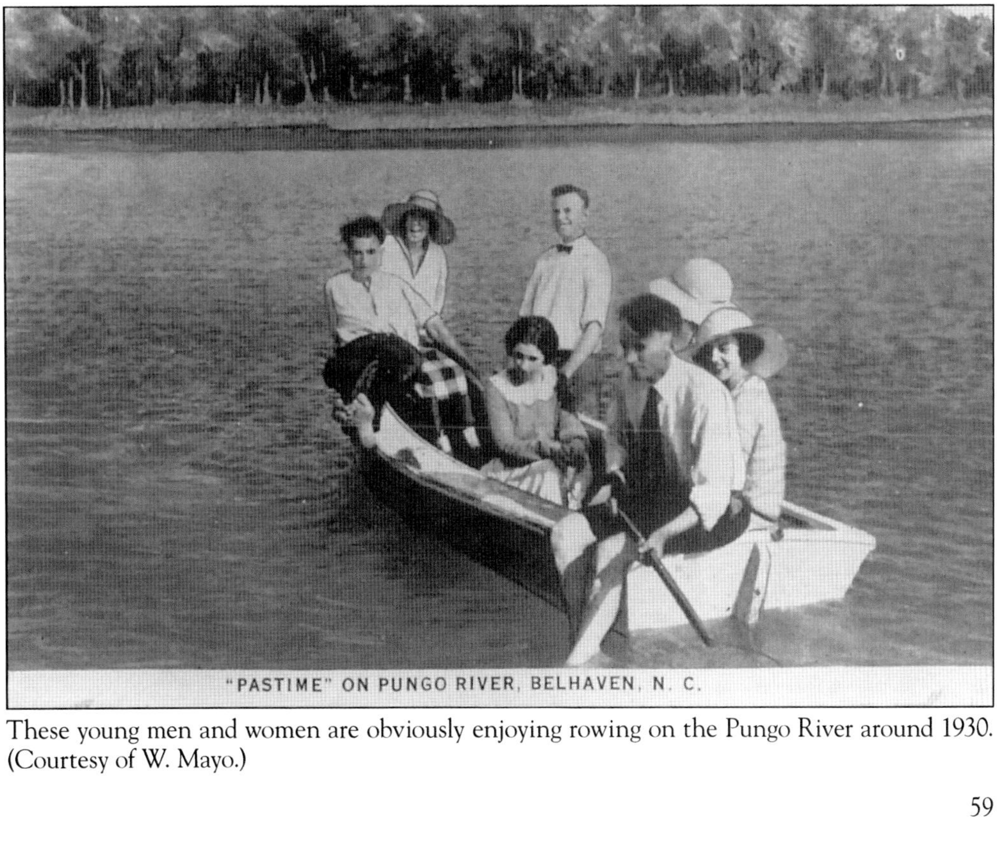

"PASTIME" ON PUNGO RIVER, BELHAVEN, N. C.

These young men and women are obviously enjoying rowing on the Pungo River around 1930. (Courtesy of W. Mayo.)

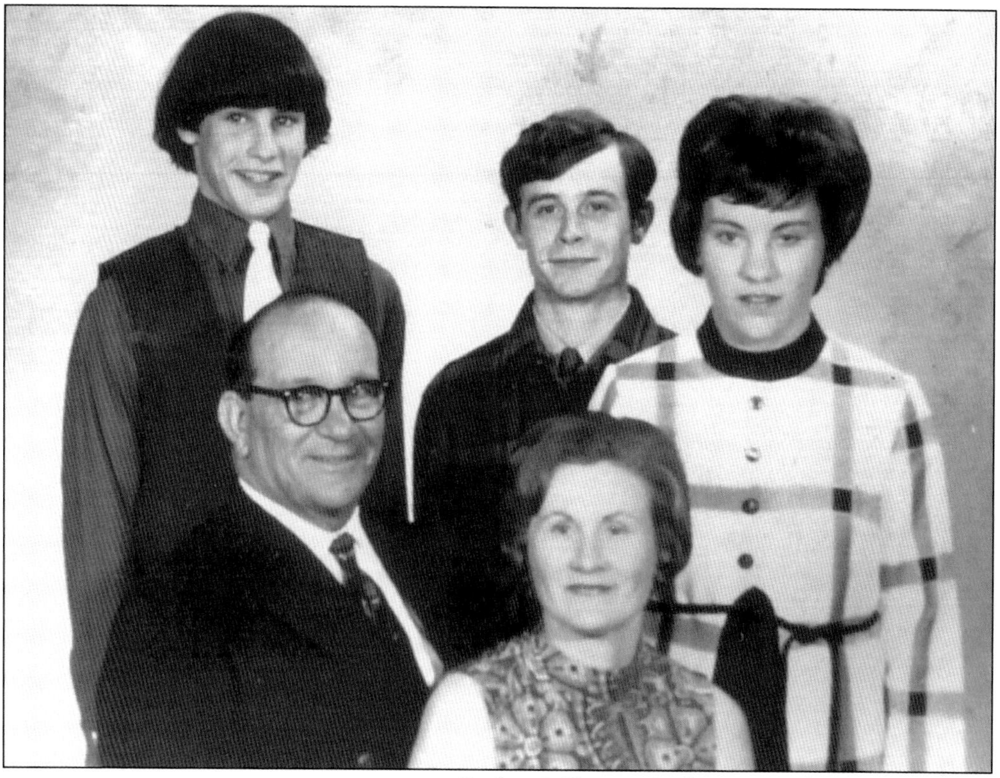

Frederick Phineas Latham started his seed and equipment company in 1917. Fred was the originator of a breed of two-ear corn stalk. His company was succeeded by the Charles Frederick Latham Co. at 147 Water Street in 1961. This friendly family can get you just about anything required for your farm equipment or lawnmower. From left to right are (top row) Seth David (1955–), Charles Frederick Jr. (1948–), and Karen Faye (1952–); (bottom row) Charles Frederick Sr. (1922–) and wife, Lyda Marie "Ann" Cuthrell (1928–). (Courtesy of C.F. Latham.)

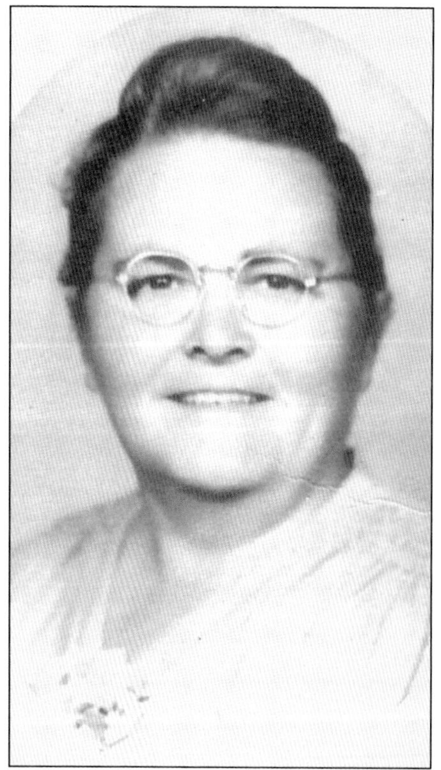

Hattie Elizabeth Everett Foreman was born in 1890 and died in 1957. Hattie married William Scott Foreman, who was a carpenter with Interstate Cooperage Lumber Co. in Belhaven. She was the sister of Robert Everett Sr., and her father was David Donaldson Everett. When Hattie and Scott were first married, Hattie licensed their home as a boarding house to accommodate Scott's fellow workers at Interstate Cooperage Lumber Co. (Courtesy of Jean Bowen.)

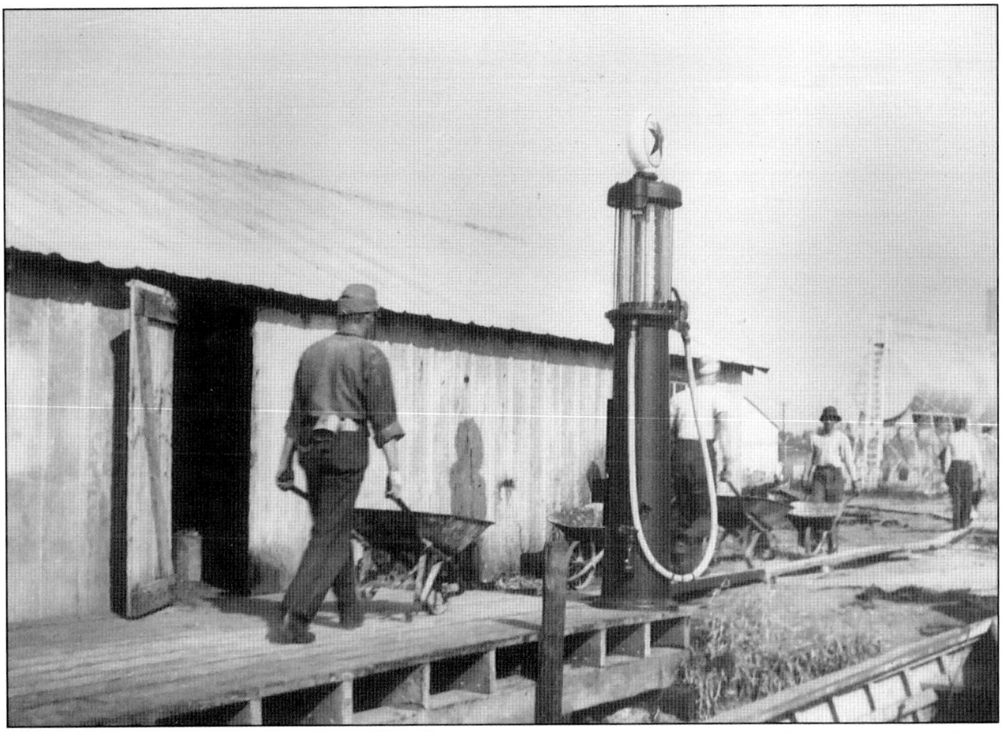

The giant Interstate Cooperage Lumber Company started operations in 1906 and was a subsidiary of the Standard Oil Company. This firm had up to 900 employees by 1914. Its main production was boxes and barrels for Standard Oil for the shipment of oil and oil products. Interstate owned several hundred thousand acres of timberland. (Courtesy of Louis G. May.)

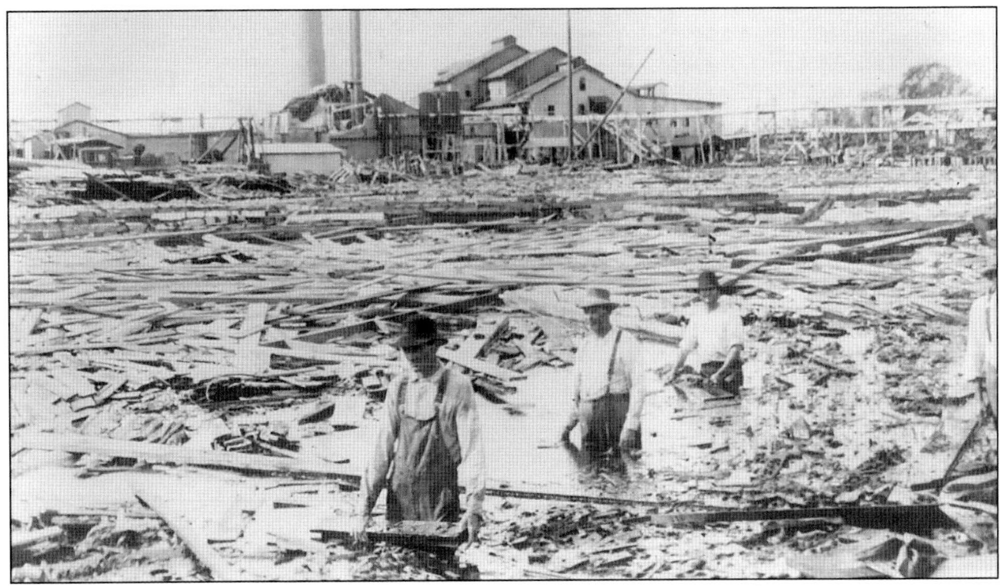

These may be the same workers shown above cleaning up the debris at the Interstate Cooperage Lumber Company after the 1913 hurricane devastated Belhaven. This was the worst hurricane ever recorded for eastern North Carolina until Hurricane Floyd in 1999. Interstate quickly rebuilt its large plant. (Courtesy of Louis G. May.)

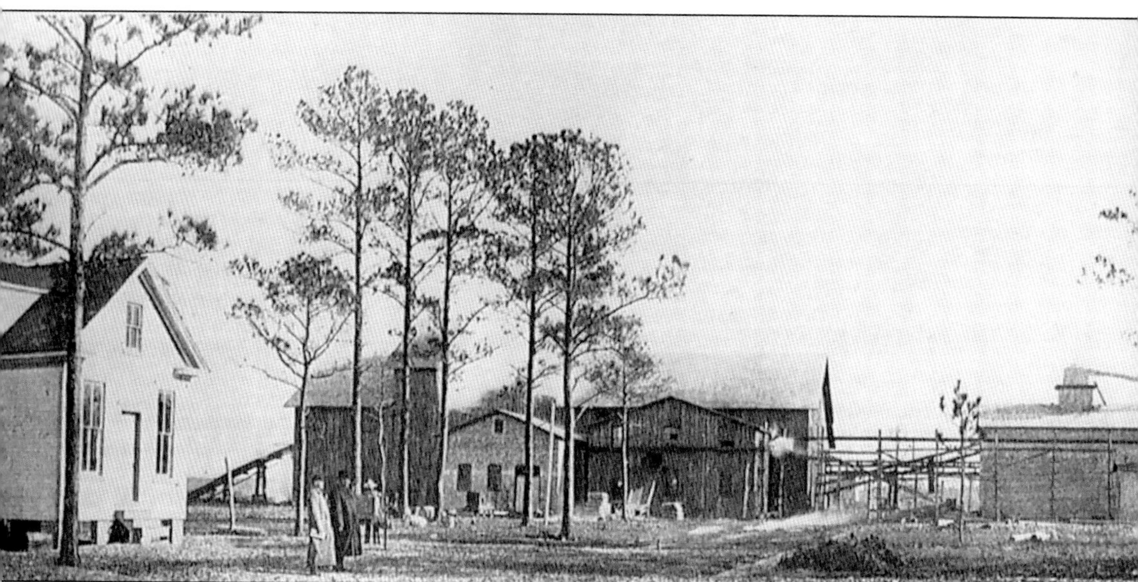

This is a panoramic view of the magnificent new plant of the John L. Roper Lumber Co. at Belhaven. "From left to right are the enormous buildings, embracing rough lumber shed, ripping mill, planing mill, dressed stock shed, and shipping tracks (throughout the entire

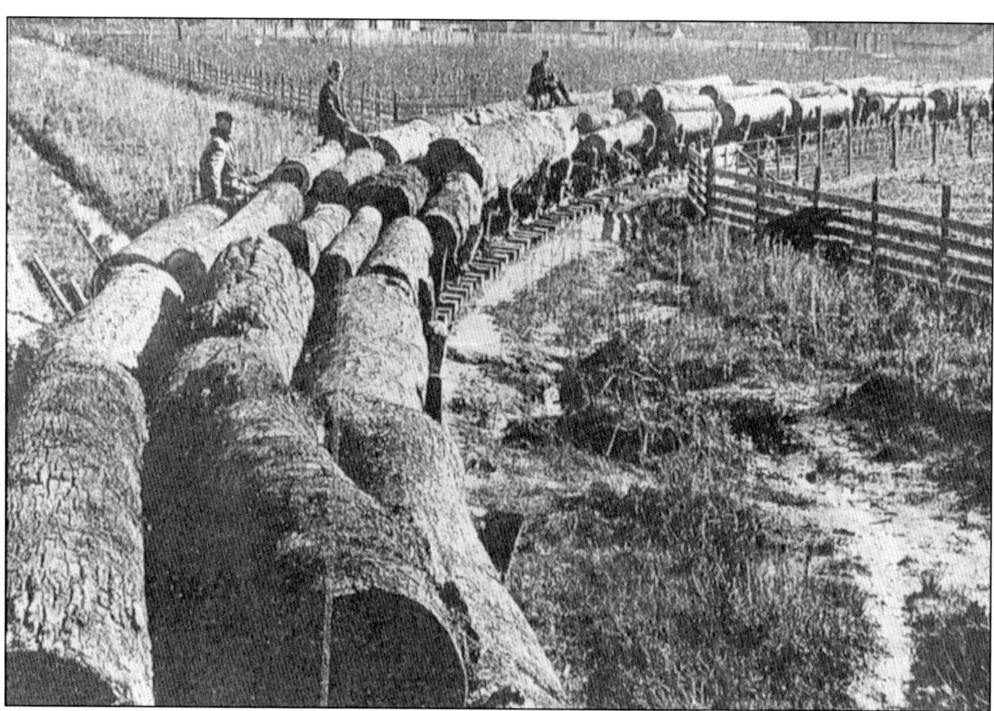

This log train is delivering sourwood trees to the John L. Roper Lumber Mill in 1913. The man in the middle appears to be Surry Parker. (Courtesy of Louis G. May.)

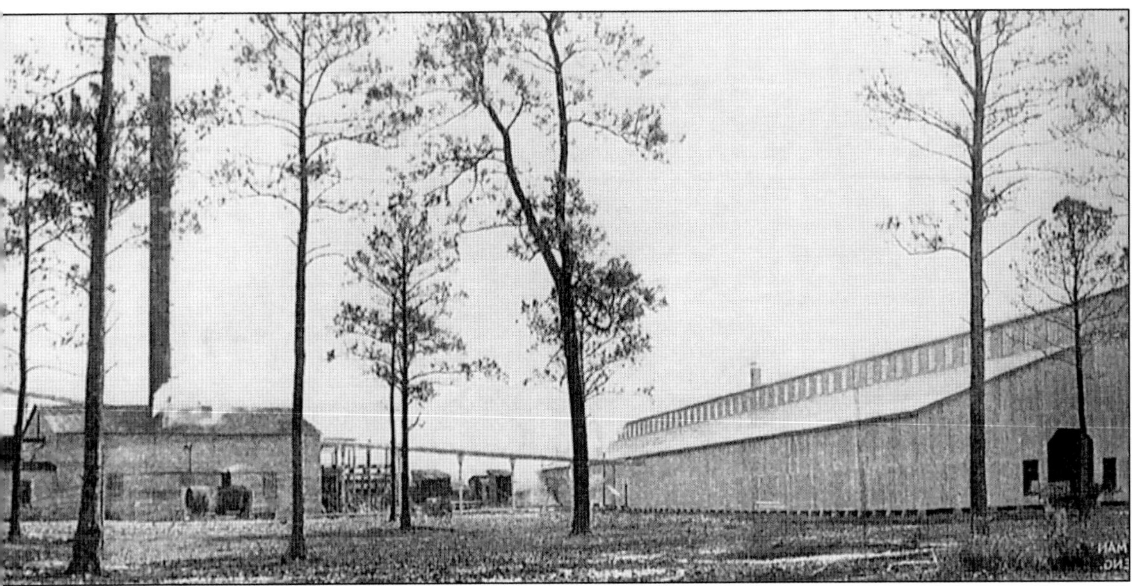

building); the power house, sawmill, and mill office are on the extreme left." (From *American Lumberman*, April 27, 1907; courtesy of Louis G. May.)

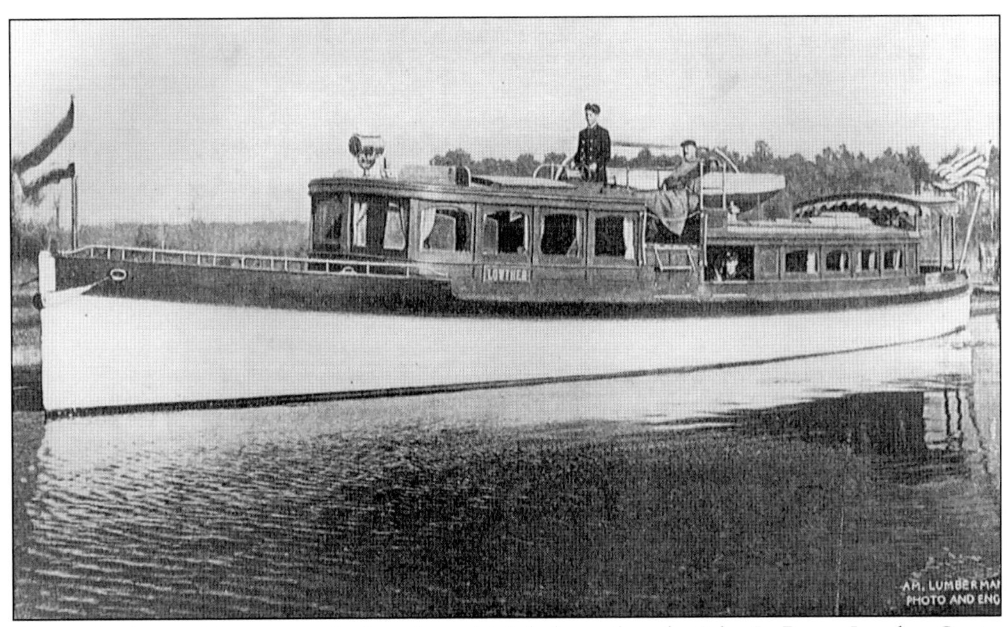

This is the beautiful motor yacht *Lowther*, which belonged to the John L. Roper Lumber Co. in 1906. The *Lowther* was used by the company officers and their guests to visit Roper mills, all of which were accessible by water. (Courtesy of Louis G. May.)

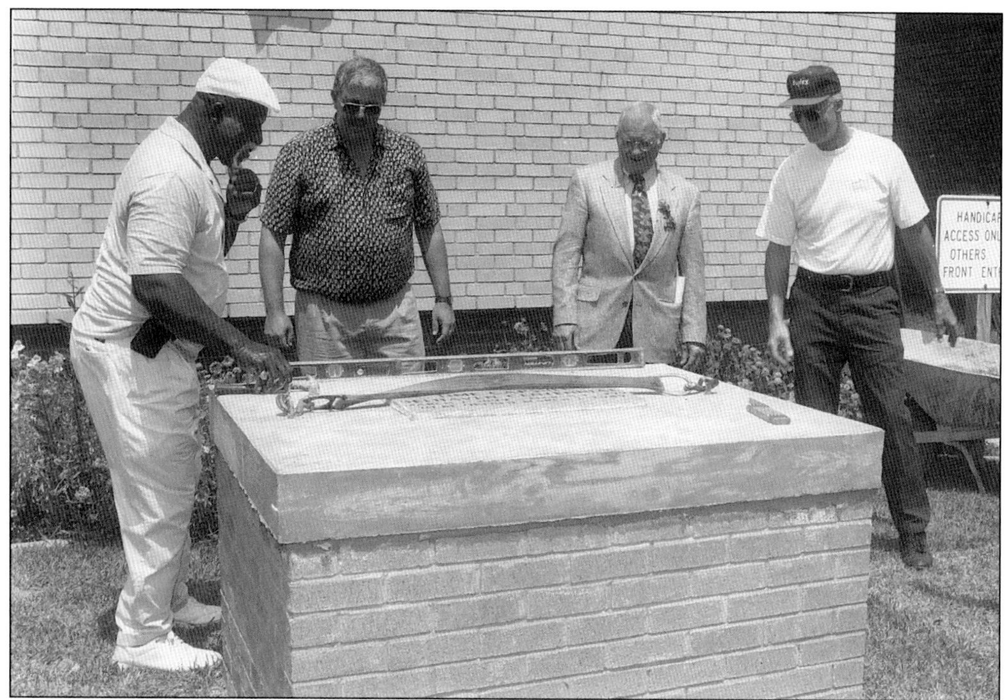

On March 7, 1999, the town of Belhaven celebrated its centennial by burying a time capsule. This tomb is scheduled to be opened on March 7, 2049. From left to right are brick mason Walter Spencer, checking the level of the cover he has just cemented on the tomb, and Town Manager Tim Johnson, Mayor Charles Boyette, and Superintendent of Public Works C. Herring watch in approval. (Photo by Louis Van Camp.)

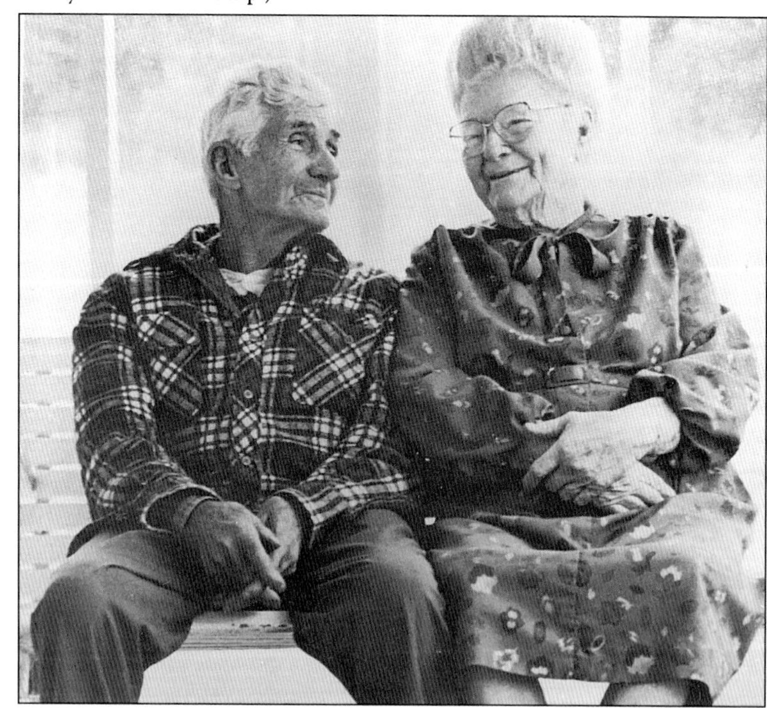

Capt. Dave Tate was a Pamlico River waterman for more than 70 years. Captain Tate and his wife, Lucy, were born and raised in the Pamlico Beach area, and they raised 12 children along the way. (Courtesy of Paul Nuremburg, BCM.)

Four

Chocowinity Township

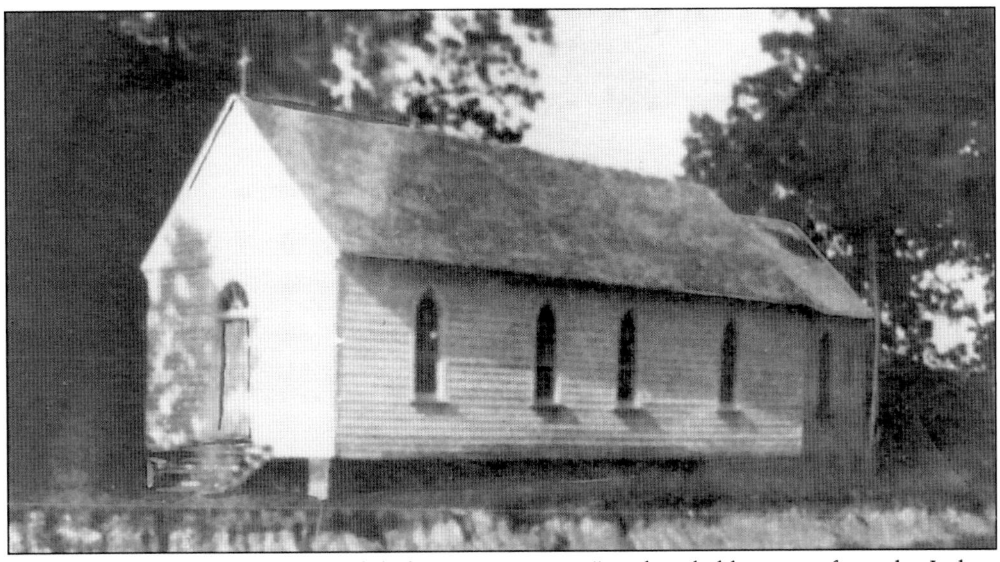

The name Chocowinity means "fish from many waters" and probably comes from the Indian spelling "chocowanateth" or "chockewinwhee." Before 1900, Chocowinity was known as "Godley's Crossroads." The Honorable N.C. Huges Jr. was the town's first mayor and town magistrate. He also founded the Trinity School, a co-ed boarding school, in 1851. Lacy Edwards was the first officer of the law. The original Blount's Chapel (now Trinity Church) was built in 1774 by Giles Shute and John Harrington for the Reverend Nathaniel Blount. The chapel was built on land donated by John and Rhoda O'Hagen that was located on Taylor Road. The chapel was moved to a new location on NC 33 west in 1939 by Richard Carrow and adjoined to the parish house. Reverend Blount served this chapel until his death in 1816. (Courtesy of Trinity Church.)

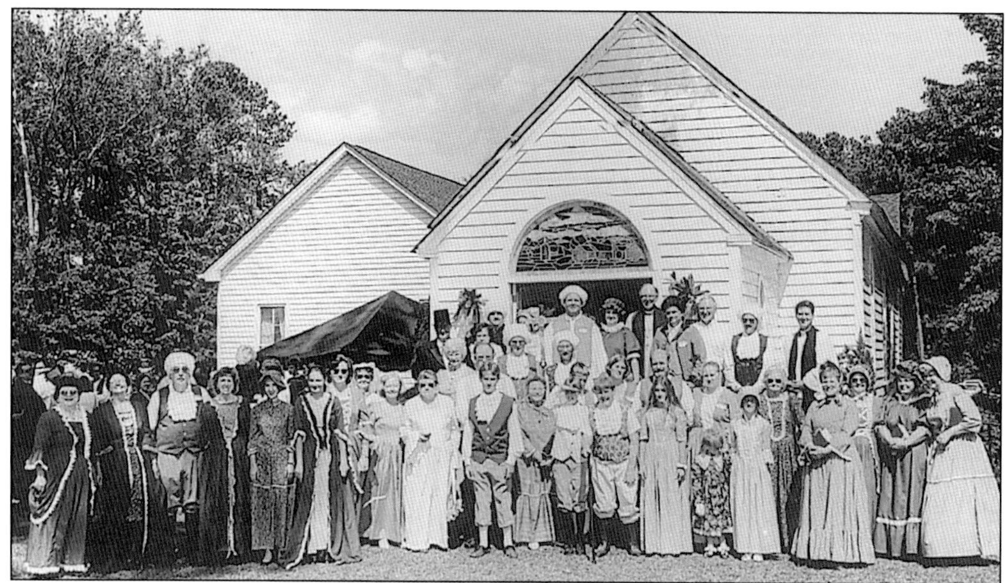

The heirs of Chocowinity's colonial past gather to announce the celebration of the 225th anniversary of Trinity Church in 1999. As part of the celebration, the church members buried a time capsule to be unearthed in 2049. From left to right are (front row) Pat Baker, Becky Deans, Hallet Deans, Donna Deans, Meridith Deans, Emily Deans, Sandy Deans, Marge Willis, Sandy Bowers, Lena Page, David Deans Jr., Estelle Guthrie, Robby Deans, Joseph Deans, Melanie Deans, Leah Rowe, Courtney Carrow, Jeanette Rowe, Gray Albritton, Linda Lewis, Michelle Sparrow, and Mary Jo Guthrie; (middle row, from edge of black tent) Louise Hill, Steve Hill, Sammy Deans, David Deans Sr., Kyle Nobles, Lou Sullivan, and Amanda Parker; (back row) Morgan Tuck, Annie Furman, David Sparrow, Daisy Bennett, Chuck Powell, Ginger Powell, Bishop Clifton Daniel III, Greg Purser, John Gray Blount, Hal Deans, and Rev. Michael C. Nations. (Courtesy of Rusty Walker.)

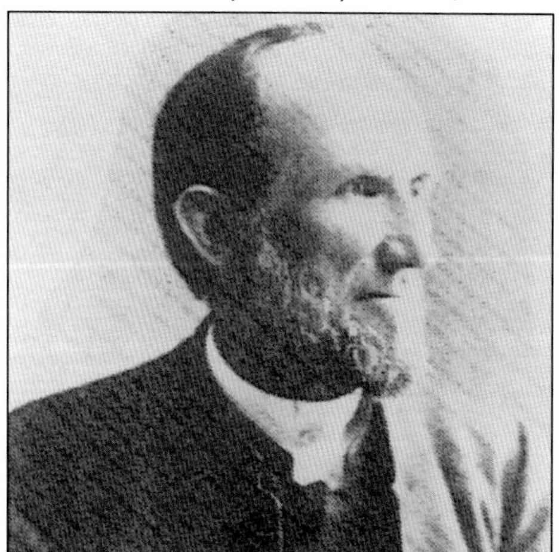

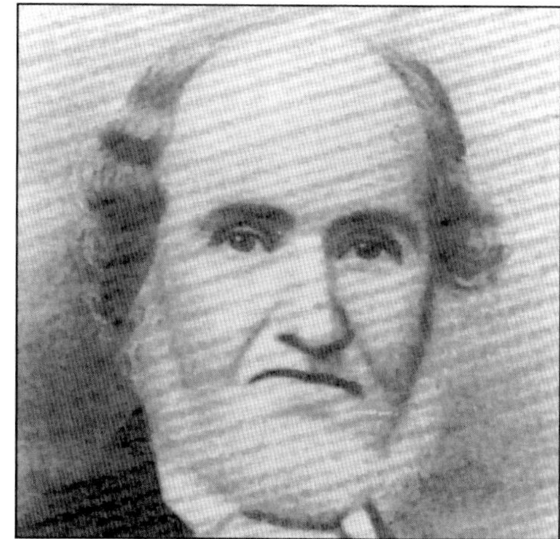

Left: The Reverend Israel Harding (1829–1891), served as rector of Trinity Church from 1868 to 1871, and again from 1873 to 1881. His wife, Susan Mary, was born in 1836 and died in 1907. (Courtesy of Trinity Church.)

Right: The Reverend Nicholas Collin Huges (1822–1893) was rector of the Chapel of the Holy Cross Church in Aurora in 1885, where he held a service once a month. Reverend Huges was rector of Trinity Chapel three times between 1880 and 1893, the year he died.

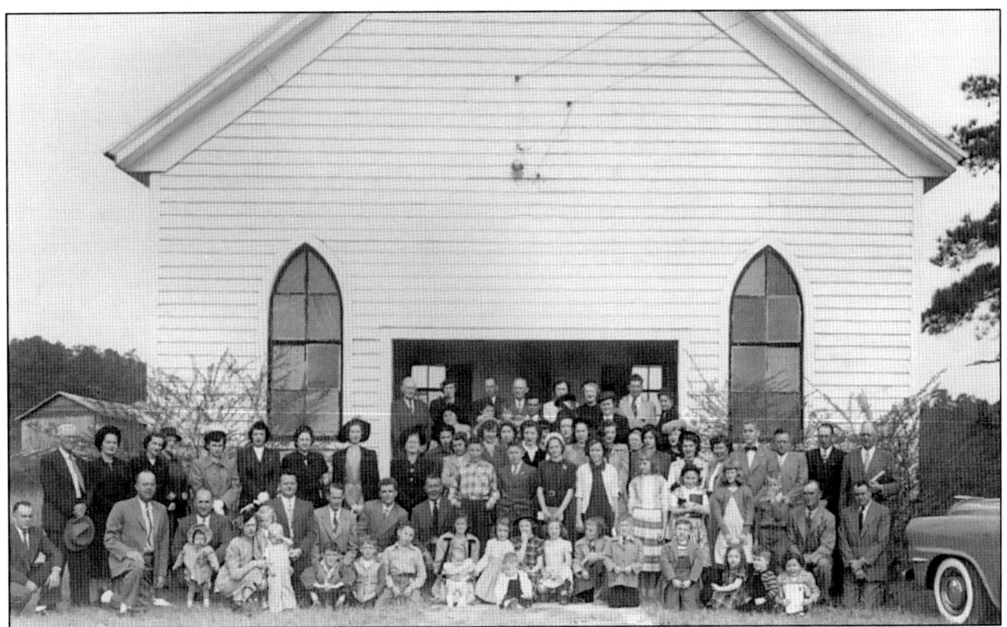

This 1948 photo of the Chocowinity Missionary Baptist Church includes Tom E. Adams, Mamie Taylor Whitley, Bobby Taylor, James D. Thomas, Bessie Jones, Mr. ? Ballance, Marjorie Sumrell, Hazel Ballance, Jake Ballance, Mrs. Lucy Smith Mill, Delores Kirkley, Sally Godley Toler, Mary Joe Ballance, Mary Lou Hill, Pet Fuller, Ester Lee Hickman, Kathleen McRoy, Mamie Taylor Powers, Rita Hicks Potter, Mary Woolard Mills, Isaac Emanuel (Simps) Taylor, Mrs. Ester (Earl) Hickman, Mrs. Pat Patrick, Ione Hays Taylor, Berth McRoy, Louise Davis Thomas, Carolyn Jones, Mrs. ? Jones, Keel Adams Mills, Francie Langley, Betsy Mills, Elvira Kirkley, Jean McRoy, Mrs. Van (Lala) Dixon, Lyndal Dixon Mills, Charles Hickman, Hillary Thomas Dumay Mills, Reverend ? Hoell, Patrica Jones, Mayhew McRoy, Earl Cutler, Joe Mills, Charlie Toler, Pat Patrick, Mary Dell, Martha McRoy, Ann McRoy, Phil McRoy, Johnnie Jones, Josh Mills, Tonnie Cutler, Raymond Ballance, Tonnice Man, Earl Hickman, Janet Ballance, Mary Etta Sawyer, Jessie Toler, Joe David, Josh (Jay) Mills Jr., Mary Helen Toler, Charles Toler Jr., and Carol Jones. (Courtesy of Marjorie Sumrell.)

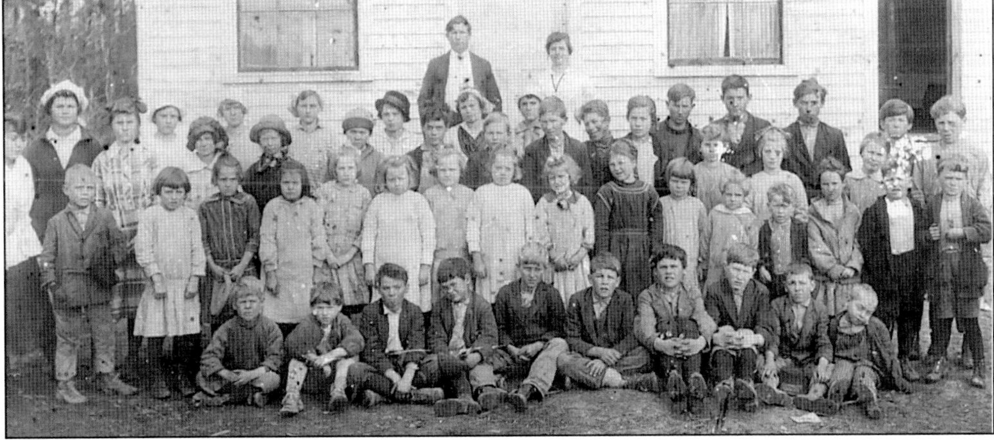

In 1923, the Marsden School (later demolished) was located next to the Dunbar Store on the southeast corner of the intersection of NC 33 and NC 17. This school accommodated grades one through seven. (Courtesy of Marjorie Sumrell.)

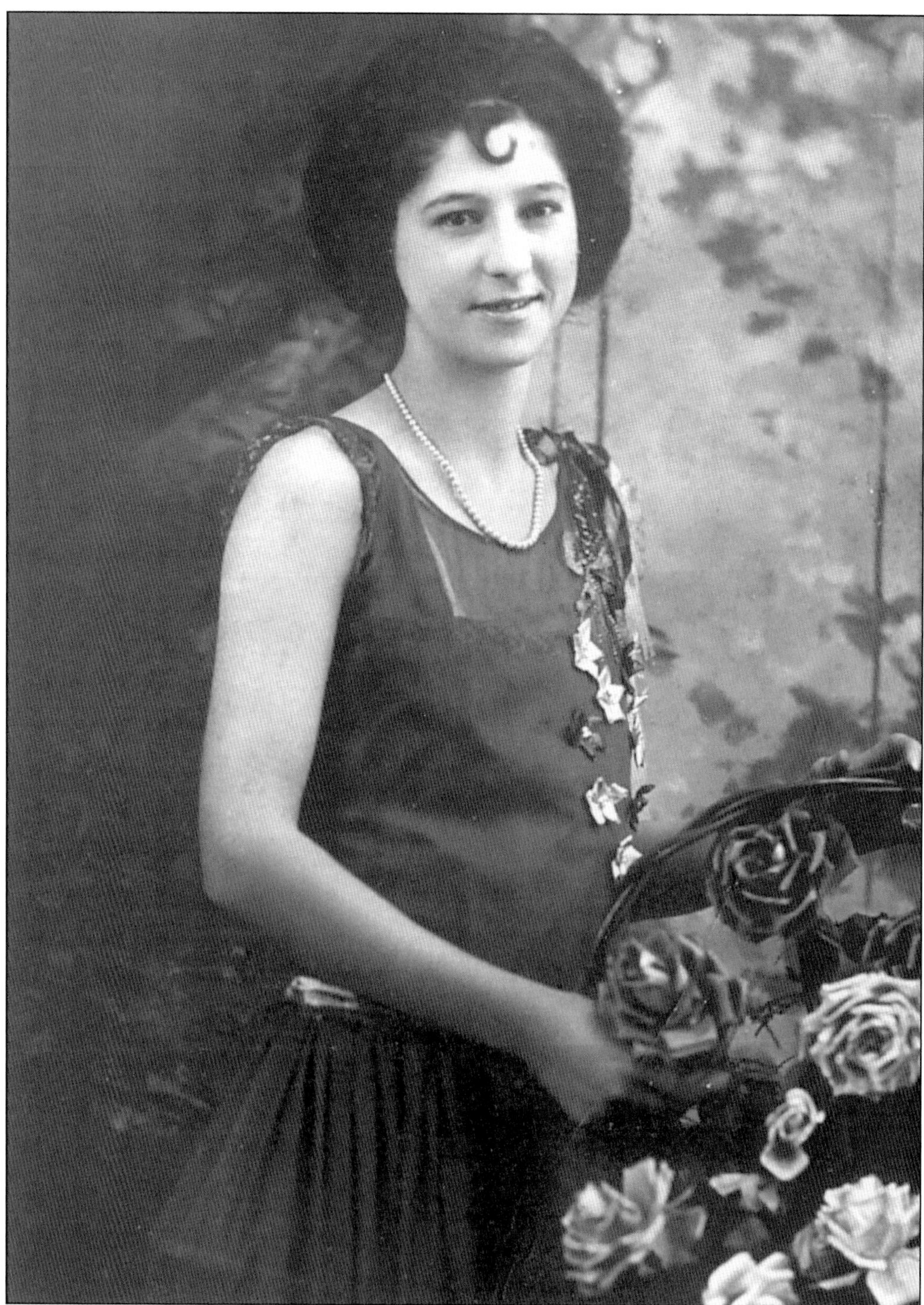

Lovely Myrtie Taylor Asby was born in 1902 and lived until 1999. She married Kenneth Asby of Pinetown in 1920. Myrtie bore twins, Maud and Kenneth, in 1921. Unfortunately, baby Kenneth died at birth and Maud survived only until 1923. Myrtie taught at the Hodges School on the Market Street Extension and later at Kings Business College in Raleigh. (Courtesy of Marjorie Sumrell.)

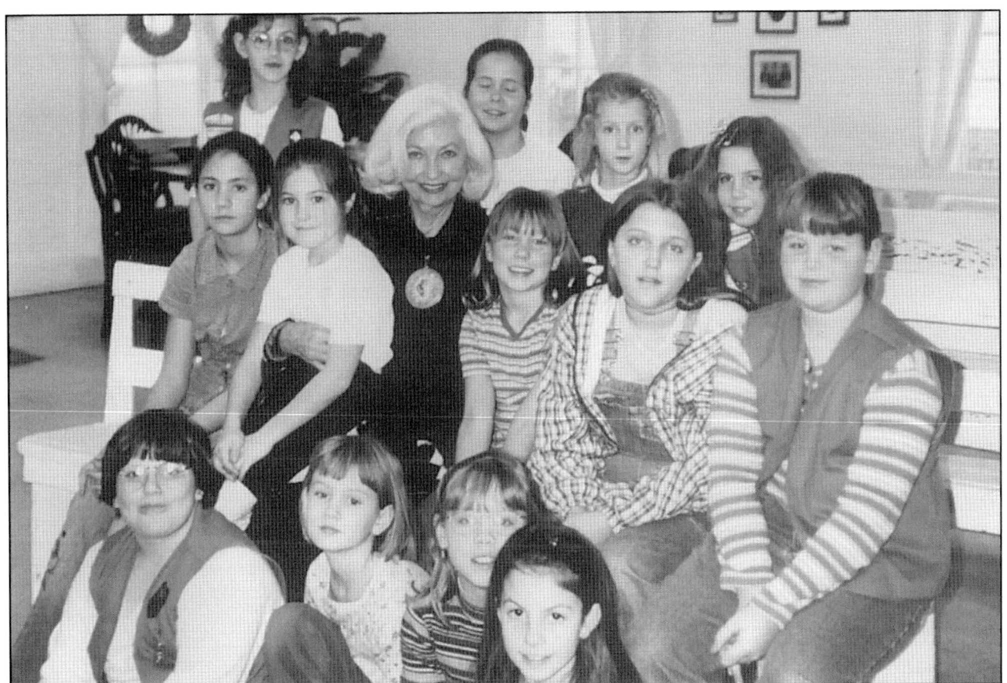

Washington resident Kay Currie shares details of her broadcasting career with the Trinity Church–sponsored Girl Scout Troop 145 on February 12, 2000. Kay showed her photos of famous people to the excited scouts. Included were interviews with Carol Channing, Joan Crawford, Pres. Lyndon Johnson, Marlo Thomas, and others. Pictured, from left to right, are (front row) Rhesa Jo Sparrow, Kelly Hardison, Dorethy Jones, and Emily Smith; (middle row) Jenifer Perez, Kaitlyn Moore, Kay Currie, Megan Bright, Lara Senteno, and Sloan Avery; (back row) Courtney Carrow, Ginnilyn Wood, Jessica Taylor, and Dawn Hill. (Courtesy of Kay Currie.)

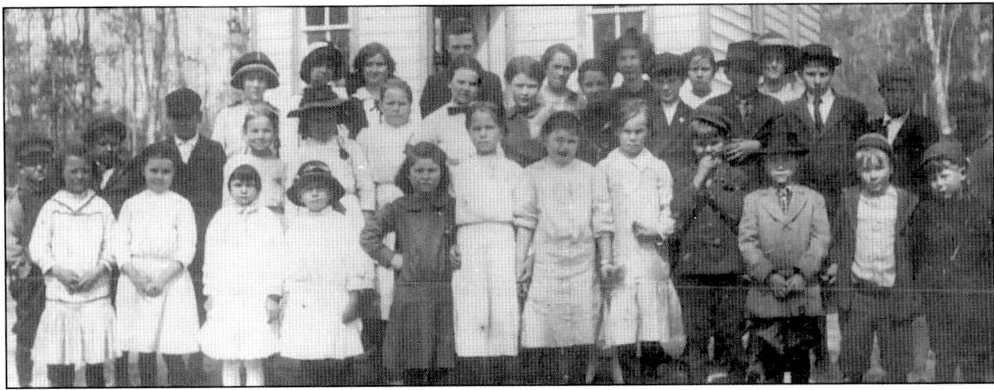

The Crow Branch School (later demolished) was located on Grey Road off SR 1129 in Chocowinity. The class of 1913 included, from left to right, (front row) Mary Clark, Myrtle Clark Jones Linton, Ruby Warren Mills, Velma Powell O'Carroll, unidentified, unidentified, Marverna Hill Edwards, Eula Clark, unidentified, Wesley Grissom, Washington Bailey Clark, and Heber Nobles; (middle row) Thurman Downs, six unidentified, Gertie Moore, Clem Clark, Oscar Clark, and two unidentified; (back row) Martha Clark, Hattie Hill Dixon, Easie Barr Waters, Barnie Barr, Viola Smithwick (teacher), unidentified, Laura McRoy Clark, Nola Porter, and Rosa Moore. (Courtesy of Marjorie Sumrell.)

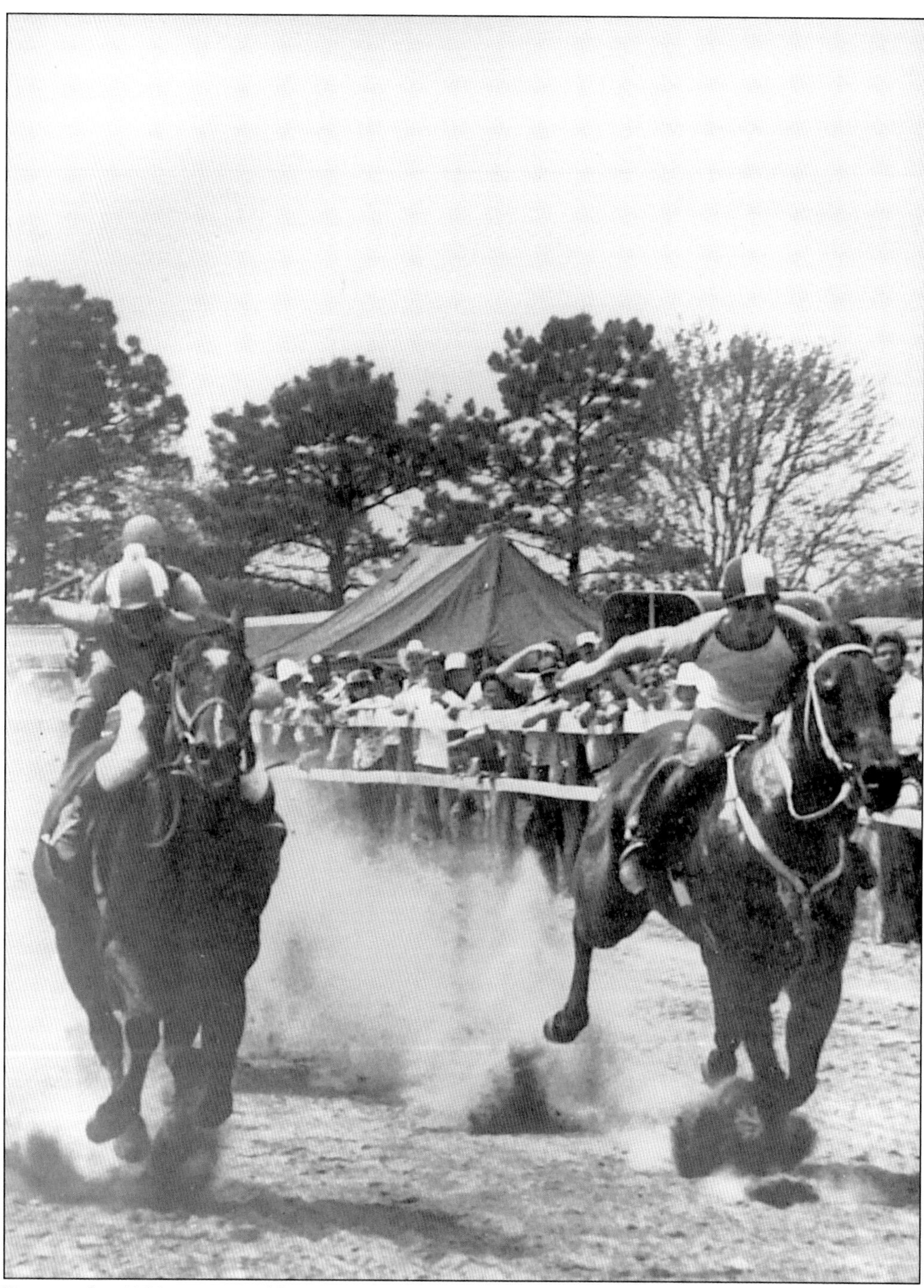

During the 1980s, you could see exciting quarter horse racing at Choco Downs Race Track, a quarter-mile race track built by the Chocowinity Saddle Clue. The track was located across from the Union Chapel Church just south of Chocowinity on NC 17. "Choco was a spin-off of weekend trail rides," said Jerome Barr, who was president of the non-profit association. "We gave all our profits to charity," said Barr. Pictured here coming down the stretch is Larry Brown on Leg Man and Frankie Piscopo (on the right) in a close match race. (Courtesy of Ric Barnes.)

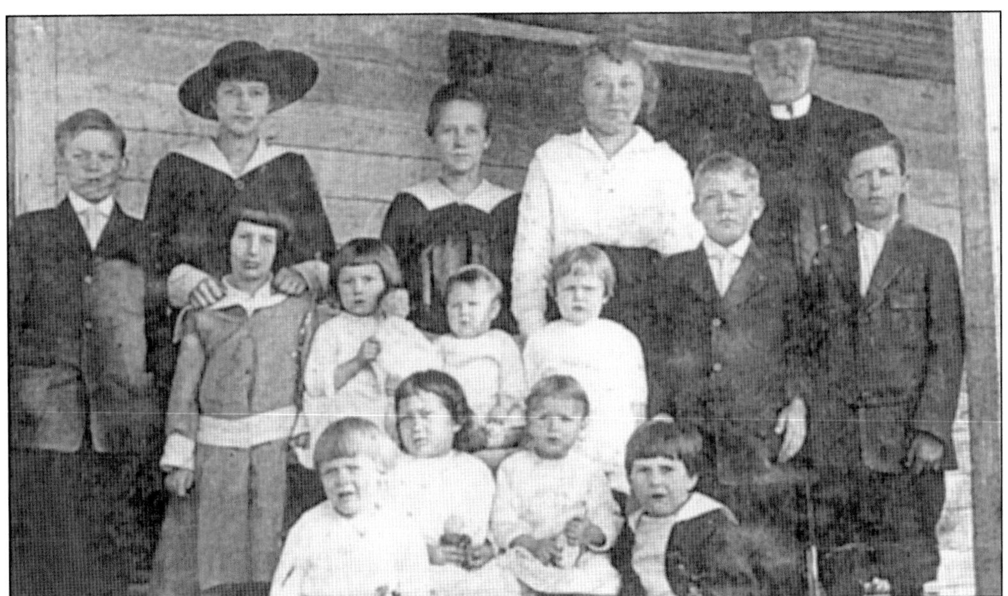

Pictured here are the descendants of Reverend Charles Daniel Malone (1845–1927) and wife Clara Elizabeth Joyner Malone (1845–1895). Reverend Malone was ordained a deacon in 1908 and led St. Thomas parish in Bath. His descendants include, from left to right, (front row) Ruby Malone, Mary Ethel Wynn, Elizabeth Wynn, and Charles Nathaniel Fuller; (middle row) Helen Lucille Fuller, Margaret Malone Fuller McKee, Clarence Blount Fuller, and Elmer Taylor; (back row) Leon Malone, Mary Elizabeth Fuller Taylor, Emily Estelle Fuller, Bessie Malone, and Rev. C.D. Malone. (Courtesy of Becky Deans.)

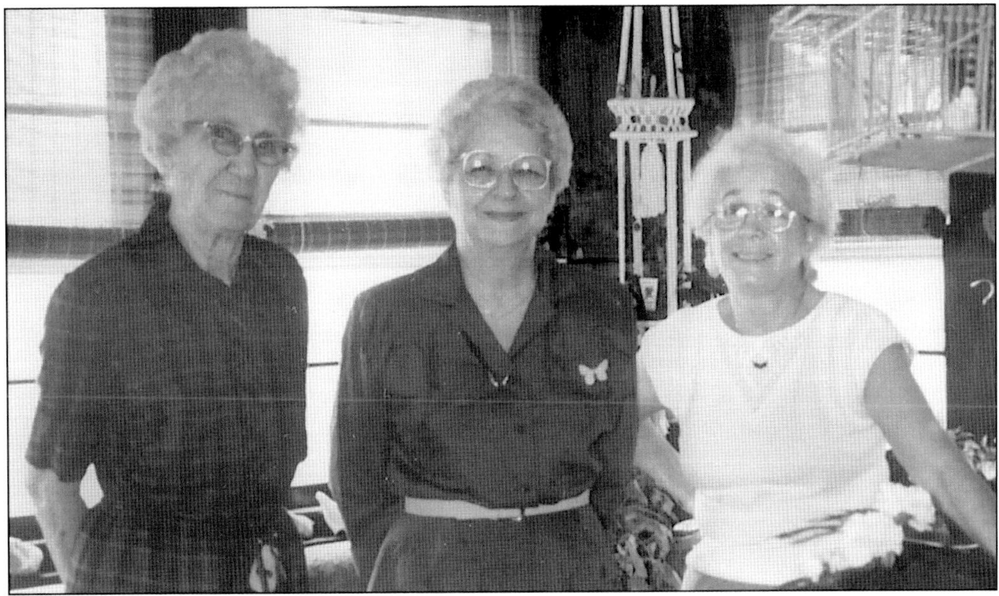

These three Chocowinity ladies were the very best of friends, and they should be because they are related. Here they are gathered together in Marjorie Sumrell's kitchen in 1986. From left to right are Marjorie's mother Mamie Taylor Whitley (1900–1991), Marjorie's sister Edna Whitley Spruill (1921–), and of course, Marjorie Whitley Sumrell (1924–). (Courtesy of Marjorie Sumrell.)

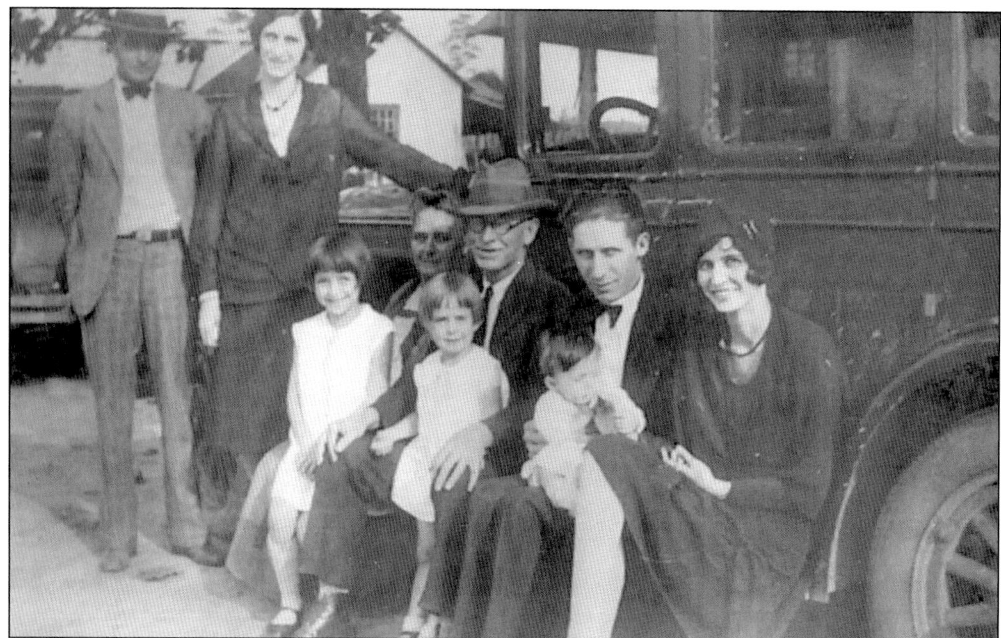

Isaac Emanuel Taylor, a blacksmith, poses here with his family in 1929. From left to right (standing) are Ed and Mamie T. Whitley; (seated) Edna T. Whitley in Rachel Taylor's lap; Marjorie Whitley in papa I. E. Taylor's lap; baby Shirley sits between Allan Taylor and his wife, Dorethy Hodges Taylor. (Courtesy of Marjorie Sumrell.)

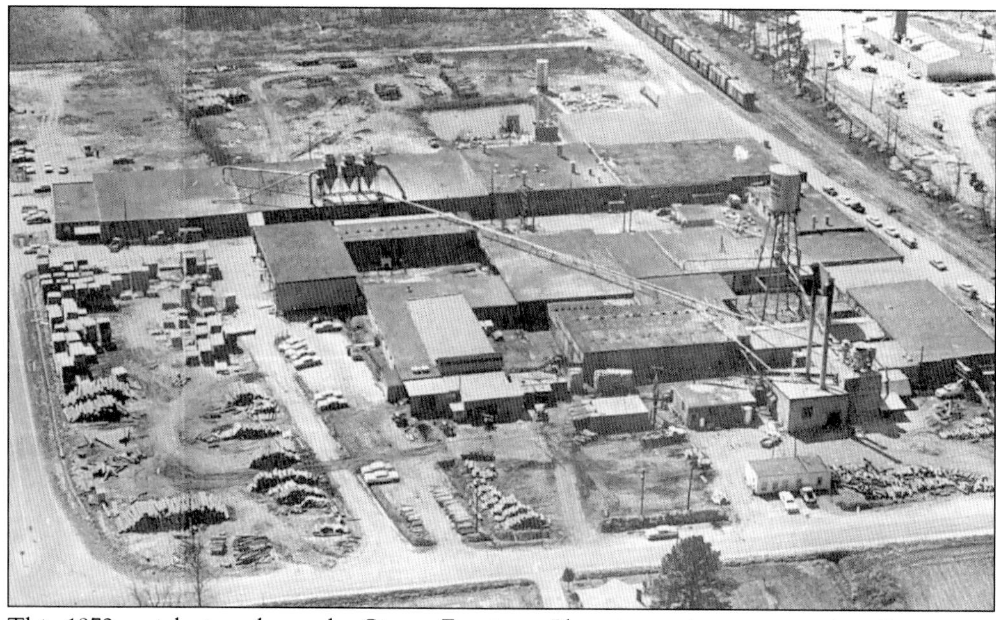

This 1972 aerial view shows the Singer Furniture Plant just prior to expansion. Singer was located on Patrick Lane off NC 17 and employed over 300 people—at least 100 of which lived in Chocowinity. The plant was originally the Edinburg Sawmill in 1948 and developed into Edinburg Industries by 1956. Later, it merged with Singer Sewing Machine Company. The Singer plant closed in 1997, and a company called Ami Lite Way occupied the building until February 2000. (Courtesy of BCM.)

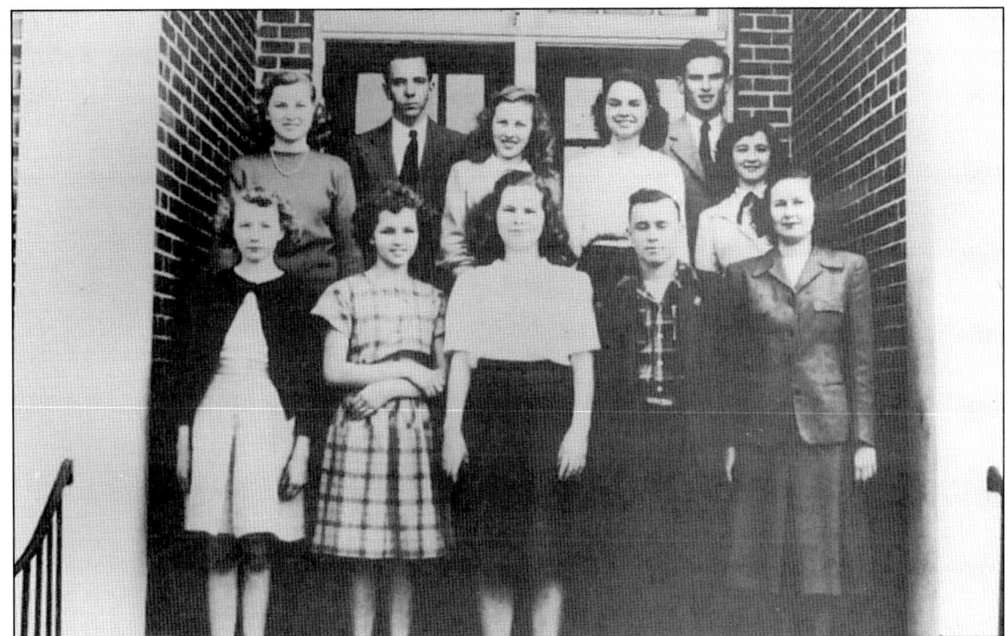

The Chocowinity High School *Chieftain* yearbook staff for 1948 included, from left to right, (front row) Lucille Smith, Beatrice Taylor, Mae Jones, Arthur Clark, and staff advisor Miss Josie Harding; (back row) Edna Paramore, Alton Taylor, Betsy Boyd, Doris Smith, David Chesson, and Estelle Carrow. (Courtesy of CHS.)

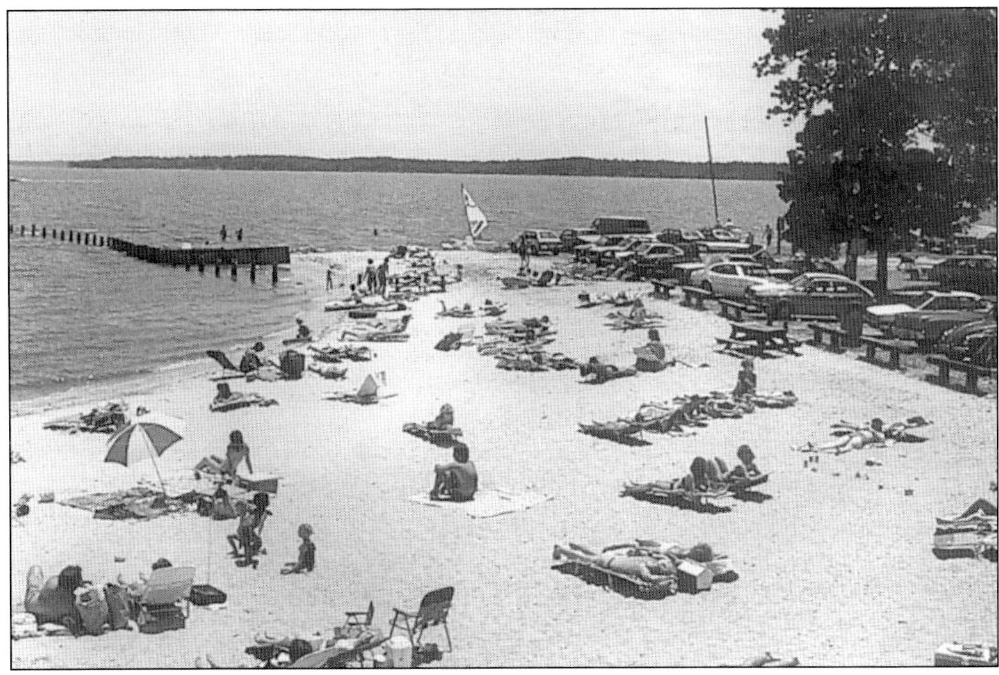

In 1945, farmer William Henry Whichard developed a portion of his peninsula property, which separates the Pamlico River from Chocowinity Bay, into a campground and full-service marina. Whichard's Beach is located at the end of SR 1166 (Whichard's Beach Road) from NC 17, about a mile south of Washington. (Courtesy of Whichard's Beach.)

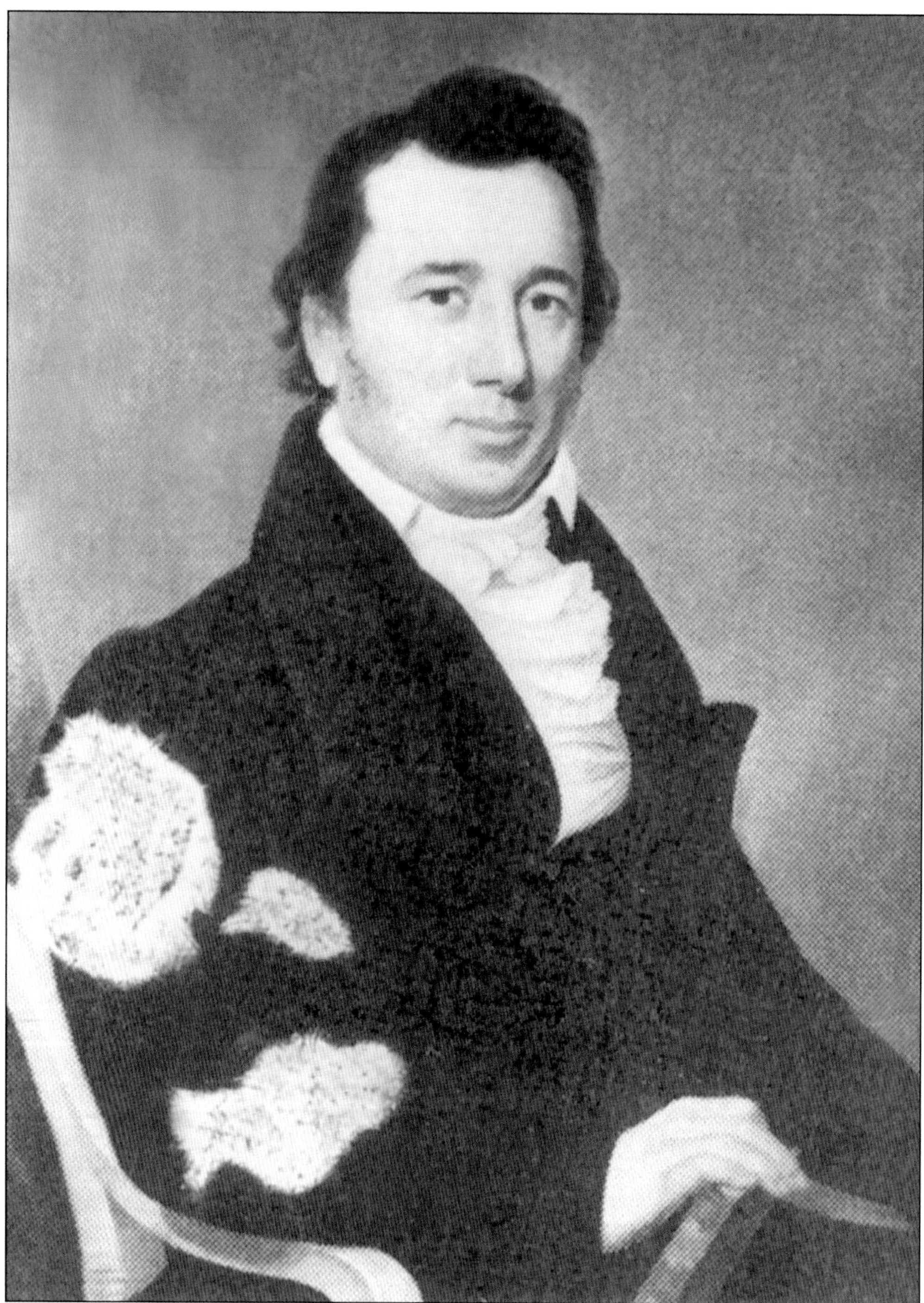

William Augustus Blount (1792–1867) was the son of John Gray Blount. He founded the 25,000-acre Meadowville Plantation in Chocowinity in 1834. At one time, this plantation required the service of some 100 slaves. General Blount was stationed in South Carolina during the War of 1812 and was elected a major general in the North Carolina militia after the war. (Portrait by Jacob Marling; courtesy of Philip Madre.)

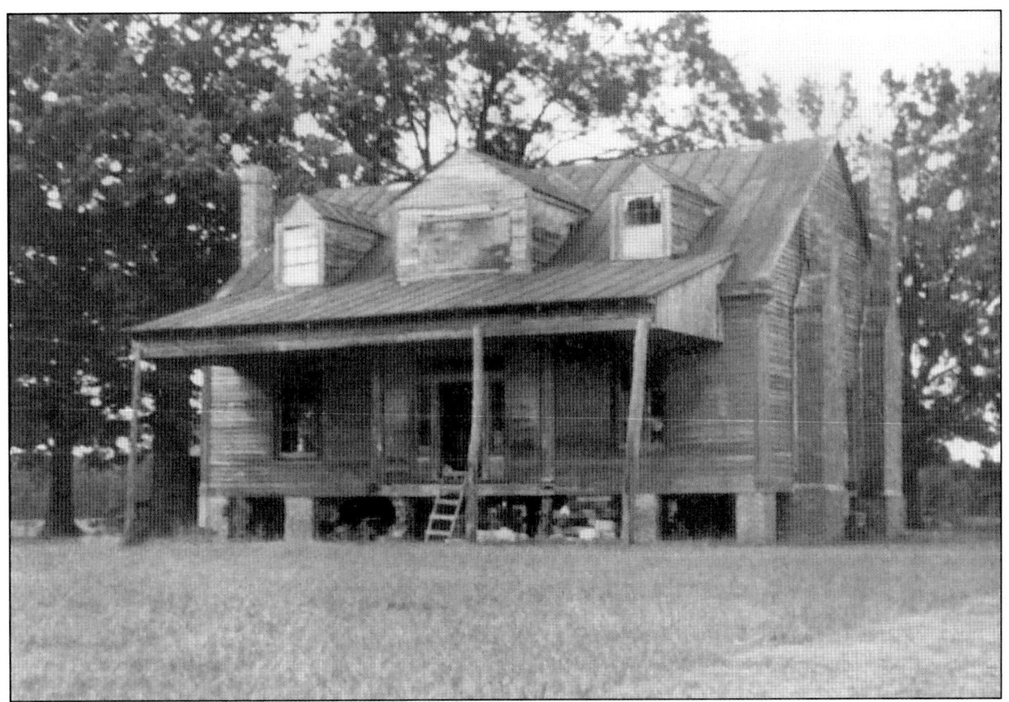

This was the condition of the William Augustus Blount Meadowville Plantation House in Chocowinity in 1982, after 50 years of neglect. Philip Madre bought and restored this fine old home and now farms a portion of the old plantation. (Courtesy of Philip Madre.)

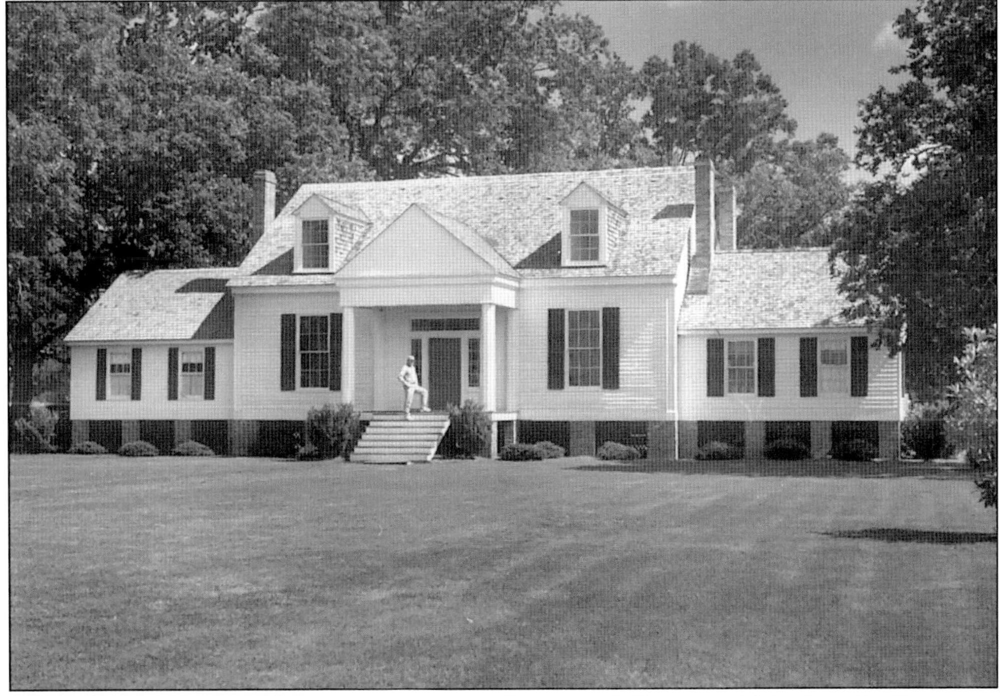

Owner Philip Madre stands on the front steps of his beautifully restored Meadowville Plantation House in the year 2000. (Photo by Louis Van Camp.)

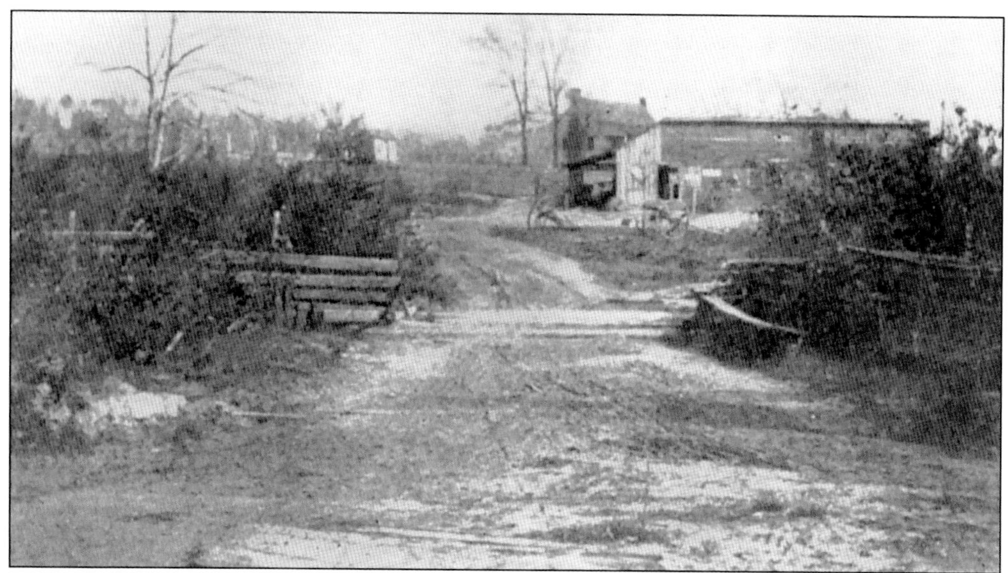

This 1890s scene shows the Southern Post Road, which was built in the early 1700s, at a point where it was intersected by Washington and South Creek Roads on the south side of the Pamlico River. Toler's Store is on the right. This road became a portion of the Southern Post Road in 1722. It ran from Edenton through Bath via a ferry crossing to Core Point and continued to New Bern. The road followed an old Native American path between the Pamlico and Neuse Rivers. The ferry crossing was eliminated in 1786 when the county seat was moved from Bath to Washington. This move was approved by the General Assembly of the State of North Carolina on December 29, 1785. (Courtesy of Jean Bowen.)

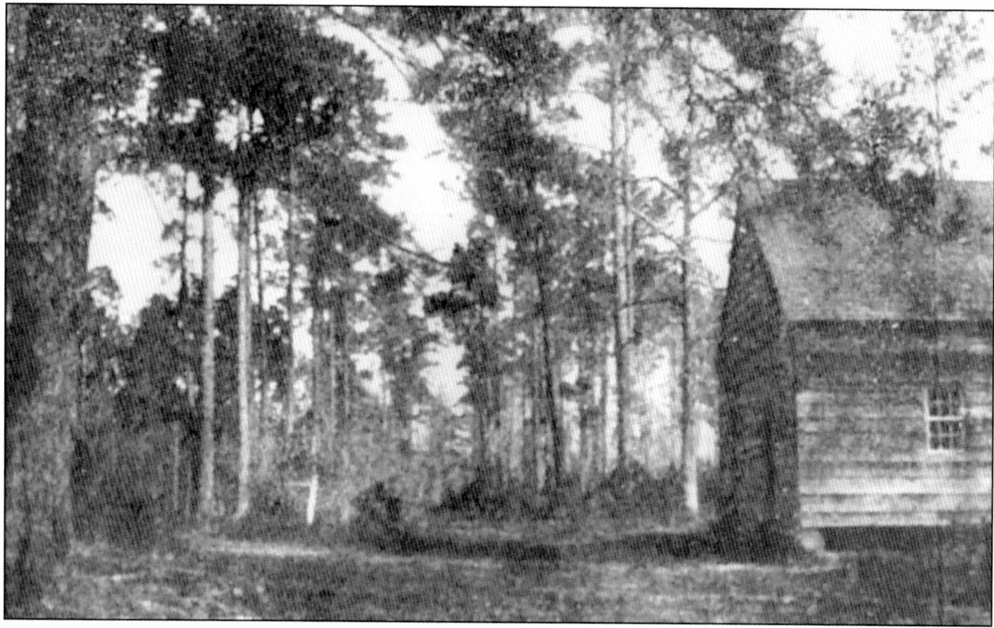

This very rare photo of the Core Point Free Will Baptist Church was probably taken in the late 1890s. The Reverend Isaac Pipkin founded the chapel in 1888 and was its first pastor. The members held prayer meetings in an old school house until 1894, when the Core Point Church was built. (Courtesy of Jean Bowen.)

Five

Aurora and Spring Creek

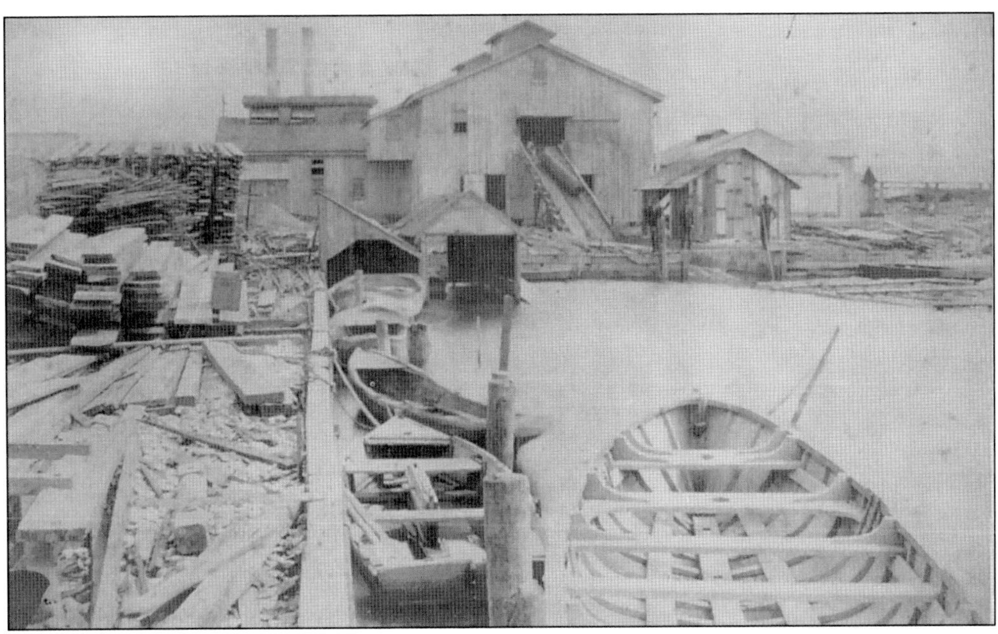

Aurora was originally called "Betty Town" and was founded on the location of a Pomouik Indian village. The land was owned by Christopher Gale, whose successors were Col. Maurice Moore, Thomas Cary, and John E. Porter. Around 1850, the Rev. William Henry Cunningham (or Cunninggim) arrived and incorporated the town in 1880 as Aurora, "the first light of dawn," to better describe the beauty of the region. In 1866, Edward D. Springer, his brother Willdin Springer, and his father, Samuel Springer, established the Springer Lumber Company on Bond Creek and made shipments of lumber to the North until the 1920s when they died. (Courtesy of BCM.)

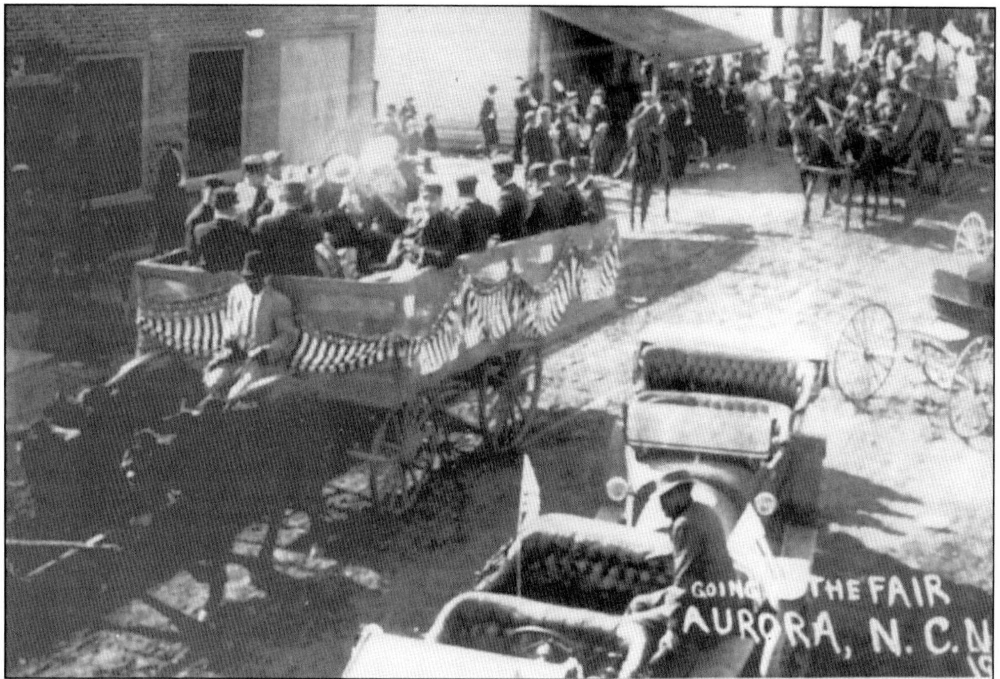

The whole town turned out for the big parade and annual fair in November 1914. The fair was held on a vacant lot behind the Methodist church. "The annual Aurora fair was very popular and successful," said resident Belinda Selby. "It always generated a great deal of excitement and enthusiasm which [this] old photograph from 1914 illustrates so well. You can practically hear their squeals of anticipation," said Belinda. (Courtesy of BCM.)

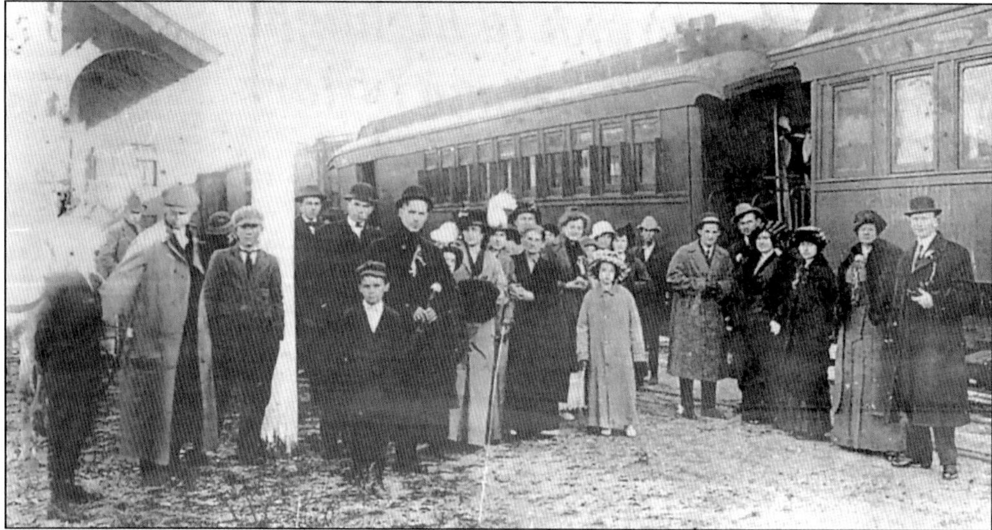

This photo shows the November 25, 1914 wedding party of Redding Aycock Thompson (1893–1966) and Rena Hooker (1892–1918). The happy couple are standing in front of the passenger car steps. Their friends came to see them depart from the Aurora station on their honeymoon. Rena was the daughter of Mr. and Mrs. William Wallace Hooker. The young lady in the long coat, in the center of the picture, is Lucille Hooker, the mother of Hooker Dough. (Courtesy of Hooker Dough.)

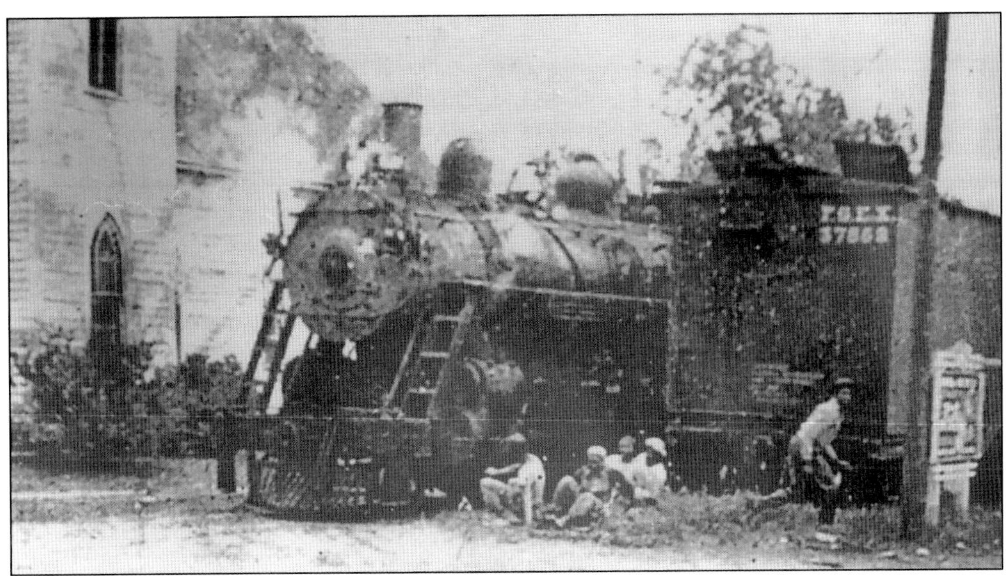

Some Aurora children sit by a train locomotive at the corner of Main and Second Streets. In the background is the Aurora Missionary Baptist Church. In 1907, John E. Porter and George T. Leach extended the Washington and Vandemere Railroad to Aurora, and by 1908, it reached its namesake destination, the village of Vandemere in Pamlico County. (Courtesy of Hooker Dough.)

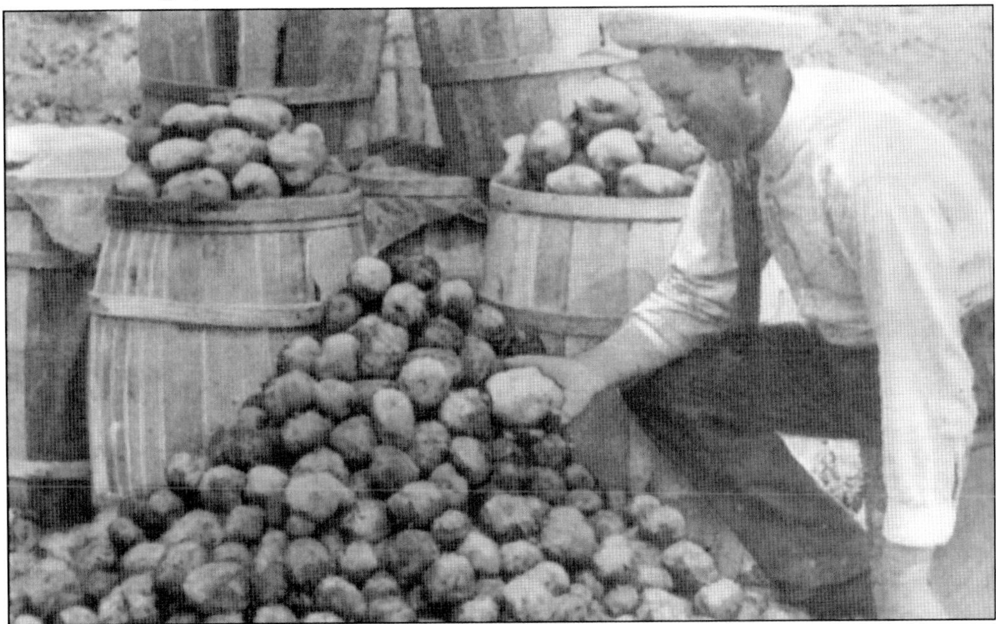

A local musician and farmer, Paul Lincke raised Irish potatoes as far back as the 1870s. By the 1900s, farmers were bringing their potatoes by horse and cart to the Aurora train depot for shipment to Northern markets. The depot was run by the Thompson family. The train was comprised of two passenger cars, a baggage and mail car, and several freight cars. Retired train engineer Bill Sellers (see page 109) says, "I remember hauling a 75-car load of Irish potatoes from Aurora to Rocky Mount, via Washington, in June 1942." (1920 postcard courtesy of Oden's Store.)

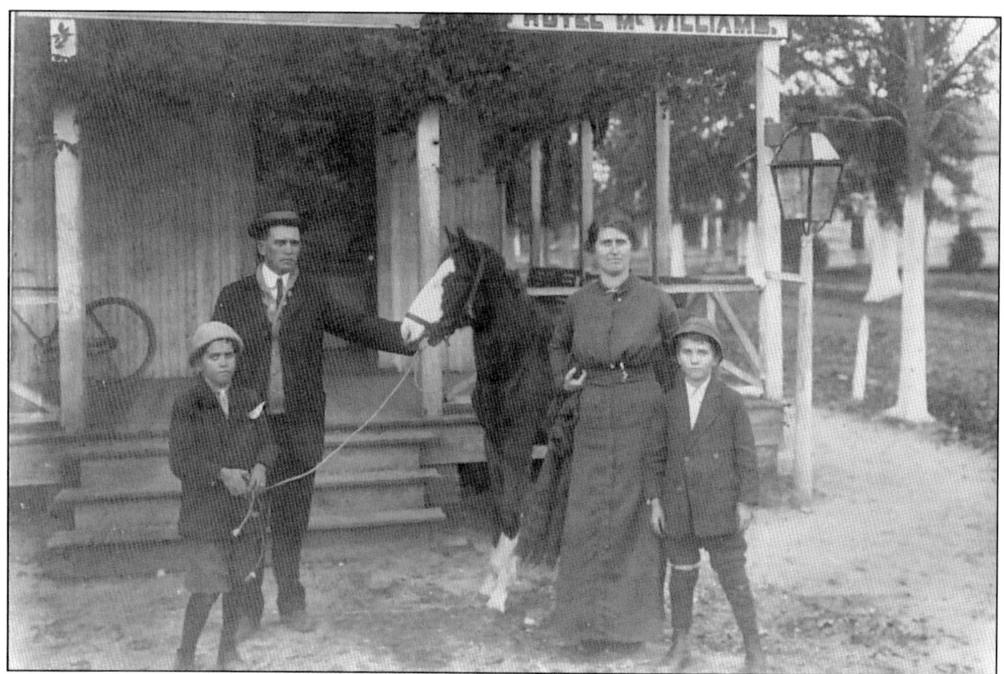

In 1914, Aurora had a fine hotel on Fourth Street that was operated by the McWilliams family. Pictured, from left to right, are William Harvey McWilliams at age 10 (1904–1939), William Jackson McWilliams at age 39 (1875–1940), Carrie Augustus Harvey McWilliams at age 37, (1877–1934), and Sidney Jackson "Jack" McWilliams at age 7 (1907–1988). Jack married Willie Crowder in 1929 and was the father of Augusta Ann McWilliams Cayton of Aurora. (Courtesy of Ann McWilliams Cayton.)

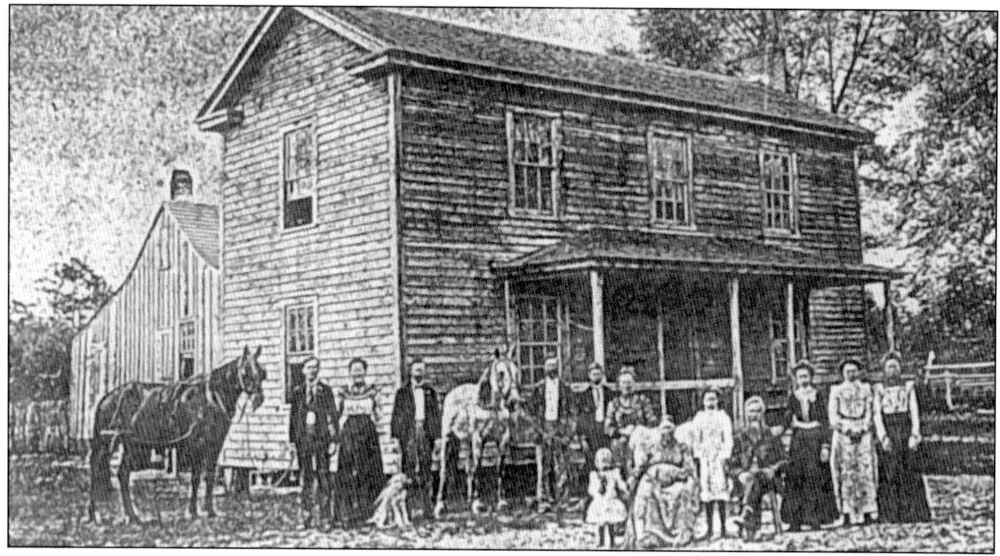

This is the Hyman R. Cayton (1840–1923) and Sydney Lewis Cayton (1847–1920) family of Small. From left to right are (between the horses) Robbie, Sue, and Yancey; (right of horse), Eddie, Zack, and unidentified; (front row) Eula Bell (small girl), Sydney (seated), unidentified, Sudie, Hyman (seated), Sally, Lena Margaret, and Mary. (Courtesy of Ann McWilliams Cayton.)

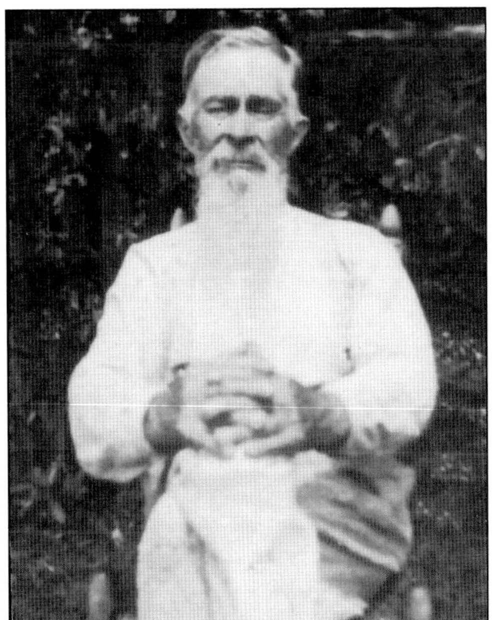
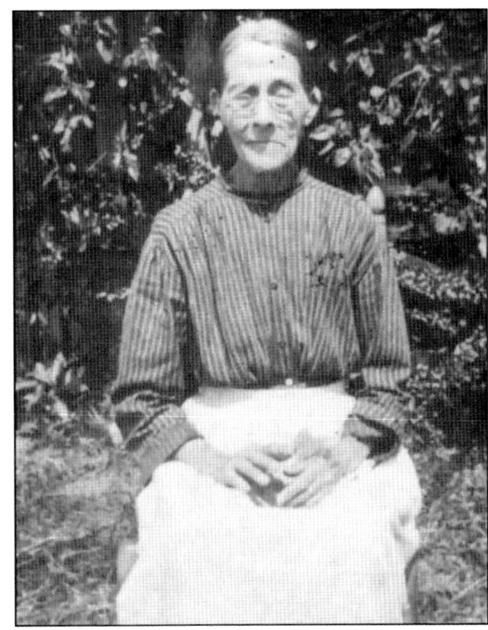

William Riley Cayton (1843–1931), at age 86, and Mary Jane Rowe Cayton (1840–1928), at age 89, are pictured in 1928. They were married in 1865, lived near Edwards, and were celebrating their 63rd wedding anniversary at the time of this picture. They raised 9 children, had 39 grandchildren, and 17 great-grandchildren. They both remembered the Mexican War and the War between the States. (Courtesy of Ann McWilliams Cayton.)

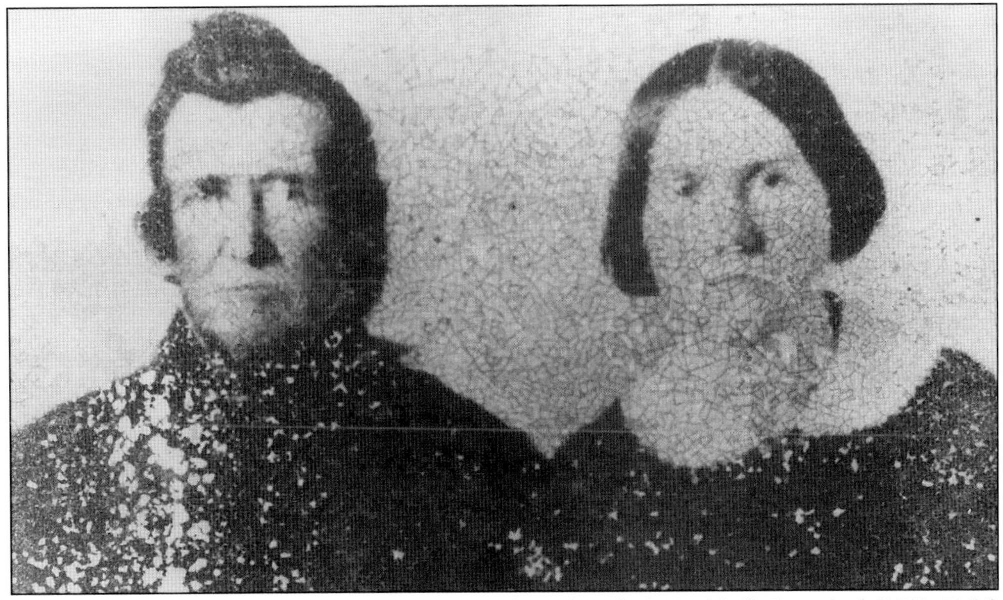

Charles Washington Crawford (1801–1872) and Emily Clark Archbell Crawford (1822–1866) were the parents of Caroline Pasteur Crawford, who married William Augustus Harvey in 1874. They were also the great-great-grandparents of Ann McWilliams Cayton. Charles was the grandson of Capt. Charles Crawford who lived at what is now known as the Whitley Plantation on the Pamlico River. Captain Crawford fought in the Revolutionary War and is buried at the old home place. (Courtesy of Ann McWilliams Cayton.)

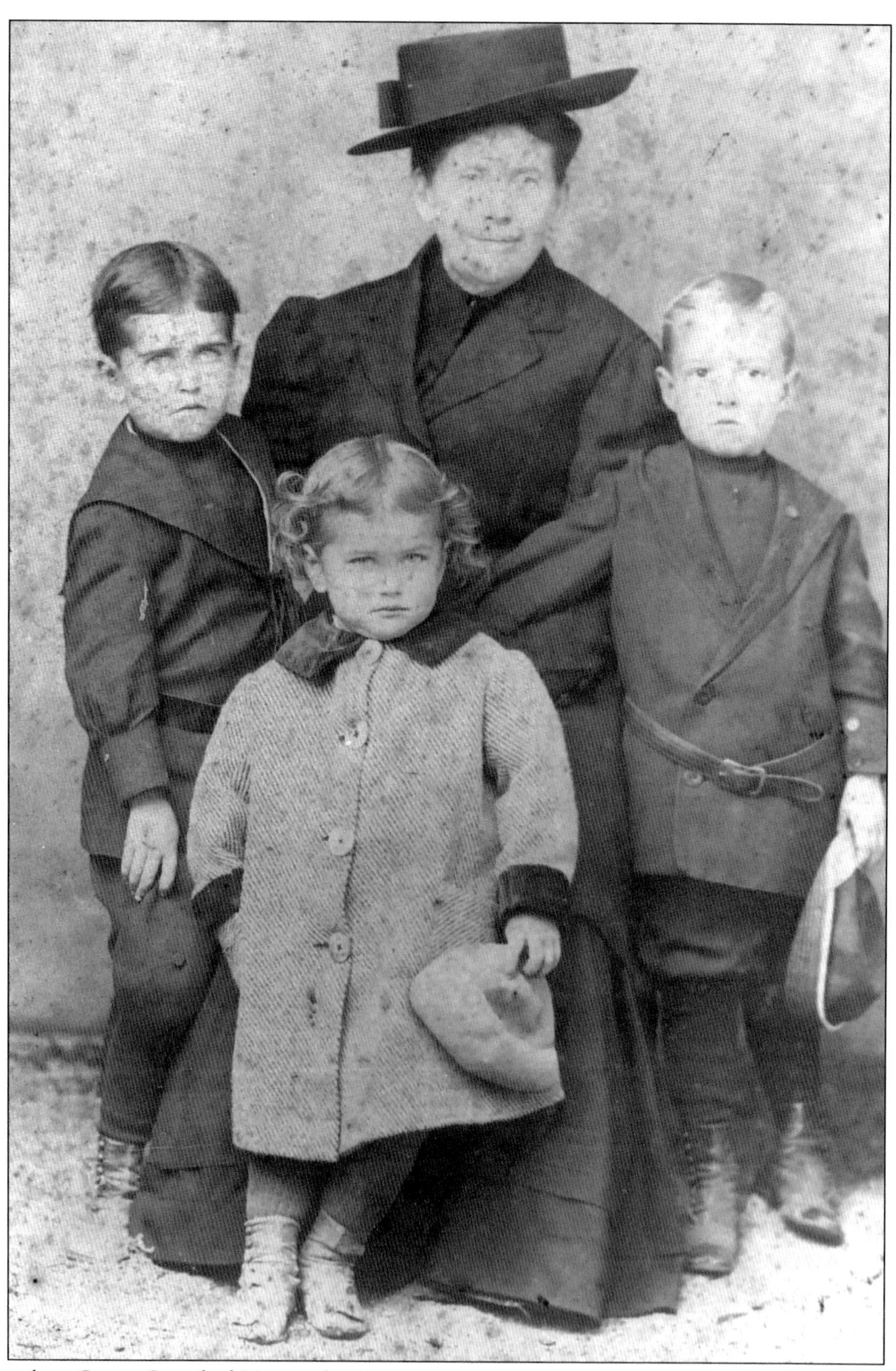

Caroline Cattie Crawford Harvey (1854–1938) was Ann Cayton's great-grandmother. Pictured with her are her grandsons, from left to right, William Harvey McWilliams (1904–1939), Jack McWilliams (1907–1988), and Halstead Bryan Alfred (1905–1951). (Courtesy of Ann McWilliams Cayton.)

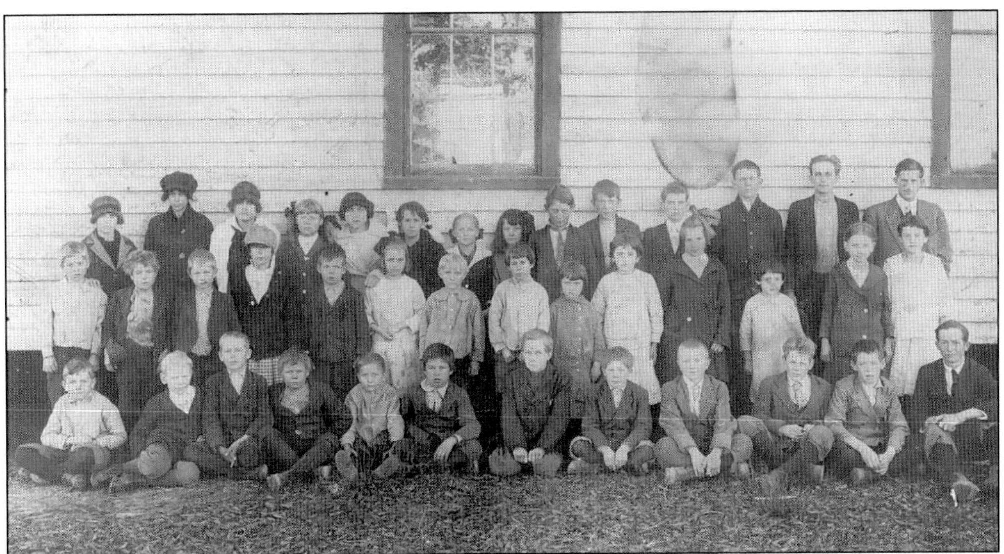

Students of the Idelia Grade School gather for a picture around 1914. Principal Redding Thompson (1893–1966) is shown on the right side of the back row. (Courtesy of Hooker Dough.)

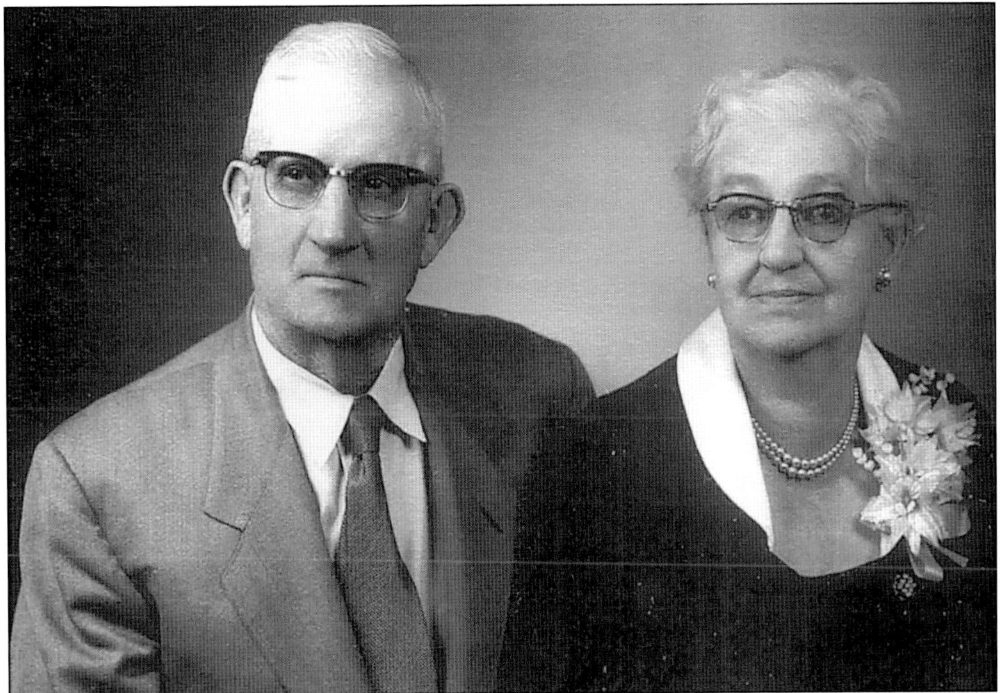

Seen here are Bryan Bonner Thompson (1875–1970) and Mattie Roberts Thompson (1878–1967). The Thompsons were married in 1895 and remained together for 72 years. Bryan worked in his father's lumber mill and cotton gin for many years before taking up farming on his own. Bryan and Mattie raised seven children, including Charles (1897–1966), Myers (1899–1963), Bonner Thompson Johnstone (1901–1926), Martha (1903–1912), Tarlton (1905–1991), Max (1907–1952), and Sally Thompson Spence, born in 1912 and still going strong. (Courtesy of Sally Thompson Spence.)

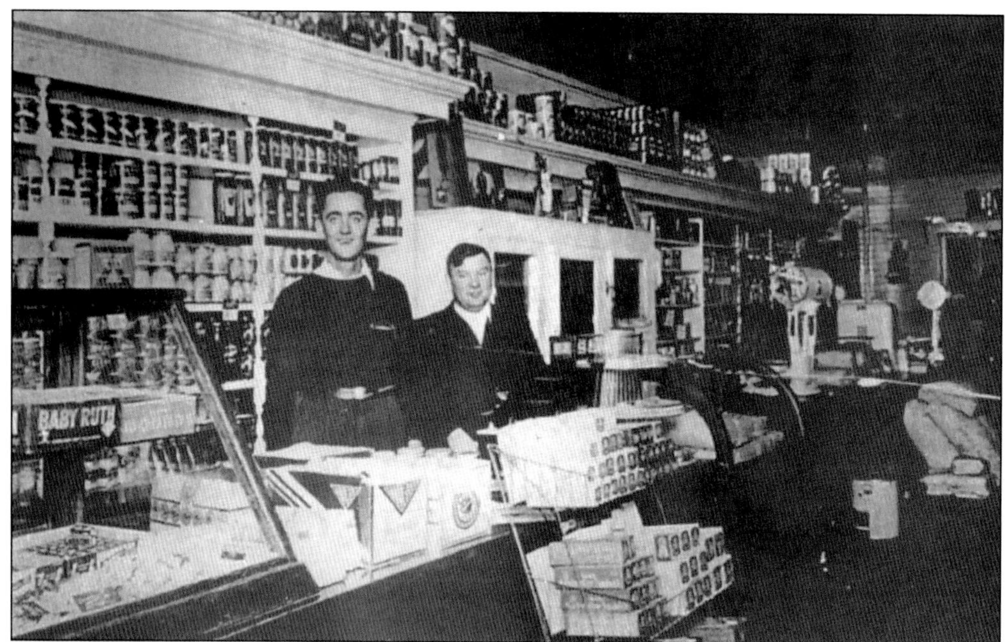

Isaac Holadia (right) opened his general merchandise store on Main Street Aurora in 1937. His son William F. Holadia still resides in Aurora. Guyan Hollowell (left) worked for Holadia, whose store was located on the vacant lot next to the Aurora/Richland Township Chamber of Commerce. (Courtesy of W. Holadia and the *Pamlico News*.)

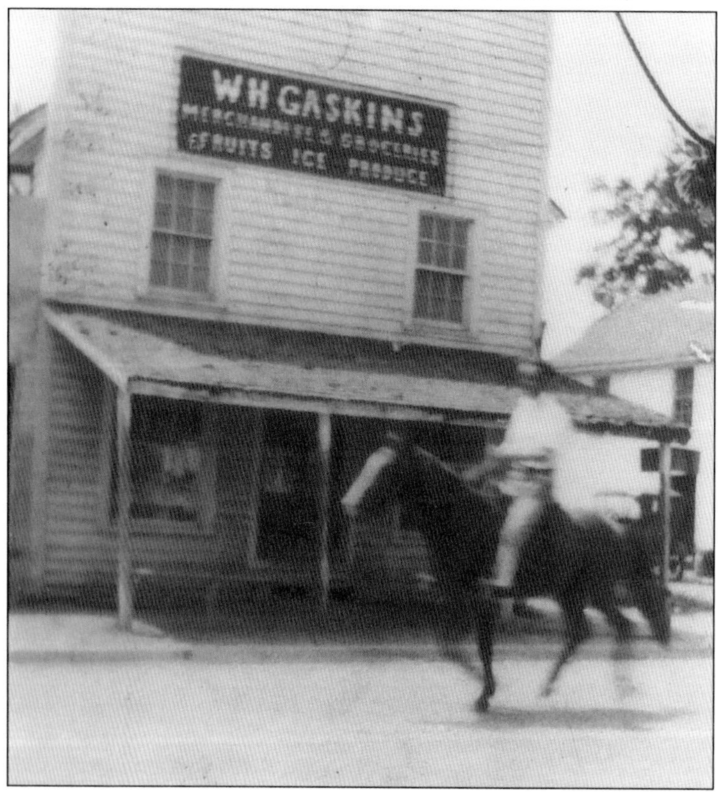

Wallace "Binky" Guilford was born in 1911. Here is Binky at age 16 riding his Texas cow pony in front of the W.H. Gaskins Grocery Store on Main Street Aurora in 1927. (Courtesy of Wallace Guilford.)

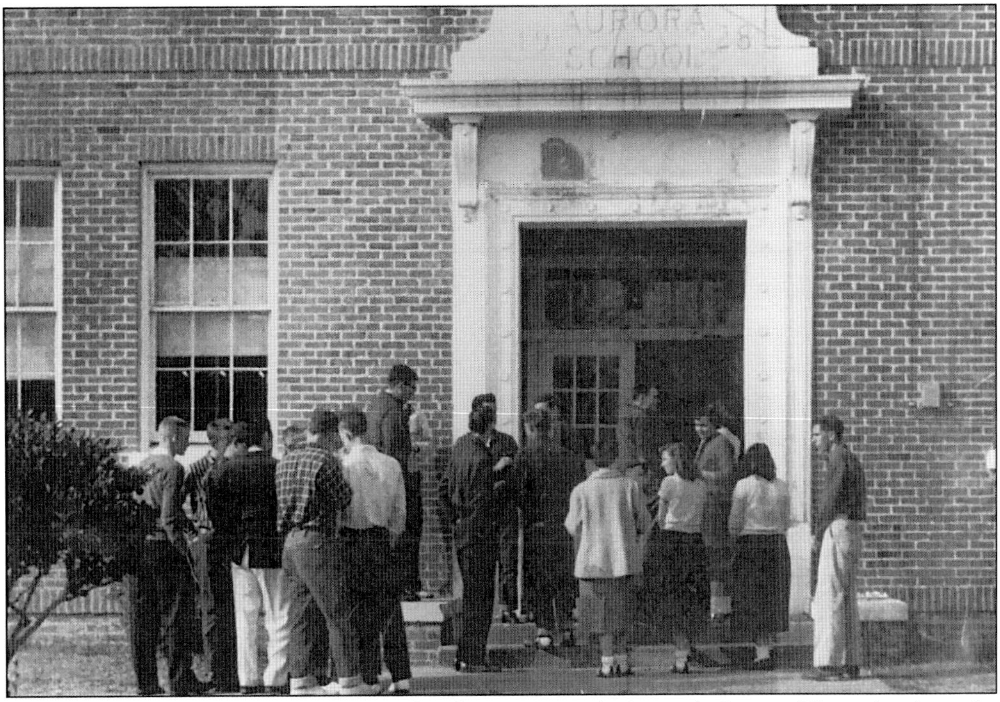

In 1928, Aurora opened a fine new school at 693 North Seventh Street. This school taught grades one through twelve until 1968, when the school was integrated. After 1968 the school taught only grades nine through twelve until 1976, when a new school was built. From 1976 until 1978 the old school building was used to teach eighth grade and some special education classes. This building was demolished by fire around 1980. (Courtesy of HWGM Library.)

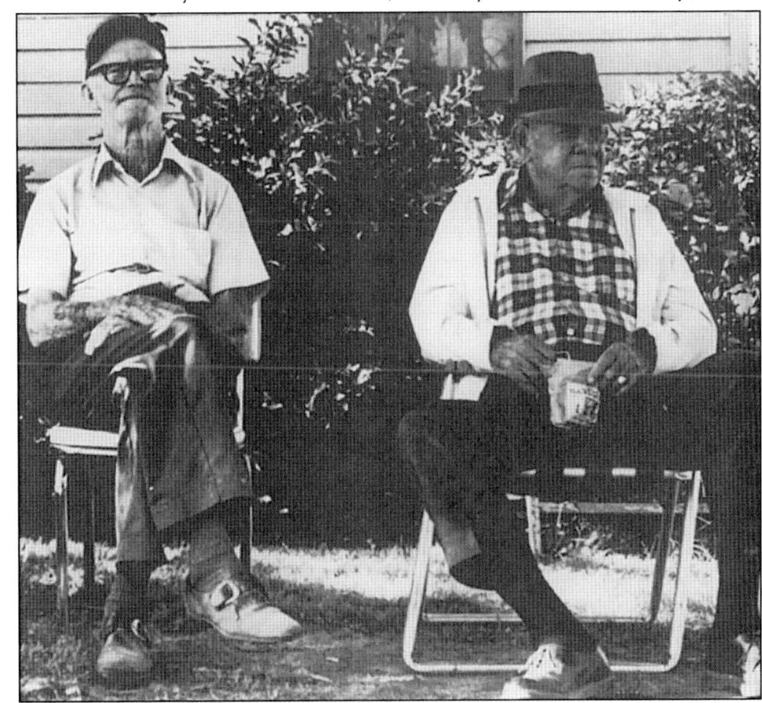

During a Main Street event in 1976, Aurora residents John McKinney (left) and Fred Buck watched the activities taking place. About such affairs of interest commentator Sinclair Lewis once said, "The significant features of all villages are whiskers . . . dogs on lawns . . . bricks, checkers." (Courtesy of HWGM Library.)

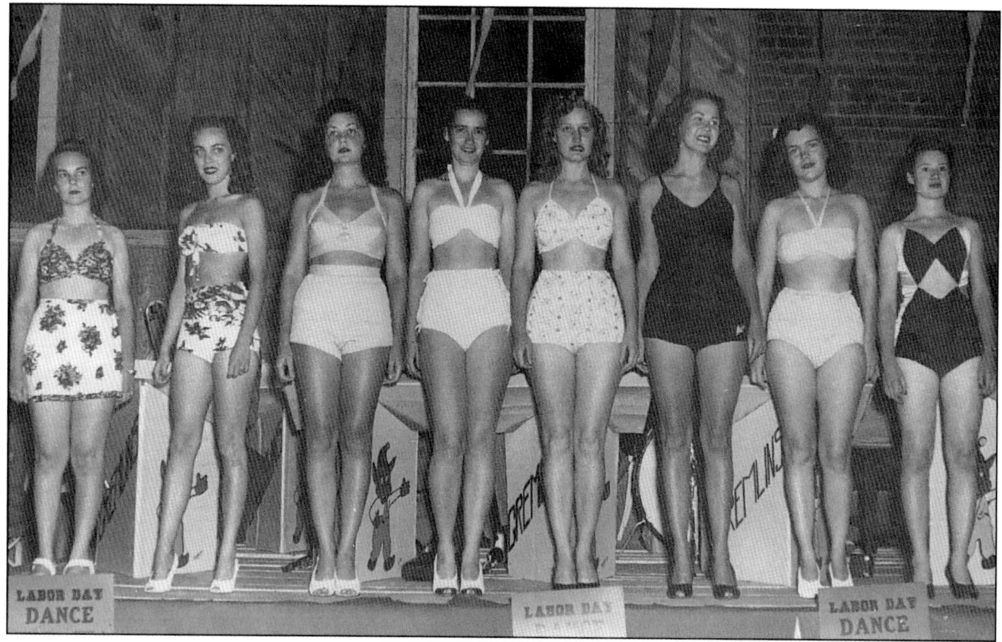

Aurora featured a beauty pageant at the Labor Day Dance on September, 2, 1946. The contestants included, from left to right, Mebaline Cayton, Hooker Dough, Harriet Hooker, Beulha Lewis, Clara Jones, Betty Jo Windley, Marie Alfred, and Evelyn Brickhouse. The winner was Harriet Hooker. (Courtesy of Hooker Dough.)

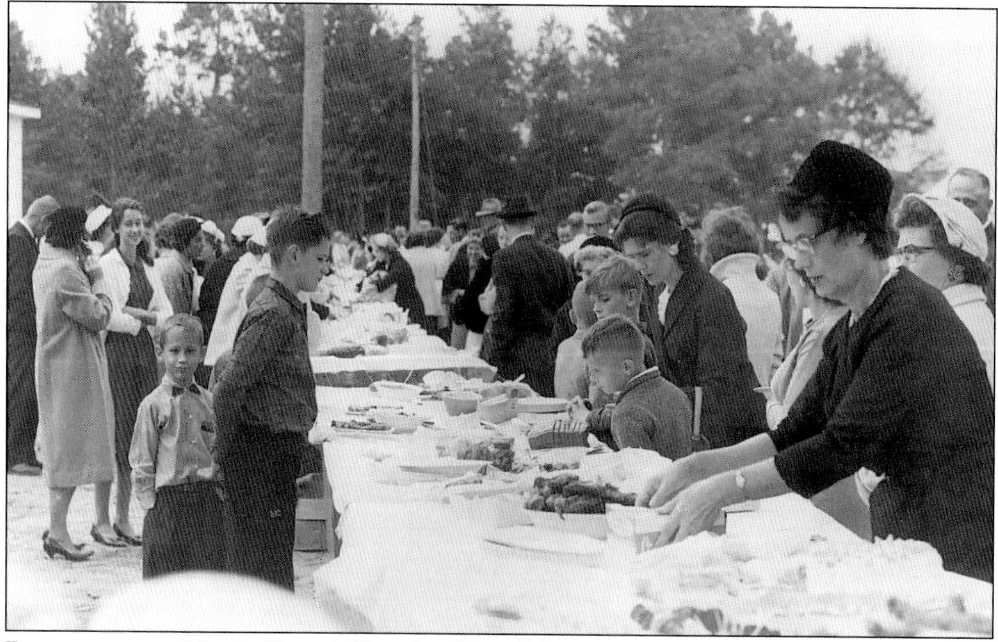

For many years, Mary's Chapel Church of Small has held a November "Homecoming" and Revival weekend for the residents of Small and Aurora. On Sunday afternoon, after morning service, a "dinner on the ground" was held with gospel singing entertainment. As you can see, this 1960 event supplied plenty of good food and fellowship for all. The church has since built a Fellowship Hall, and the annual event is now held indoors. (Courtesy of Ann Cayton.)

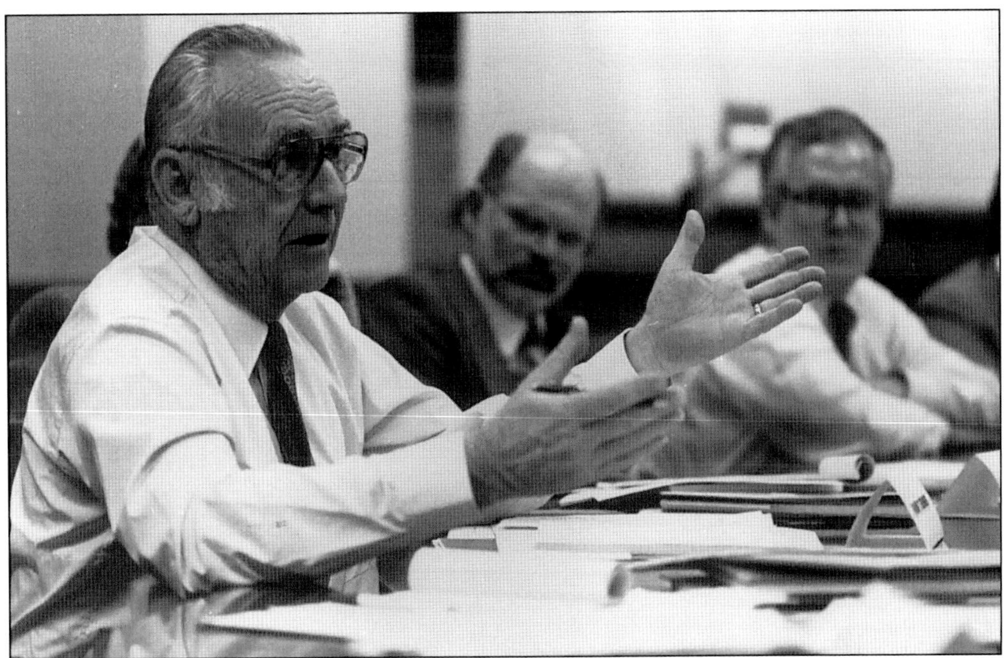

Beaufort County Commissioner Frank T. Bonner addresses the "Risk Control Committee" at the Washington, North Carolina Agriculture Department meeting in 1988. (Courtesy of F. Bonner.)

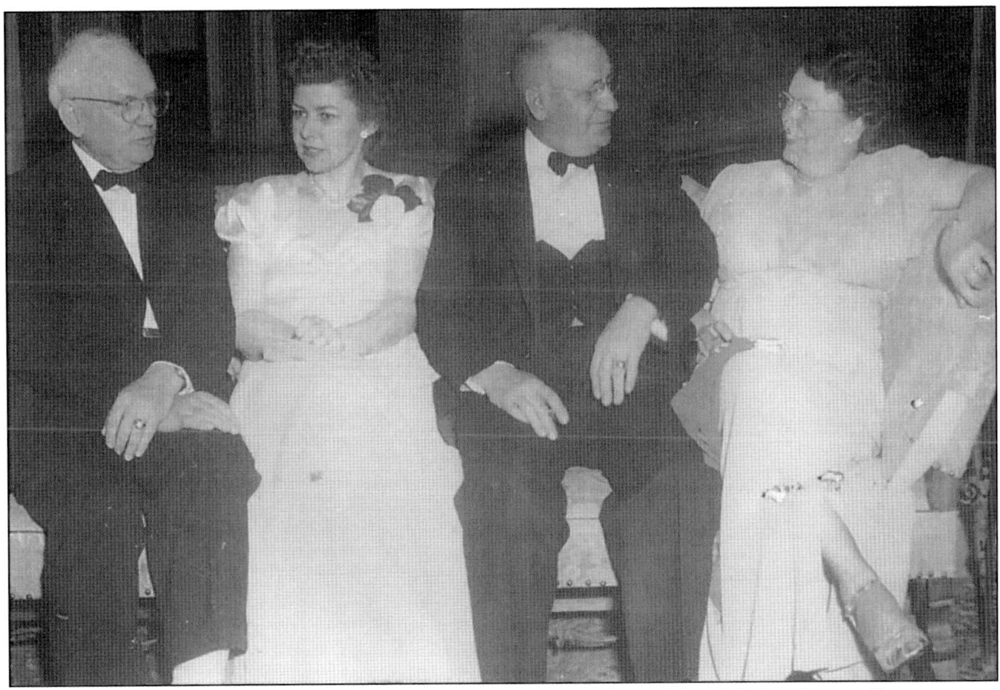

From left to right are Dr. ? Crutchfield, Mrs. Oleta Deal Litchfield, John Bryan Bonner, and Ruth Taylor. This distinguished group is pictured attending an Atlantic Coast Line Surgeons Convention in Savannah, Georgia in 1945. (Courtesy of F. Bonner.)

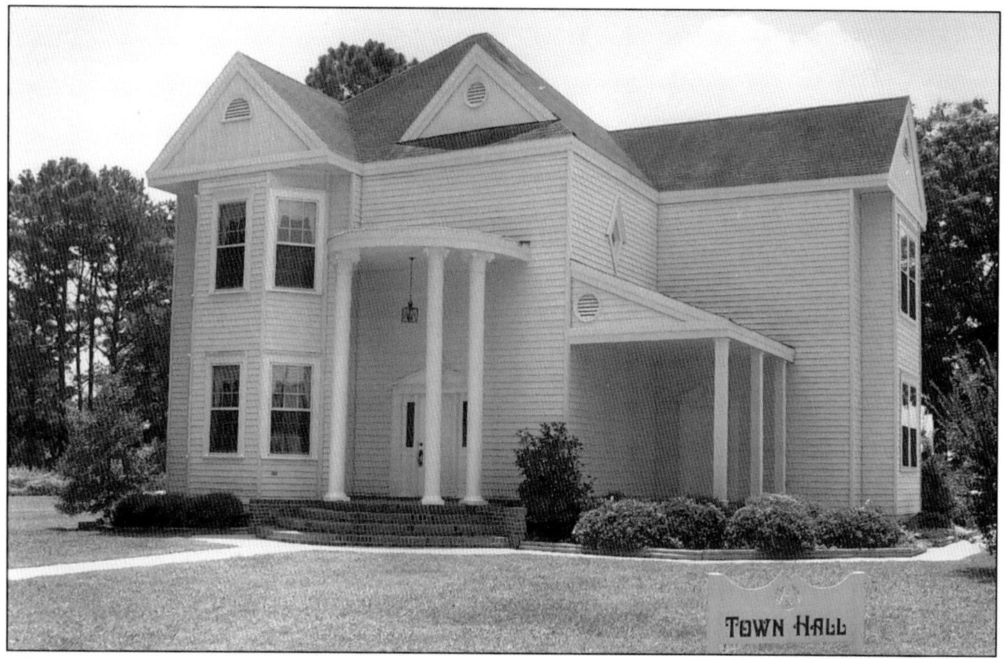

The Rutledge House was built in 1902. The town purchased this fine old house in 1976, and renovated it to become the Aurora Town Hall. Aurora is governed by a mayor and four commissioners. In the year 2000 the mayor is Joe Hooker, and the commissioners include Brad Lee, Water and Sewer; Jess Peed, Streets; Lewis Leaming, Building; and Royce Hamm, Police. (Photo by Louis Van Camp.)

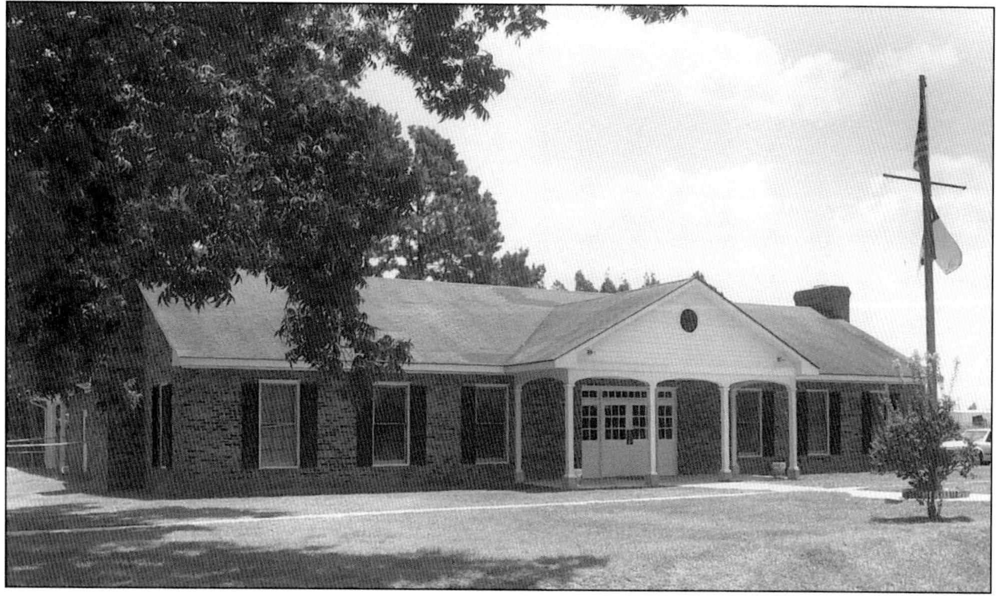

The Aurora Community Center is located at 442 Third Street. The center has a day care, a playground, and features an aerobics class weekly. A large recreation hall is available for party rental and is used during the last Saturday in May for the annual Fossil Festival. At Christmas, the Woman's Club sponsors a community party and the senior group helps with entertainment. (Photo by Louis Van Camp.)

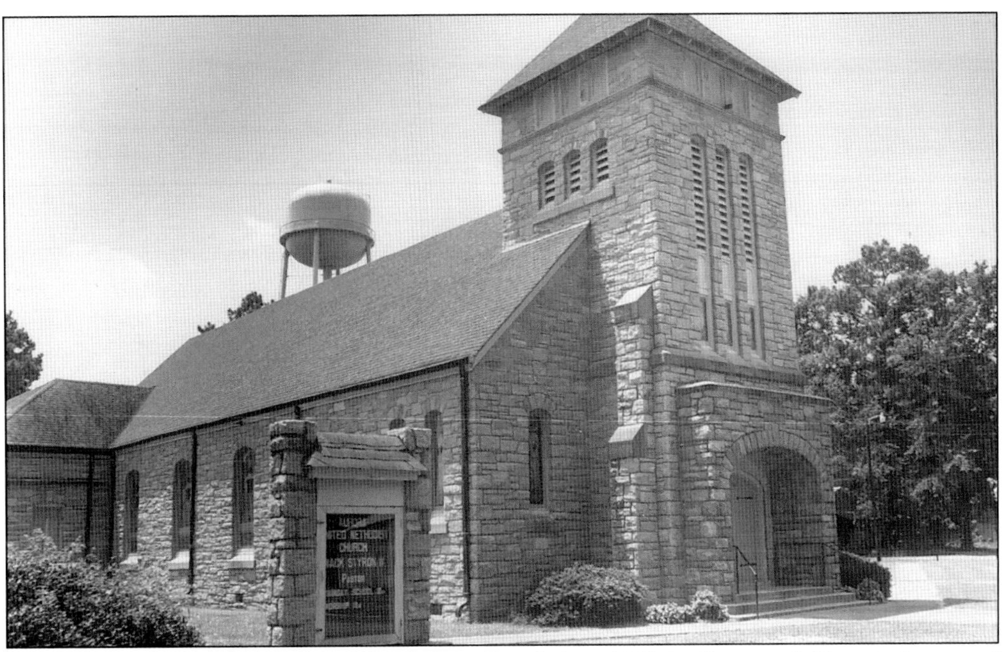

The Aurora United Methodist Church was founded in 1860 by Reverend Cunningham and Rev. John W. Litchfield. The first pastor was Rev. D.O. Wyche in 1886. The present-day pastor is Mack Stryon II. (Photo by Louis Van Camp.)

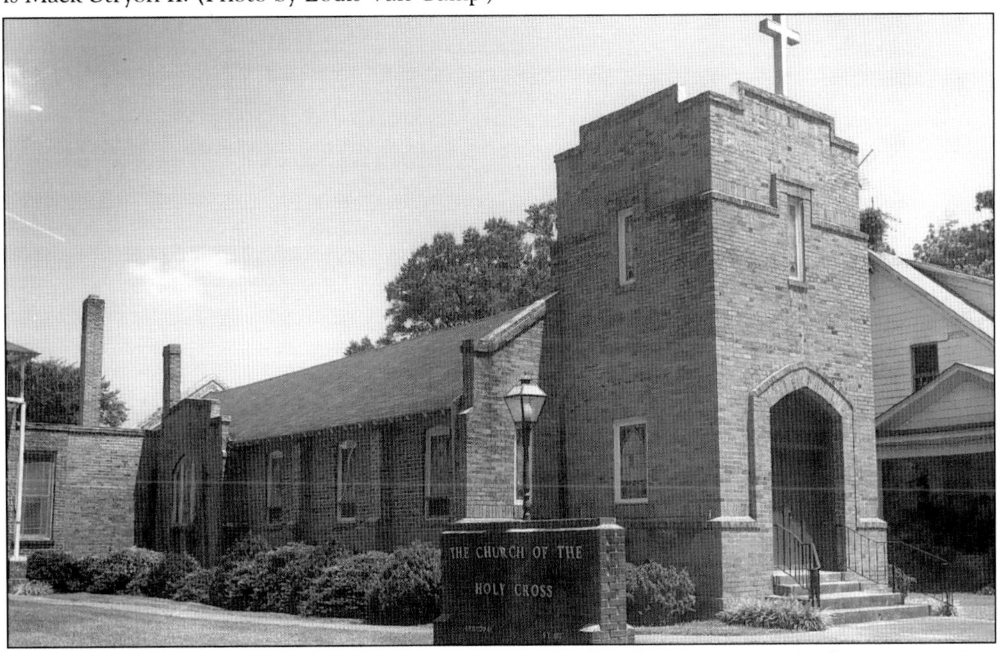

The original Aurora Chapel of the Cross Episcopal Church was a frame building erected in 1885 on land donated by Mr. and Mrs. J.B. Bryan. Trustees of the church were J.B. Bryan, J.B. Bonner, C.S. Dixon, Joe Peed, and F.C. Buck. The first rector was Rev. Francis Joyner; he was succeeded by Rev. N.C. Huges of Chocowinity, who came once a month. A new brick church was built in 1917 and consecrated by Rev. T.C. Darst, bishop of East Carolina. The name was then changed to the Episcopal Church of the Holy Cross. (Photo by Louis Van Camp.)

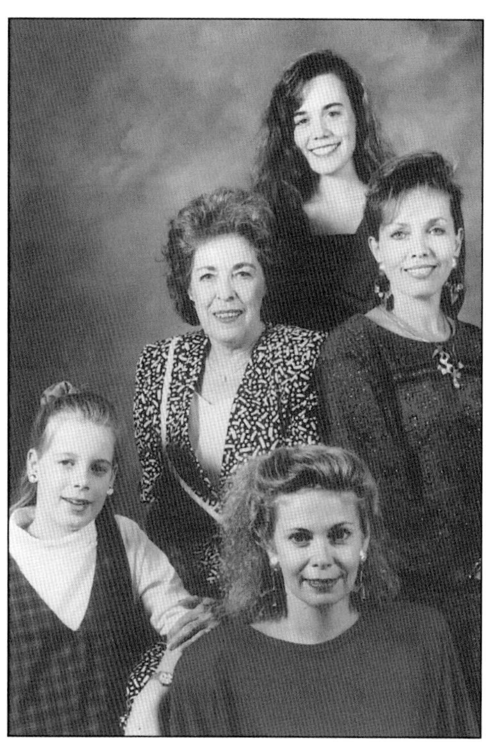

The 1990 generation of the Hooker Dough family includes, clockwise from bottom left, Lindsey Meyers, Hooker Dough, Valrie Vincent Ramsey, Sandra Vincent, and Emily Meyers. (Courtesy of Hooker Dough.)

The Caytons of Aurora are shown here at their daughter Lynn Crowder's wedding in April 1992. From left to right are Dawn Ann Cayton Broome (1960–), Ann McWilliams Cayton (1937–), Linwood L. Cayton (1934–), daughter Lynn Crowder Cayton Ferguson (1964–), and Sidney "Sid" McWilliams Cayton (1962–). (Courtesy of Ann McWilliams Cayton.)

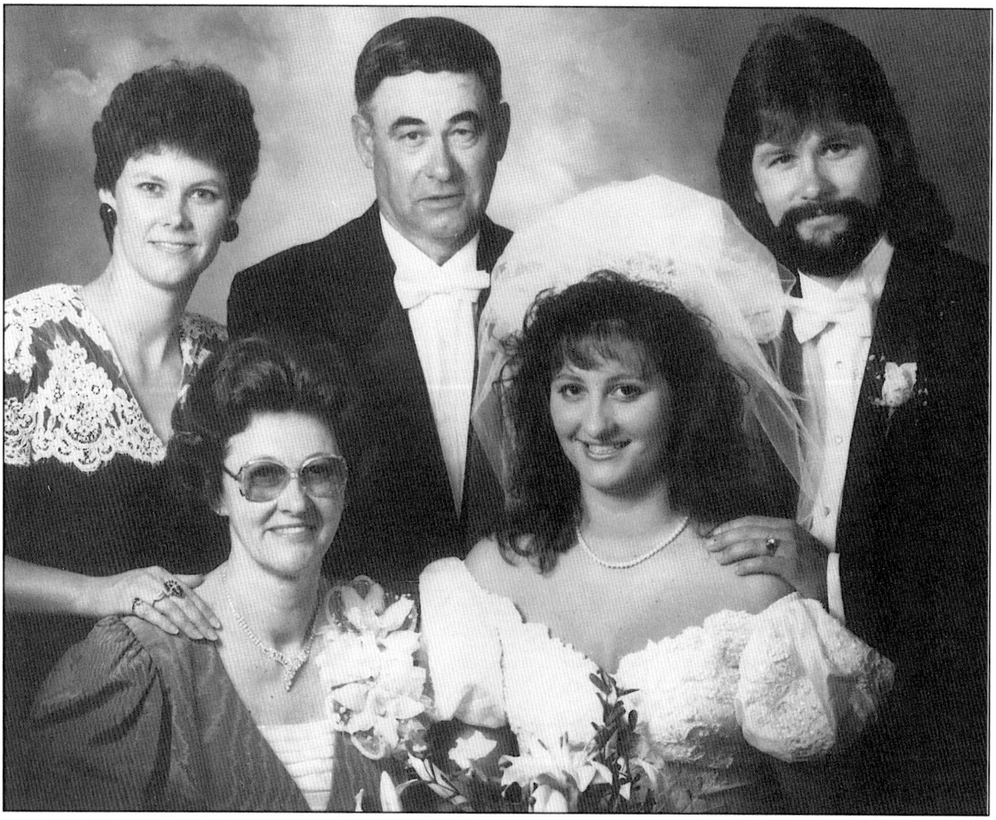

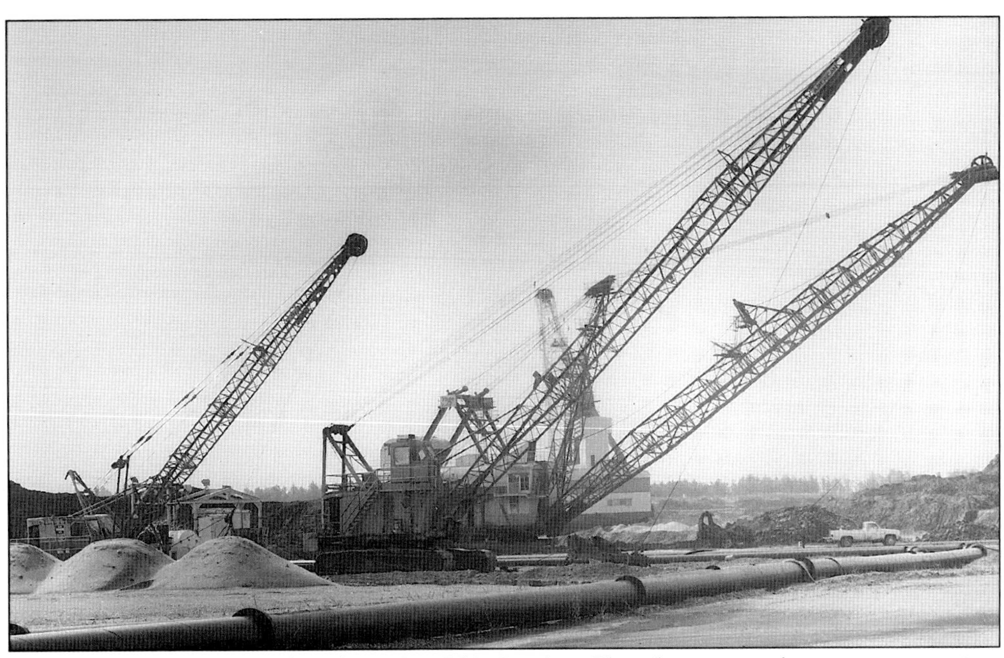

These cranes are mining phosphate. In 1954, Carolina Phosphate opened a mining operation, which became Texas Gulf Company around 1964. In the late 1980s it was purchased by the PCS Phosphate Company. (Photo by Louis Van Camp.)

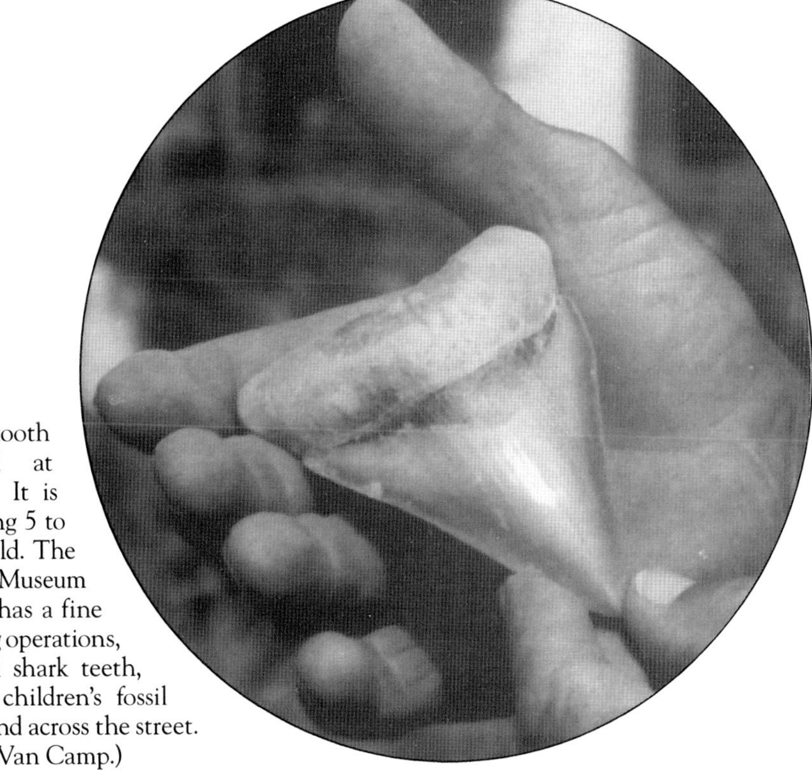

This shark's tooth was uncovered at PCS Phosphate. It is estimated as being 5 to 6 million years old. The Aurora Fossil Museum on Main Street has a fine exhibit of mining operations, fossil shells, and shark teeth, and there is a children's fossil digging playground across the street. (Photo by Louis Van Camp.)

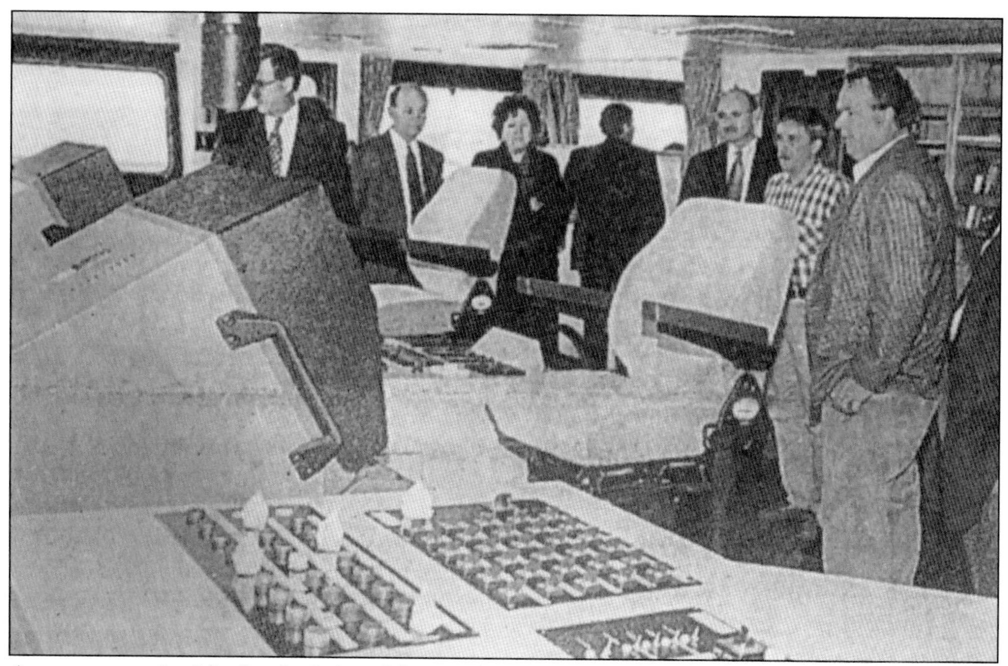

Aurora mayor Joe Hooker (right) and former Aurora mayor Grace Bonner (center) look over the captain's deck instrumentation on the new PCS Phosphate tanker *Aurora*. (Courtesy of Rusty Walker.)

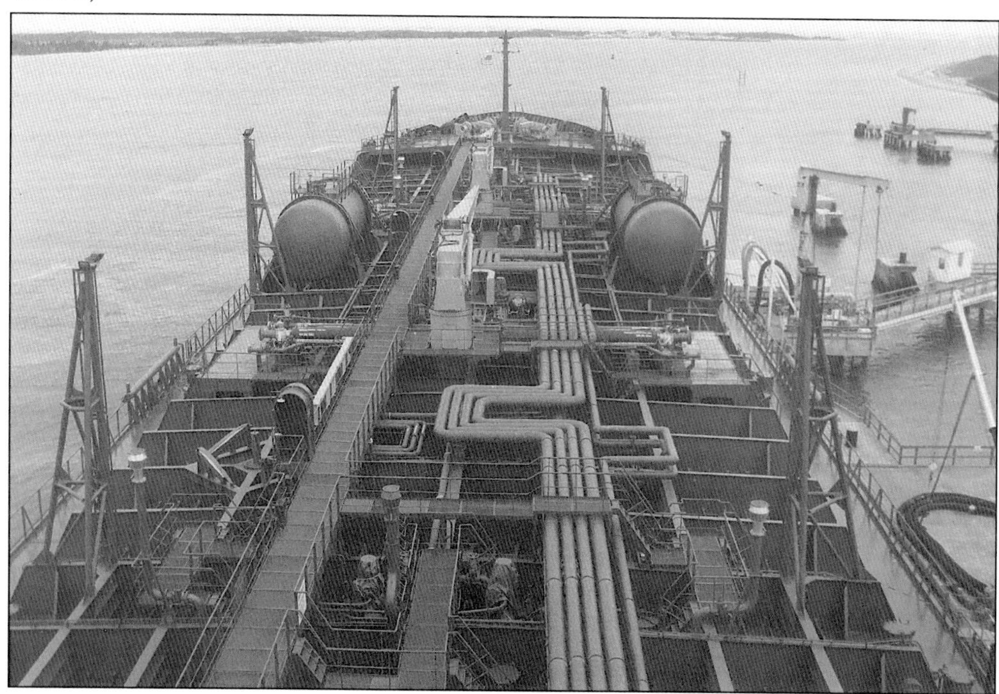

PCS Phosphate now operates an ocean-going tanker called the *Aurora*. The *Aurora* is "the most unique in the world for its cargo capabilities," said company president Tom Regan. The *Aurora* is a $42-million, high-tech tanker that carries PCS raw materials including molten sulfur, sulfuric acid, and PCS product phosphoric acid. (Courtesy of Rusty Walker.)

Six

Washington Revisited

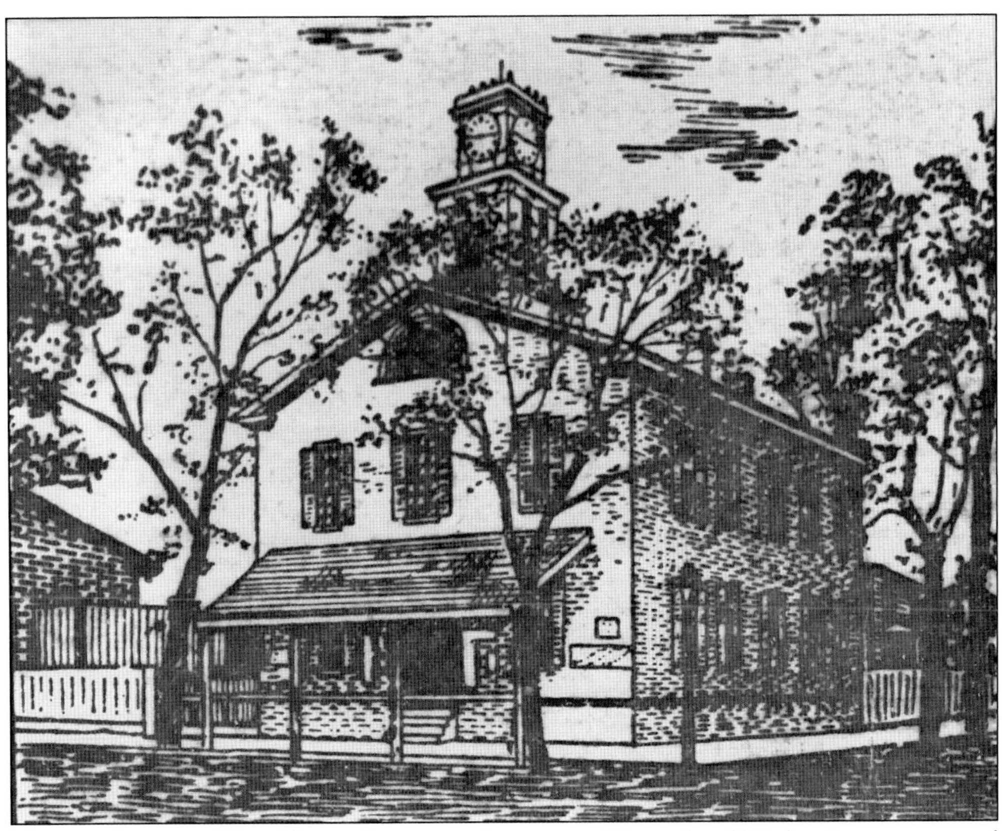

This rare drawing of the old court house, on the corner of Second and Market Streets, appeared in the *Washington Gazette* in 1889. It shows an extended roof, or lean-to shelter, across the front. Sometime between 1889 and about 1900 this shelter was removed. (Courtesy of Vance Harper Jones.)

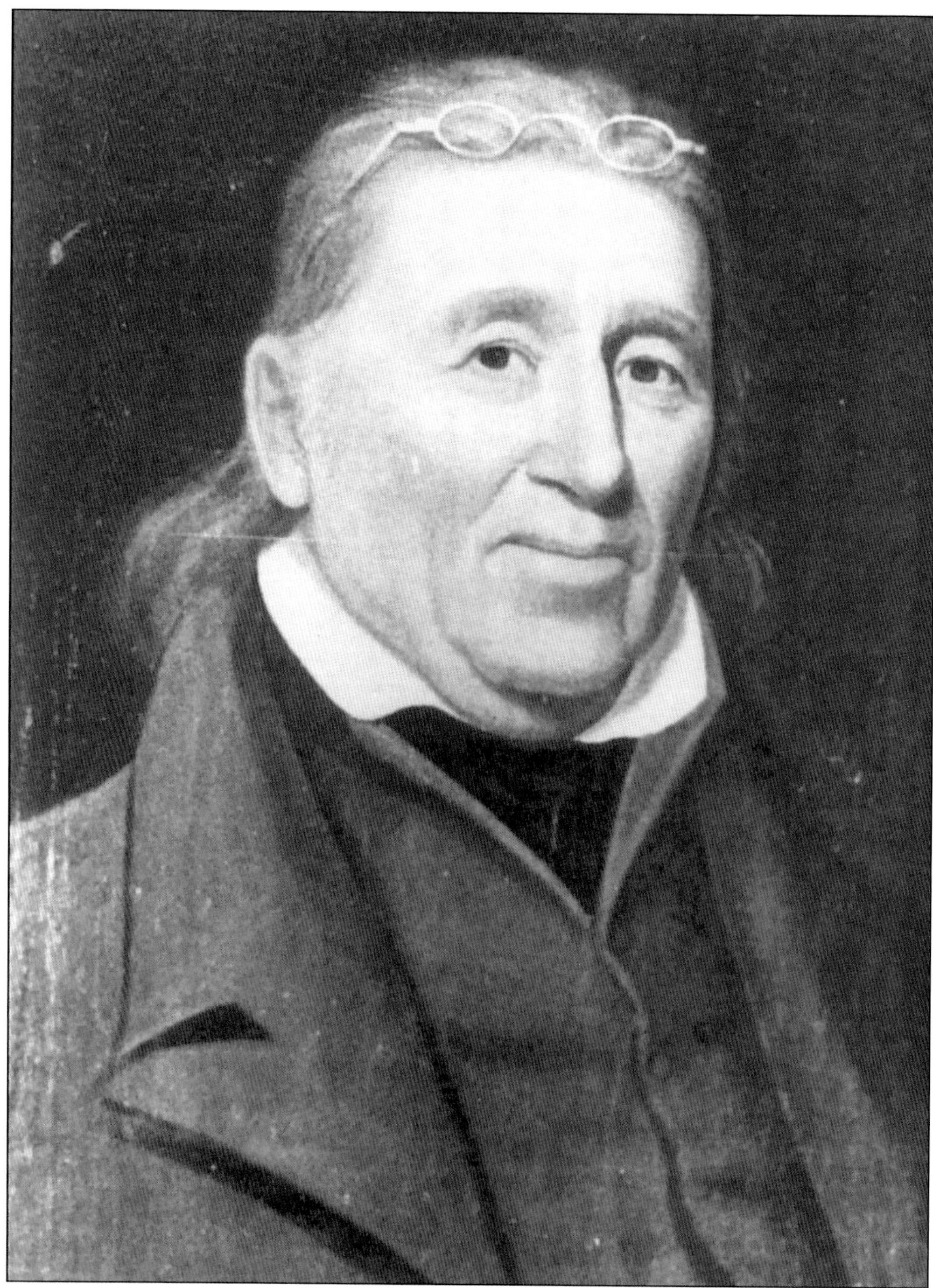

John Gray Blount (1752–1833) was the largest ever private land owner in the United States. Early in his career, Blount was a chain bearer (surveyor's assistant) for Daniel Boone. Blount was appointed commissioner for the Port of Bath in 1783 and maintained a home on Main Street in Washington. John Gray Blount and his brother Thomas, who lived in Tarboro, were commission merchants and owned warehouses and saw mills in Tarboro and Washington in the 1780s. (Portrait by Jacob Marling; courtesy of Philip Madre.)

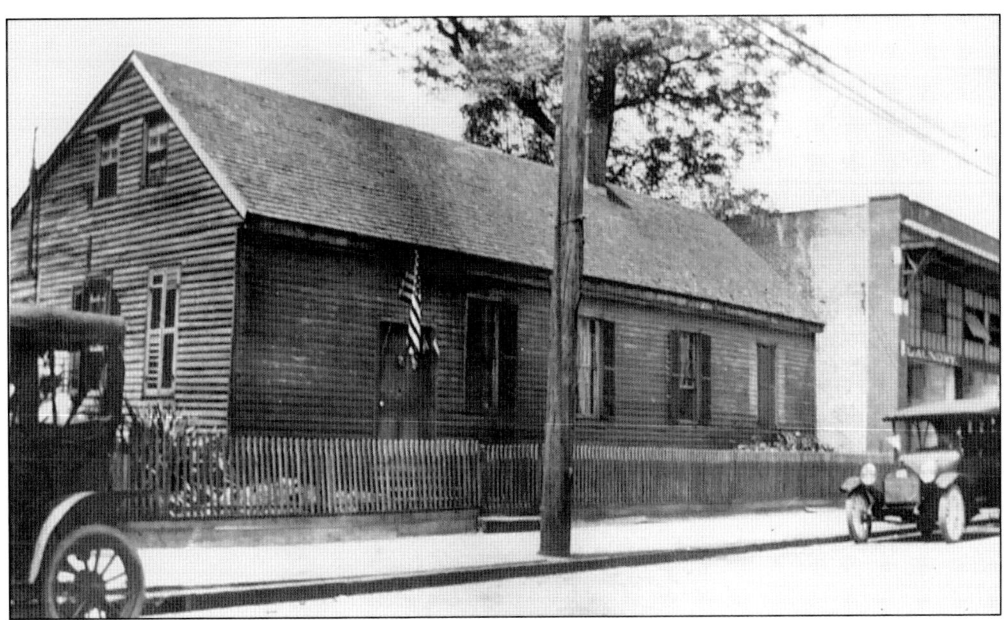

The John Gray Blount House (c. 1778) was the sixth house built in Washington and was located on the south side of Main Street near Market Street. His home was demolished in 1923. "John Gray was the brother of Major Reading Blount," wrote Lida Tunstall Rodman on the back of this picture of his home. (Courtesy of Philip Madre.)

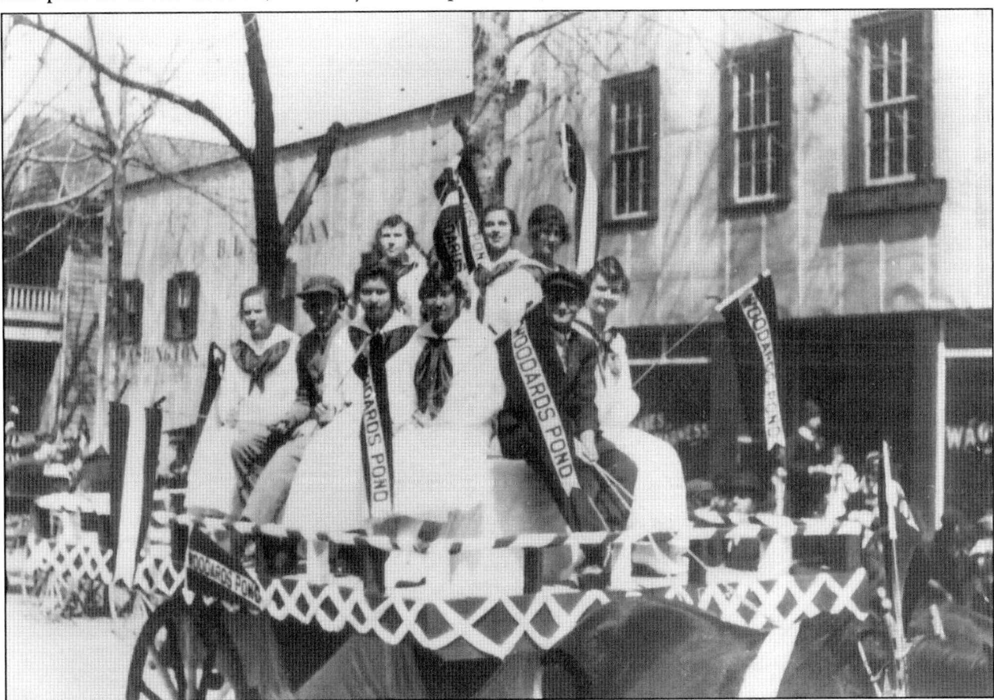

The Woodard's Pond School float passes along Main Street in Washington in an early 20th-century parade. This school was located at the junction of NC 264 and Harvey Road No. 1, where the Woodard's Pond Church is located in the year 2000. Woodard's Pond School was active from 1909 to 1935. (Courtesy of Evelyn Cutler.)

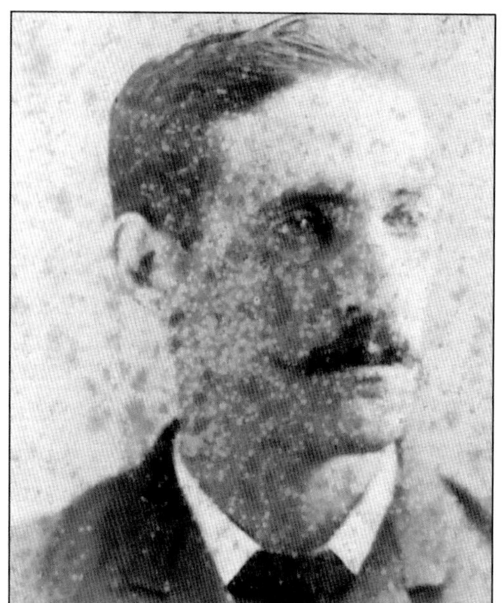

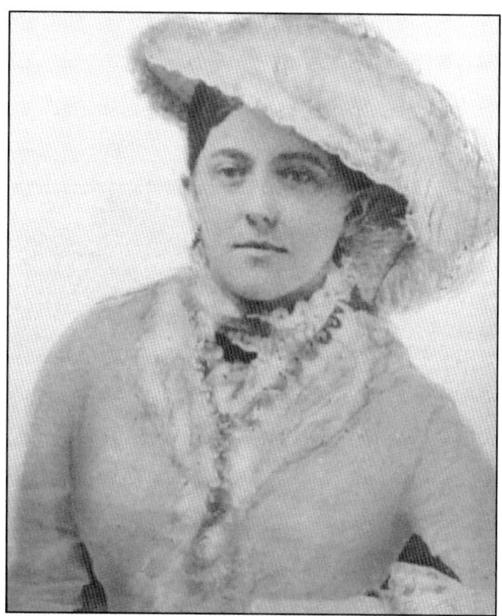

Left: Samuel Richardson Fowle (1856–1946) married Mary Adeline Payne of Lexington, North Carolina, in 1881. Samuel worked in the S.R. Fowle Hardware Store from about 1880 until the 1920s, when he retired. (Courtesy of Sadie Fowle.)
Right: Mary Adeline "Mamie" Payne Fowle (1859–1938) was the daughter of Dr. R.L. Payne of Lexington, North Carolina. Mamie was very active in the First Presbyterian Church of Washington. (Courtesy of Sadie Fowle.)

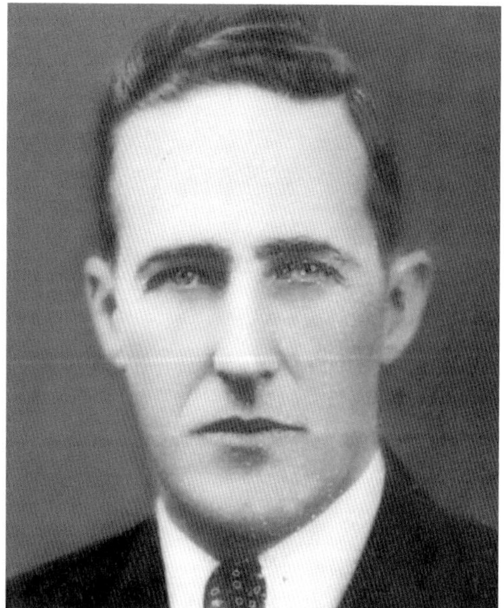

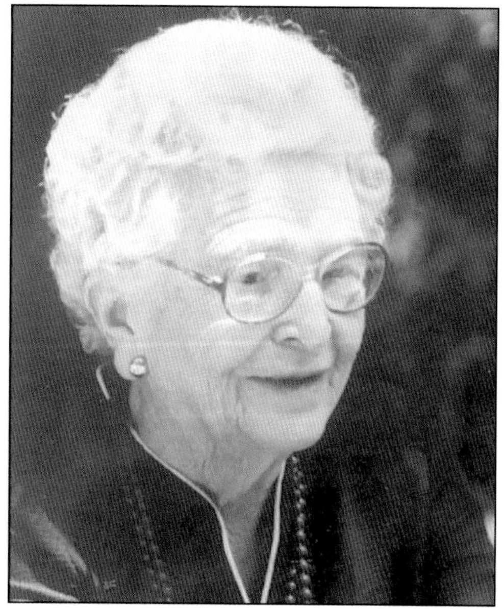

Left: Samuel Richardson Fowle Jr. (1896–1963) was the tenth generation of Fowles to bear the name Samuel Richardson. He was mayor of Washington from 1932 until 1938 and postmaster from 1935 until his death in 1963. (Courtesy of Sadie Fowle.)
Right: Elizabeth Tayloe Fowle (1895–1982) was the daughter of Dr. David Tayloe. Samuel and Elizabeth were married in 1919, and they had three children: Samuel Richardson III, (1925–), Elizabeth Tayloe (1921–), and David Tayloe (1933–). (Courtesy of Sadie Fowle.)

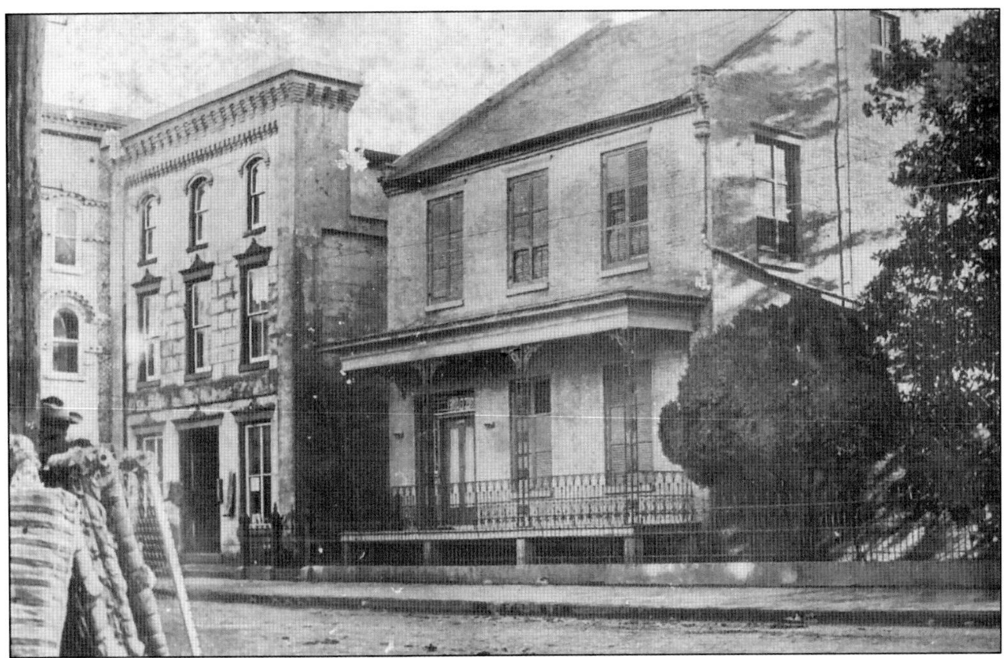

The original Samuel Richardson Fowle House (c. 1839) was located on West Main Street next to the S.R. Fowle & Son store. Their store was located on the southwest corner of Main and Respass (now Respess) Streets. In 1902, Fowle & Son built an additional store and warehouse on the southeast corner of Main and Respass Streets. (Courtesy of Sadie Fowle.)

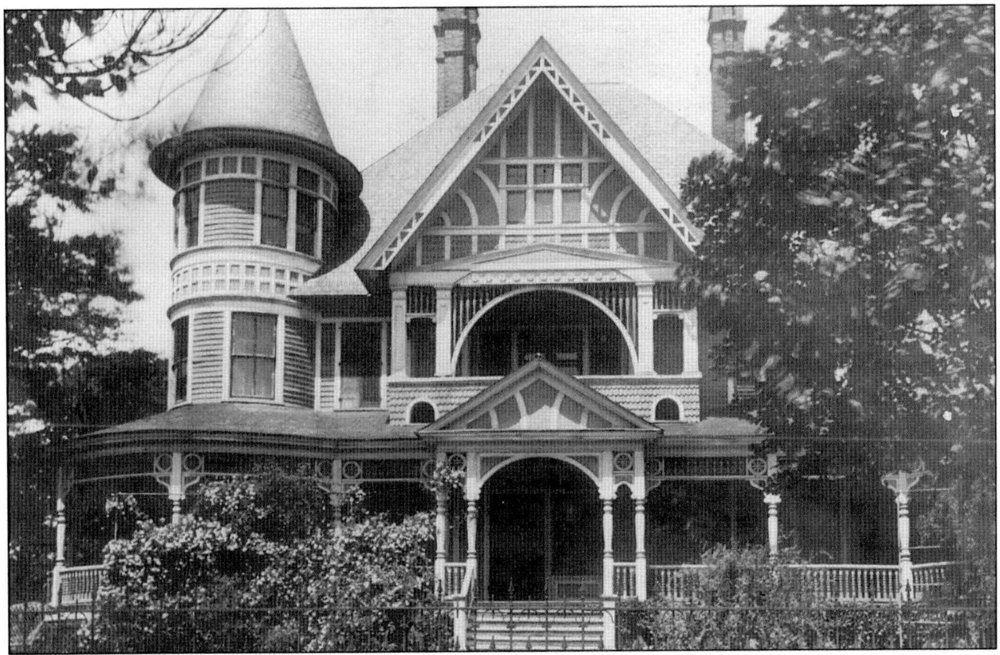

The second Samuel Richardson Fowle House was built in 1899 on the corner of Van Norden and West Main Streets. It was a stately mansion and greatly admired. However, time took its toll and this once proud home, which was no longer being used, was demolished in the 1960s. (Courtesy of Sadie Fowle.)

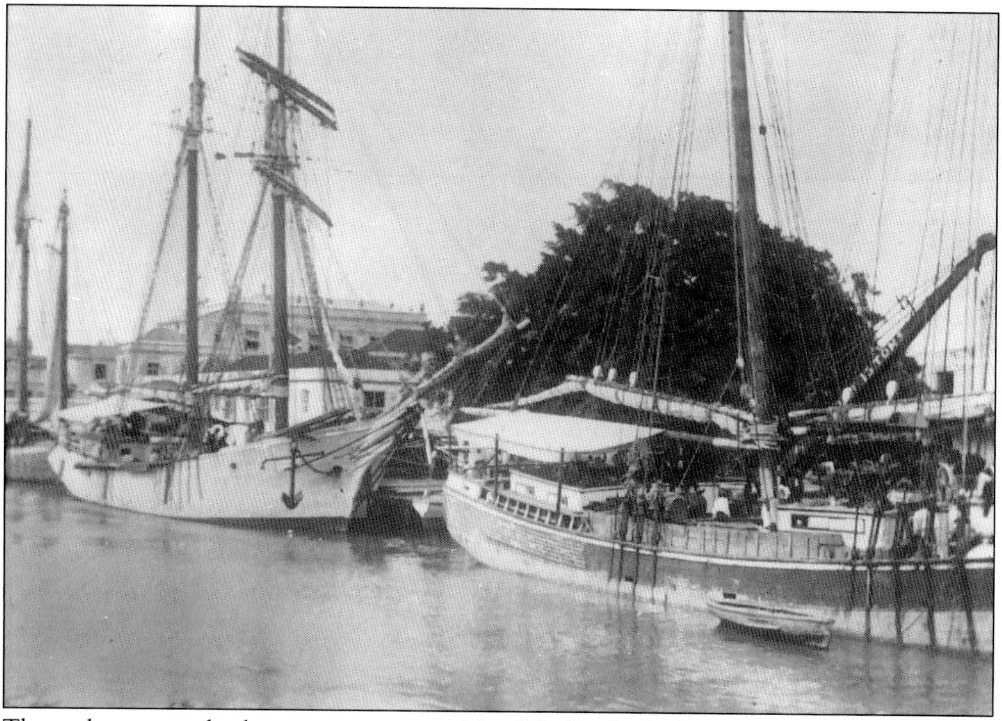

These three-masted schooners were owned by S.R. Fowle & Sons in 1895. They sailed to the West Indies and Cuba and returned laden with hogsheads of molasses, which were sold throughout eastern North Carolina. One schooner was the *Cora*, under the command of Capt. David Gaskill. (Courtesy of Sadie Fowle.)

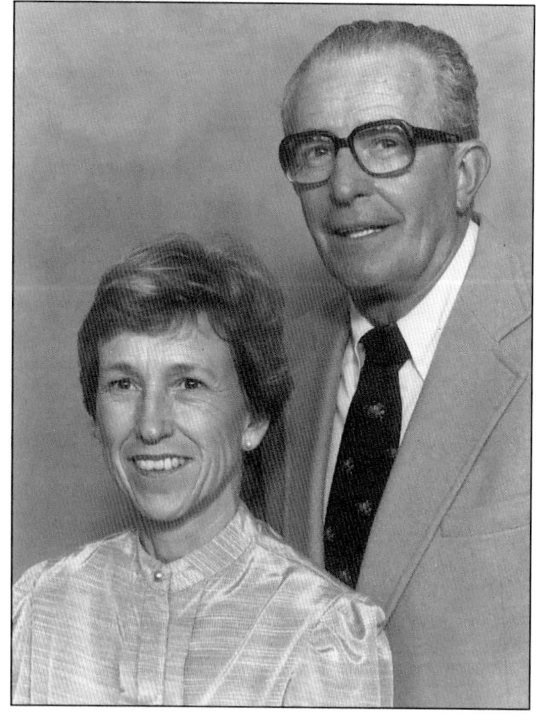

Samuel Richardson Fowle (1925–1991), was the fifth generation to carry the S.R. Fowle name since the family moved to Washington in 1818. Samuel worked as a farm equipment salesman until he retired in 1985. He served on the Washington City Council until 1987 and was mayor of Washington. He died while in office in 1991. Sadie Francis Fowle (1934–) was a teacher in the Beaufort County School system from 1973 until she retired in 1994. Sadie then worked as an education supervisor for Eastern Carolina University in Greenville for several years. Samuel and Sadie were married in 1957 and raised three children, Samuel Richardson IV (1958–), John Marshall (1961–), and Sadie Francis (1966–). (Courtesy of Sadie Fowle.)

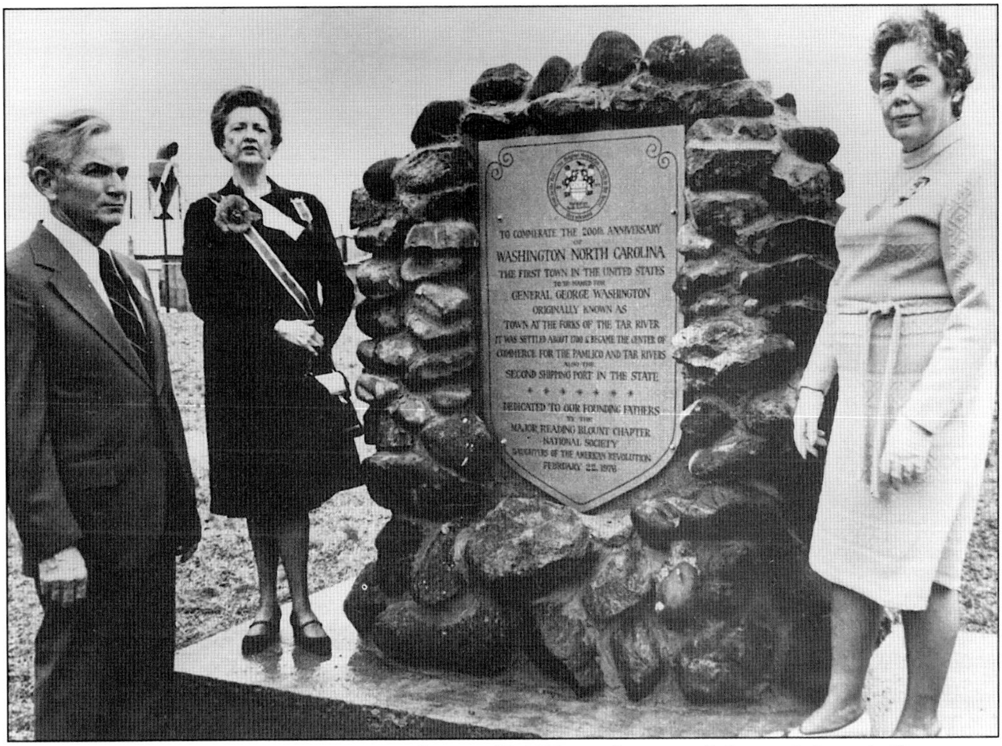

This Daughters of the American Revolution (DAR) marker was fashioned from ballast stone brought in by early sailing ships. The monument, erected on Stewart Parkway at the corner of Water Street in Washington, was dedicated on February 23, 1976 and reads, in part, "To commemorate the 200th anniversary of Washington, North Carolina, the first town in the United States to be named for General George Washington." Pictured here, from left to right, are Mayor Richard Tripp; Mrs. John Blount MacLeod, state regent of the DAR; and Mrs. W.P. McLean, regent of the Major Reading Blount chapter of the DAR. (Courtesy of the DAR.)

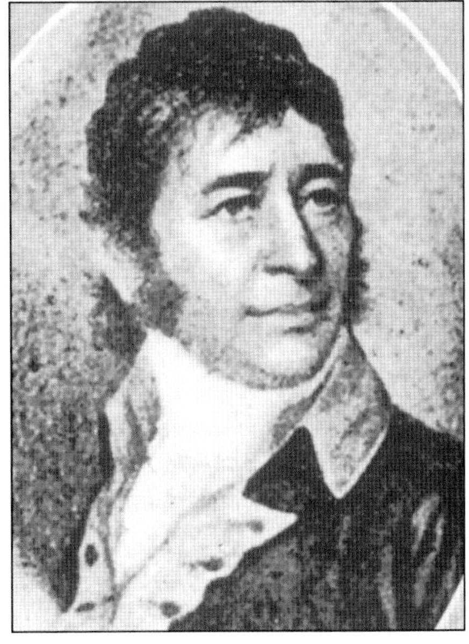

Maj. Reading Blount (1757–1807) was captain of the fifth regiment of the North Carolina Continental Troops from April 1776 until May 1788 during the Revolutionary War. He served successively under Generals Jethro Sumner and Nathaniel Greene in their brilliant Carolinas campaign. Blount was cited for bravery in the battles of Guilford Court House and Eutaw Springs and was promoted to major in 1778. After the war, he was appointed major general of the North Carolina Militia by the North Carolina Legislature. Major Blount resided in "Bellefont" off NC 264, west of Washington. He was a charter member of the Society of the Cincinnati. The Major Reading Blount Chapter of the DAR was organized in 1910 by Miss Lida T. Rodman, the first regent. (Courtesy of NC Historic Bath.)

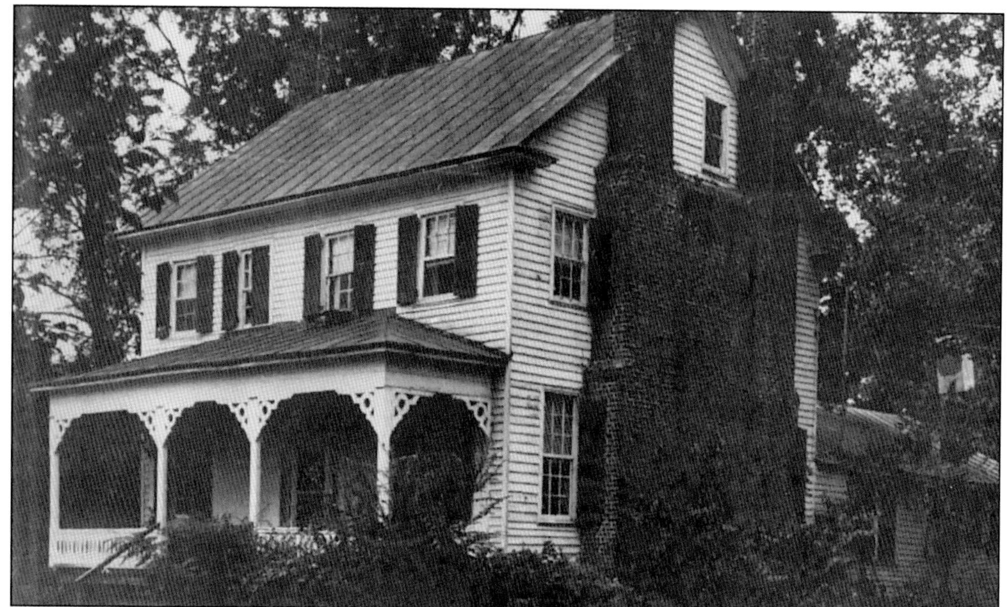

This is the Bellefont Plantation house (c. 1790), the home of Maj. Reading Blount. Bellefont is located in the Tranters Creek area on a side road off NC 264. In the year 2000, this house was "in remarkably fine condition . . . there's not a crack in the twin chimneys . . . and the interior paneling has been lovingly restored," said Philip Madre, who is knowledgeable in restoration work. Maj. Reading Blount is buried in the graveyard behind his house. (Courtesy of WDN.)

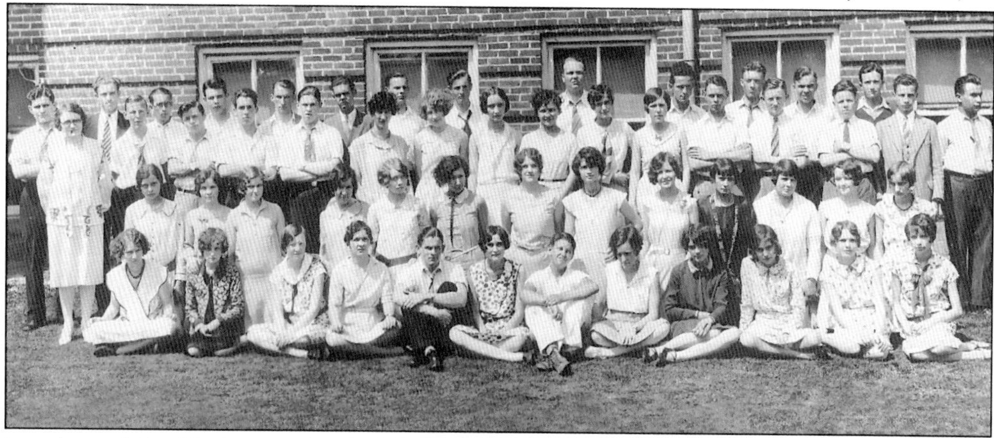

Members of the Washington High School Class of 1929, pictured from left to right, are (front row) Eleanor Shelton, Minnie T. Ross, Elizabeth Flynn, Nellie Stewart, Fenner Phillips, Lillian Birch Ellison, William A. Oden, Carlotta L. Waters, Erma McLean, Laura Butler, Margaret Sparrow, and Annie Mae Pledger; (second row) Elizabeth Alligood, Margaret Patrick, Hattie Carrow, Mildred Leggett, Josie Covey, Louise Williams, Nina Way Credle, Dera Parvin, Helena Russ, Minnie Lee Gurganus, Alice May Elks, Evelyn Cutler, and Sina Scott; (third row) homeroom teacher Mrs. E.T. Campbell, John Williams, Rufus Shackelford, George Phillips, George Fulford, Betsy Harding, Mildred Harrison, Helen Parker, Louise Paul, Pauline Stilley, Mary Whit Matthews, Milton Brown, Charlie Alligood, Johnnie Jones, Alfred H. Hodges, and Cleveland Duke; (fourth row) Wendell Tyson, Principal E. S. Johnson, Fred Alligood, Dumay Gorham, Bill Daniels, Ed Mallison, Ras Daniel, Norwood Simmons, Leon Watson, Norman Waters, Bruce Alligood, Oliver Credle, and Bill Waters. (Courtesy of Vance Harper Jones.)

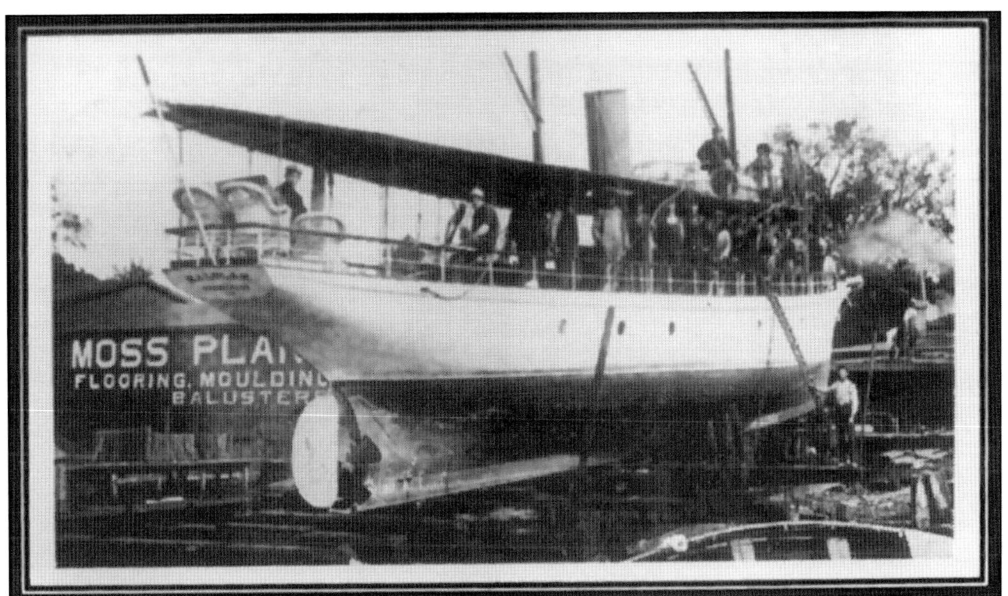

This beautiful steam yacht sits in dry dock at the Moss Planing Mill awaiting some bottom work around 1909. Beverly G. Moss started the Moss Planing Mill in 1907. (Courtesy of BCM.)

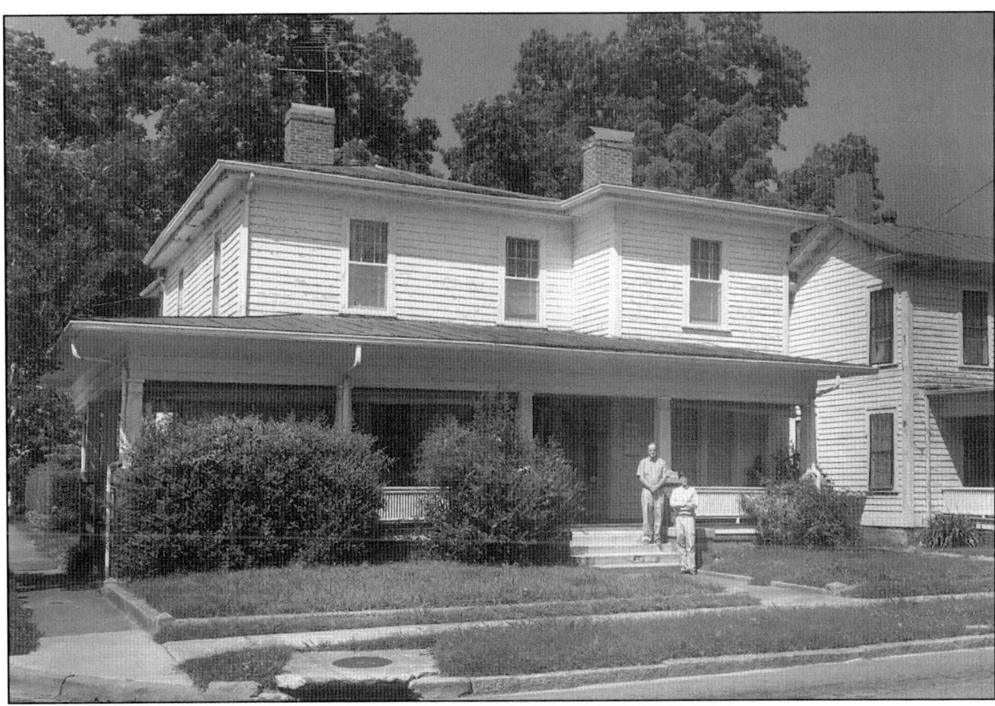

The Capt. Milton "Mick" S. and Susan W. Mayo House was built on Lot 52 at 202 East Second Street in 1873. This home replaced the original 1830 George Hobbs house that burned during the War in 1864. Henry A. and Lucille Harper Jones purchased this fine home in 1944. The Mayo House is a pleasant blend of late 19th- and early 20th-century architectural styles. Shown standing on the steps are (front) Vance Harper Jones and (back) Rev. William Donald Harper Jones of Dry Ridge, Kentucky Presbyterian Church. (Photo by Louis Van Camp.)

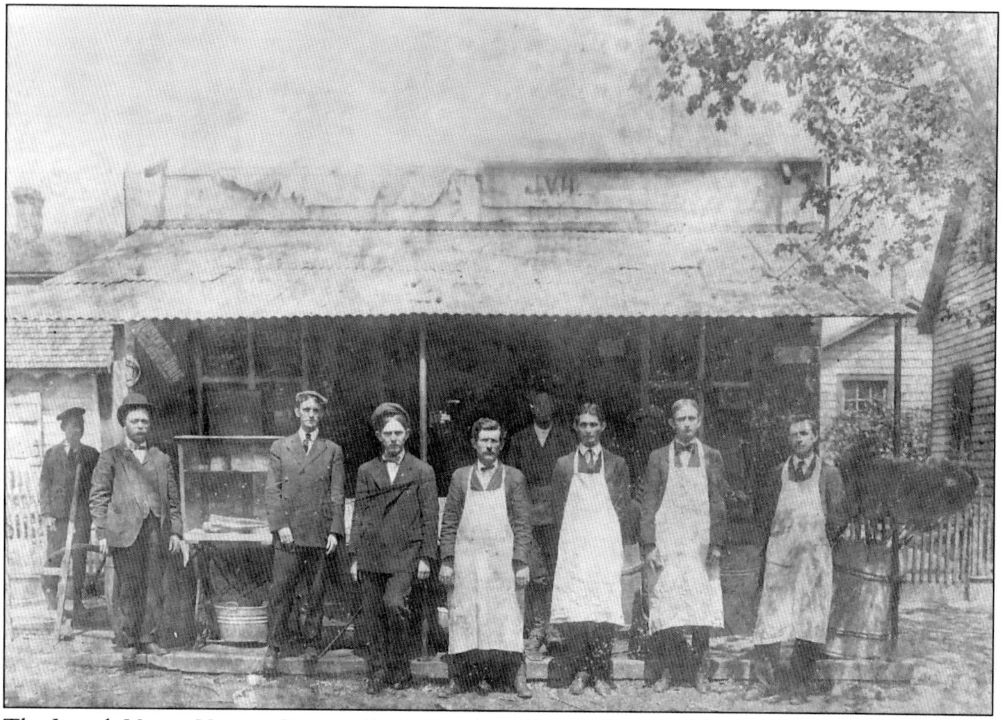

The Joseph Vance Harper Grocery Store stood on the north side of the 500 block on West Third Street in the late 1800s. Pictured in this early 1900s photo are, from left to right, unidentified, Mr. ? Rhodes (in derby), Dave Shelton, unidentified, Joseph Vance Harper (Saturday clerk), unidentified (in background), Fernando Lilley (regular clerk), Charles Dudley, and Zoph Leggett. (Courtesy of Vance Harper Jones.)

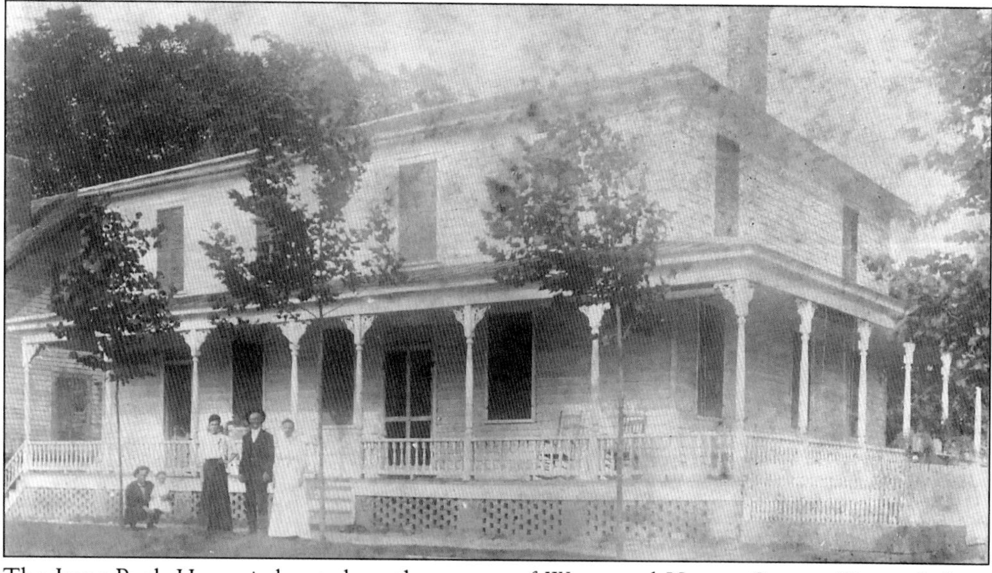

The Isaac Buck House is located on the corner of Water and Harvey Streets. Pictured, from left to right, are Mr. ? Daniels and his son, Sarah Jones (the sister of Angeline Turner Buck), Isaac Buck, and Angeline Turner Buck. Isaac Buck was Vance Harper Jones's great-grandfather. (Courtesy of Vance Harper Jones.)

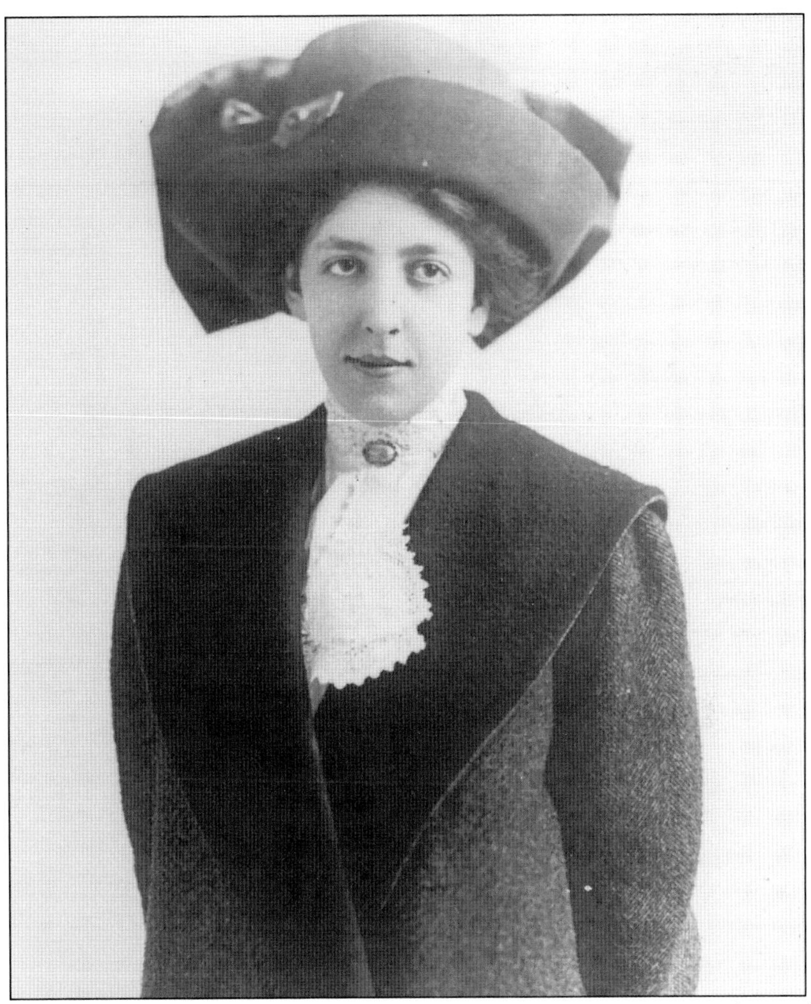

Anne Blackwell Payne (1887–1969) was a poet born in Concord, New Hampshire. The Payne family moved to Washington when she was six months old. Anne graduated from Flora McDonald College and was a member of the Writer's Club of Columbia University. Anne wrote a poem about Washington titled "My Little Town."

My little town, that has not yet attained,
The height and breadth of cities, oh, stay small !,
What profit is the vastness they have gained,
Their strength of stone and steel; when, growing tall,
They lose the singing company of leaves;
And growing wide, they have no room for grass;
No rose vines reaching for contented eves,
No space to watch the seasons as they pass.
No lure have cities to entice a thrush,
Nor yards for children, carpeted and sweet;
With all their pride and gaiety and rush,
They bear the burden of a million feet.
You have your gardens, friendliness, and trees,
My little town, be satisfied with these.

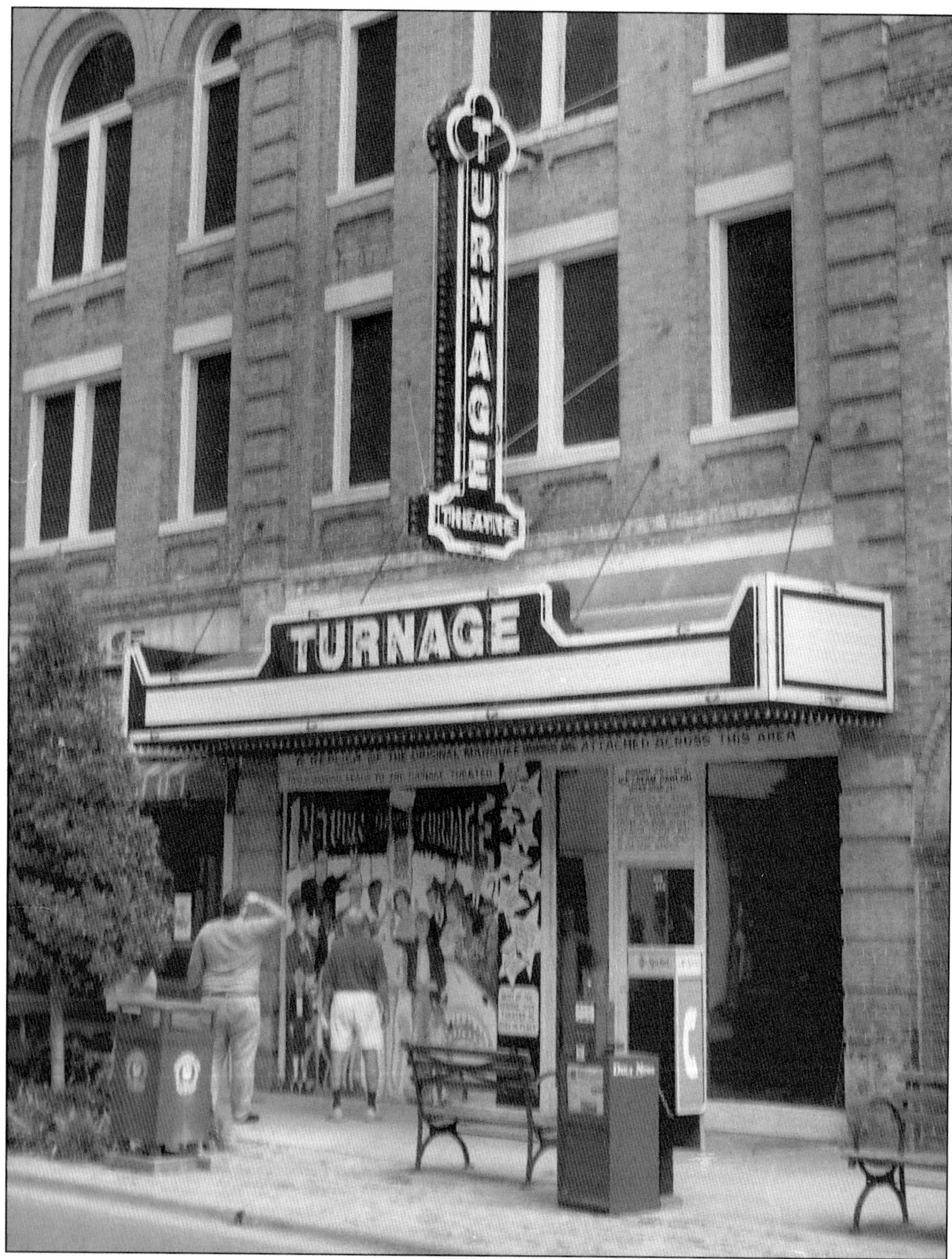

On the evening of July 29, 2000, some 300 people gathered to see the ceremonial lighting of the new Turnage Theater marquee. This event kicked off the annual weekend Summer Festival. The Turnage Theater, originally a vaudeville house, seated 400 people and operated from 1930 to 1976. The Turnage Theater Foundation is working to reopen soon. (Photo by Louis Van Camp.)

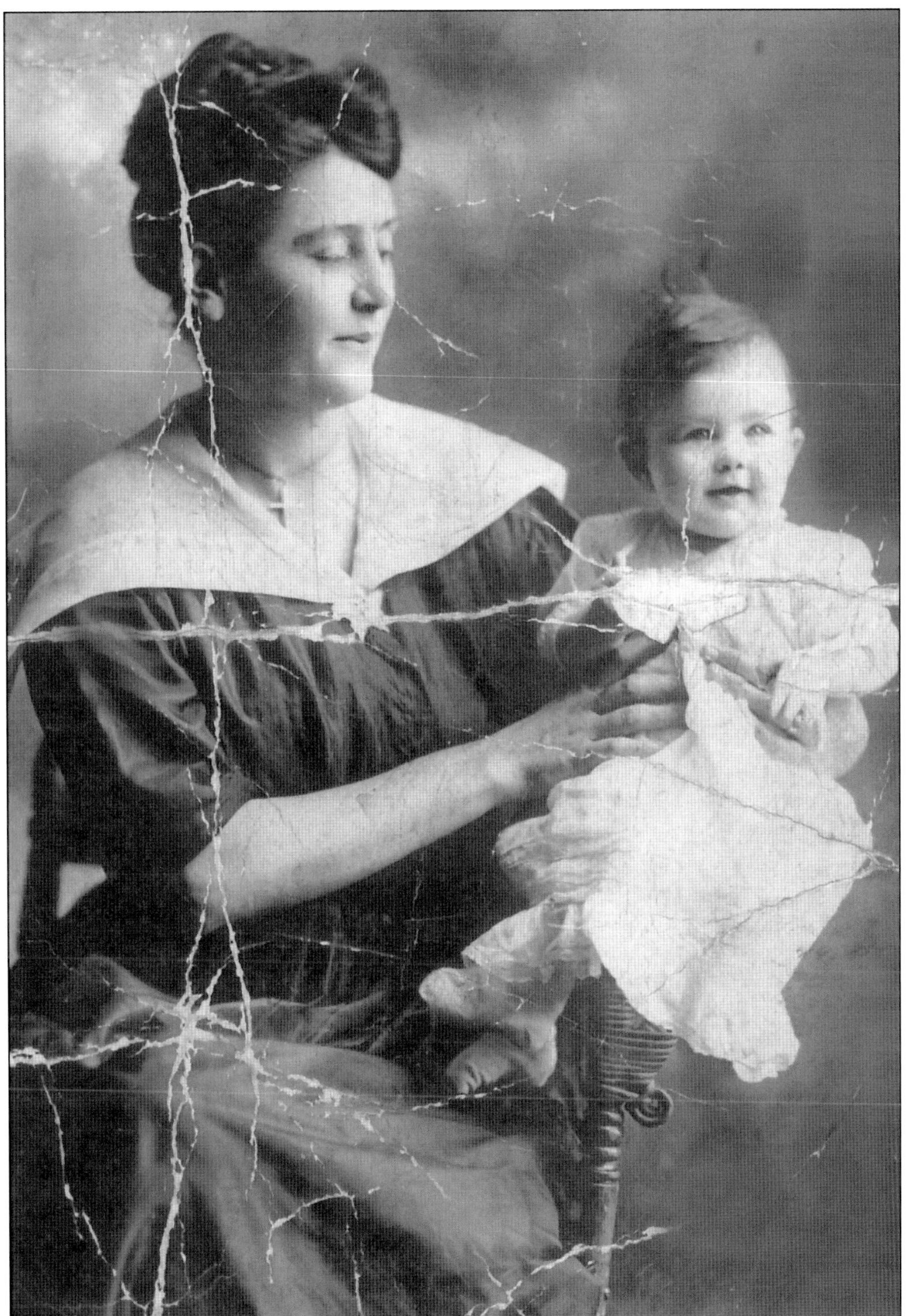

This portrait of lovely Annie Elizabeth Mitchell, at age 29, with her daughter Fannie Mae Singelton Clark, at age 2, was made in her home at 611 Charlotte Street in Washington in 1916. Annie was born in 1887 and died in 1967 at age 80. (Courtesy of Pat Clark.)

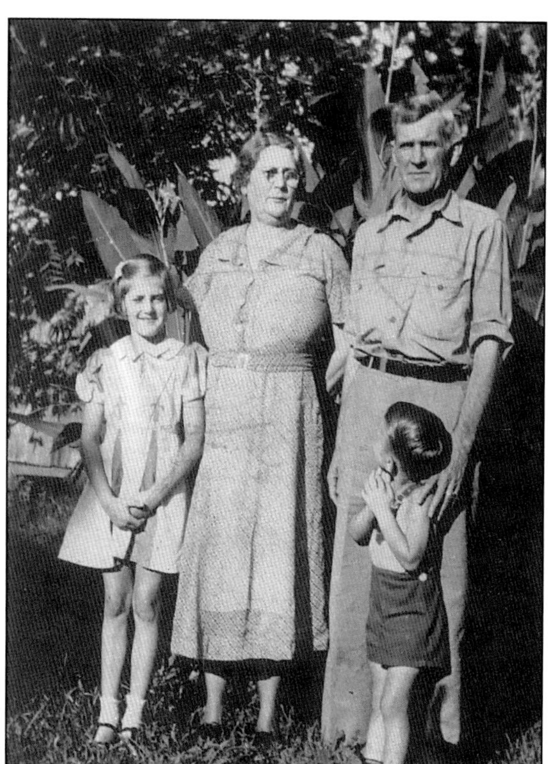

This 1937 photo shows, from left to right, Helen Irene Singelton at age 9, Annie Mitchell Singelton, James Ellison Singelton, and their neighbor Hubert Fodrey Jr. at age 4. (Courtesy of Pat Clark.)

Thomp Litchfield of Washington is shown at the controls of his P-47 Thunderbolt at an English airstrip in World War II in 1944. Litchfield was shot down over France and held as a prisoner of war. After the war, he returned to Washington and, along with two other partners, purchased the Moss Planing Mill Company. Litchfield was one of the original founders of the Washington Yacht and Country Club, which opened in December of 1949. (Courtesy of BCM.)

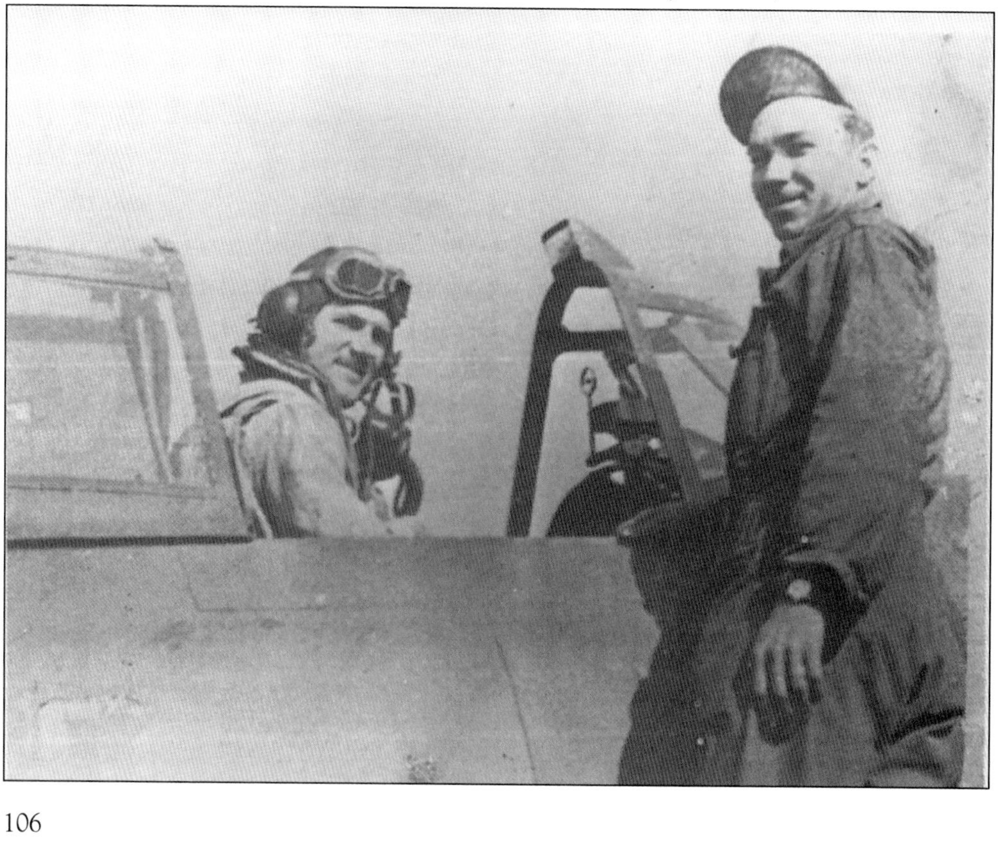

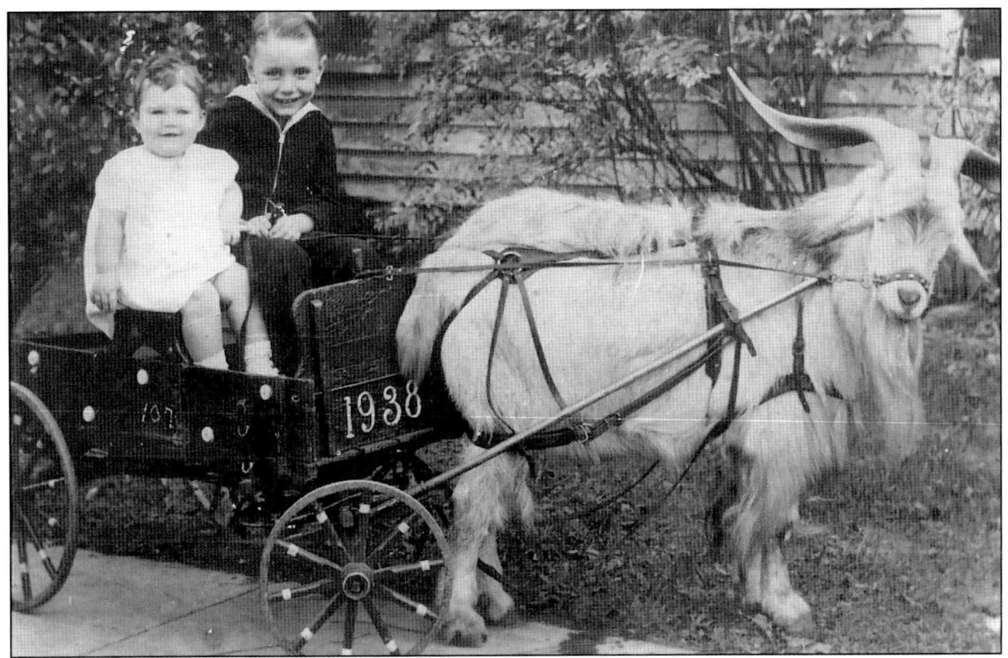

Shown here in 1938 is Patricia Ann Clark, born in 1937, and Hubert Fodrey Jr., born in 1933, with their pet goat. (Courtesy of Pat Clark.)

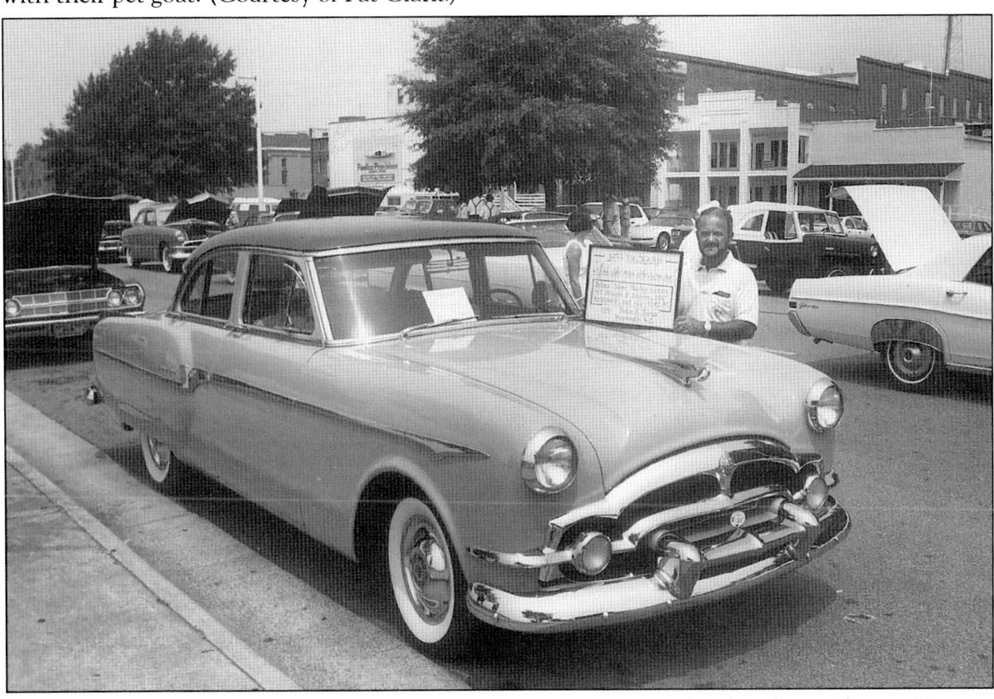

Preston K. Turner of Washington proudly displays his 1953 Packard Deluxe Clipper Touring Sedan at the August 1999 annual Antique Automobile Club of America Show held on Stewart Parkway in Washington. "This Packard has a 327 straight S engine which produces a 160 horsepower. This beauty sold for $3,192 in 1953," said Turner who restored it around 1987. His classic car took first place in Class 26D. (Photo by Louis Van Camp)

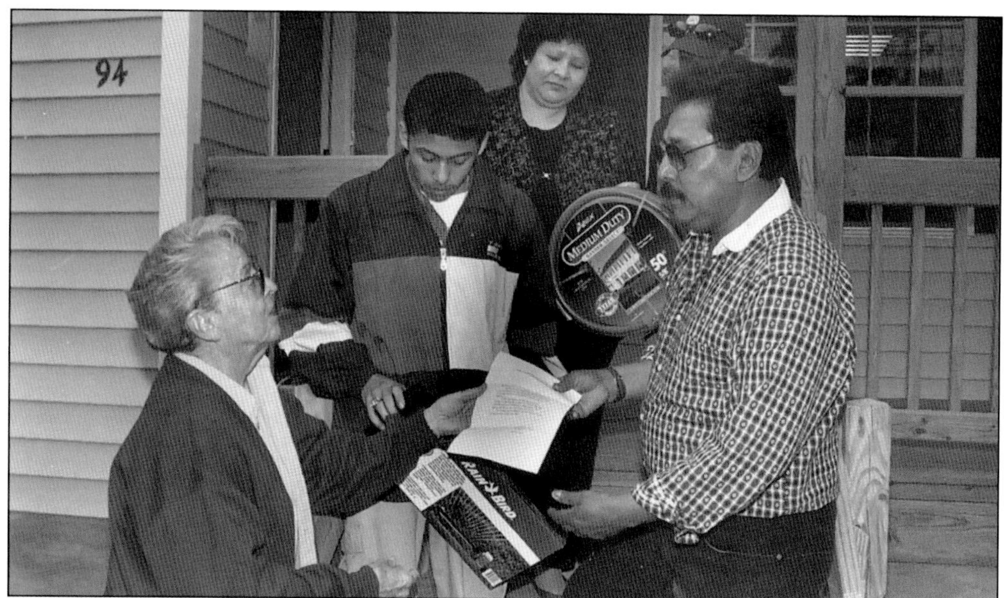

On March 4, 2000, Nancy Nash, the civic beautification chairperson of the Washington Garden Club, presented Gino and Izabeth Pelagio and their son a garden hose and sprinkler for their new Habitat for Humanity home. Habitat is not a welfare charity, but a non-government volunteer project that helps responsible, low-income families become homeowners. "This is my dream come true," said Izabeth Pelagio with tears welling in her eyes. (Photo by Louis Van Camp.)

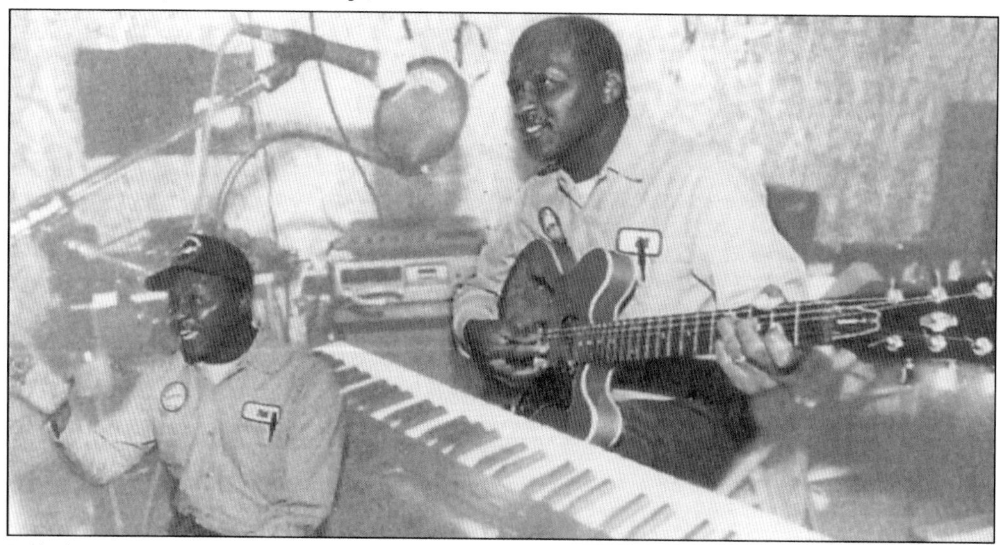

Bill Ebison, a native of Washington, is a multi-talented musician who has written songs about restless youth and the desire to leave home, only to return again. "I've lived in Massachusetts, New Jersey, and Virginia," recalls Ebison, "but I like Washington best. I love it here. I've always loved this city, that's why I came back." Ebison's first recording in 1986 was a catchy tribute to Washington called "I Like Your Style, Washington." The song as it is recorded sounds like a group of singers accompanied by a band. However, Ebison plays all of the instruments and sings all four of the vocal renditions. He put the entire piece together in his home studio on a digital recording. (Courtesy of Rusty Walker.)

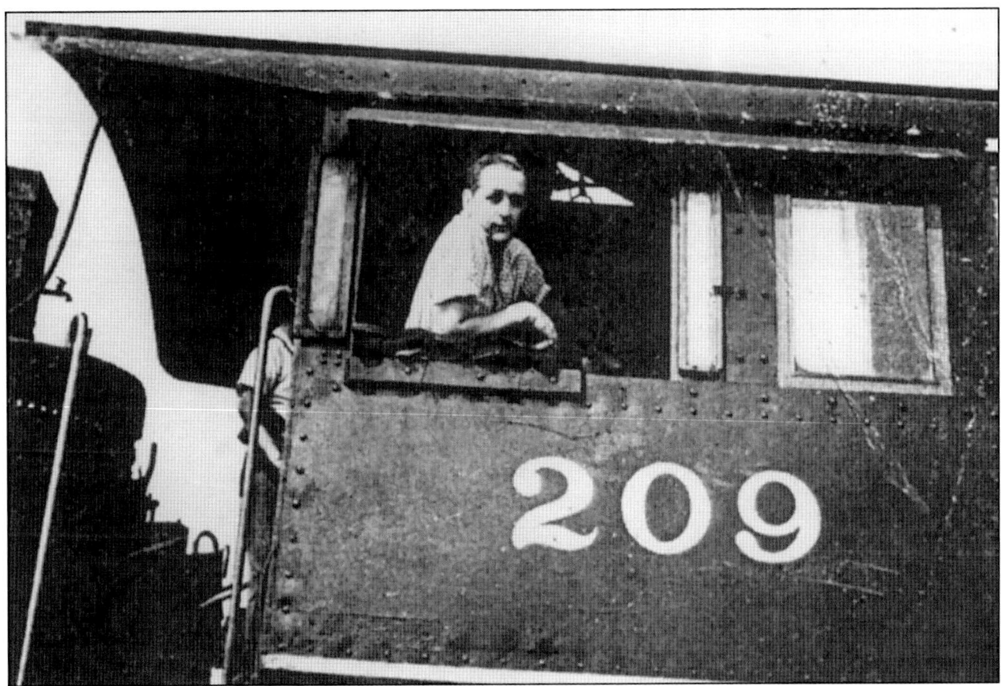

In the engineer's seat of Gainesville Midland steam locomotive 209 is William "Bill" Sellers of Wilson, at age 37. As a young lad, Bill would come to Washington every chance he had and stay at his aunt Mae Alligood's home. "Billy just loved trains," said Aunt Mae. About Washington Bill says, "In the 1930s, Washington was a magic river town of sawmills, steam railroads and gingerbread houses. My young days there were as close to a Tom Sawyer life as was possible without going to Missouri." (Courtesy of Bill Sellers.)

The Farmer's Market was originally located downtown off Respess Street where the covered stalls are located. When business slowed down in the late 1990s, the market was moved to the corner of Whispering Pines Road and West Fifteenth Street. For farm-fresh produce, residents shop at this fine market, which is open Saturdays from 7 a.m. until 1 p.m., most of the year. A group of regulars is pictured in 1991, including, from left to right, Hazel Moore, Paul Wilson, Willis Pippin, Terrance Moore, Willard Daniels, and Adelene Gurganus. (Courtesy of WDN.)

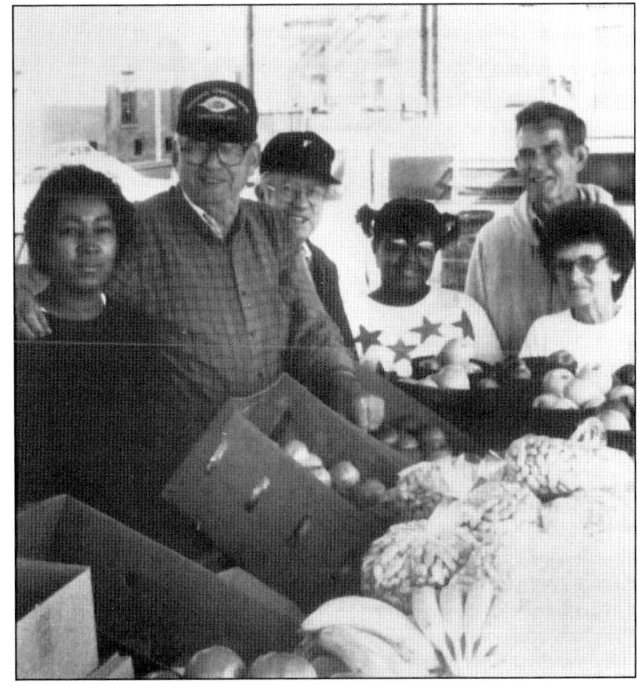

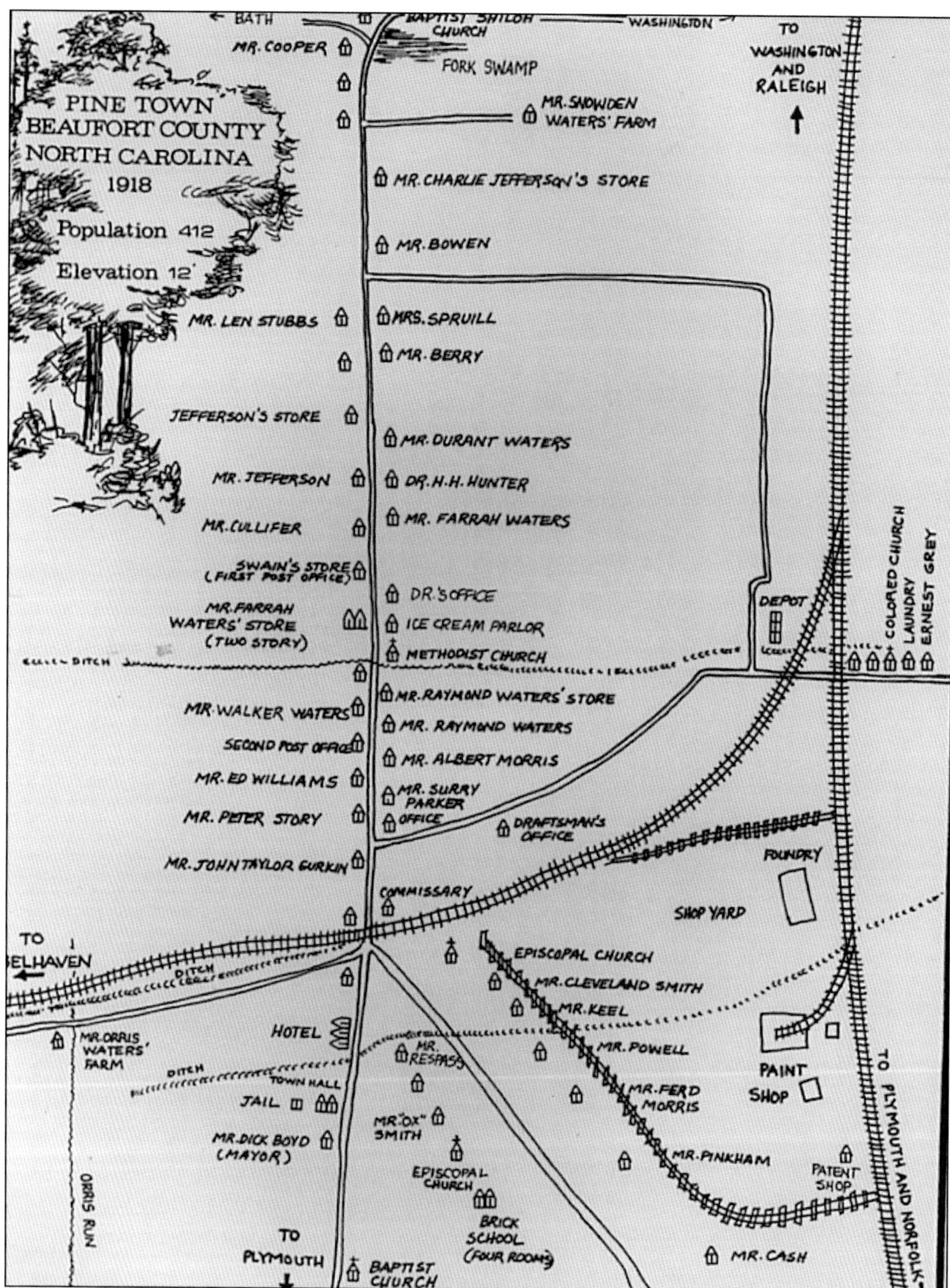

This 1918 street map of Pine Town indicates a population of 412 residents. Pine Town was incorporated in 1907 by founder Surry Parker and is located about 3 miles west of Acre, off NC 32. The post office was established in 1894 next to the saw mill commissary, and Ferdinand L. Morris was the first postmaster. The town name was shortened to "Pinetown" in 1930. (*)

Seven

PINETOWN, YEATESVILLE, TERRA CEIA

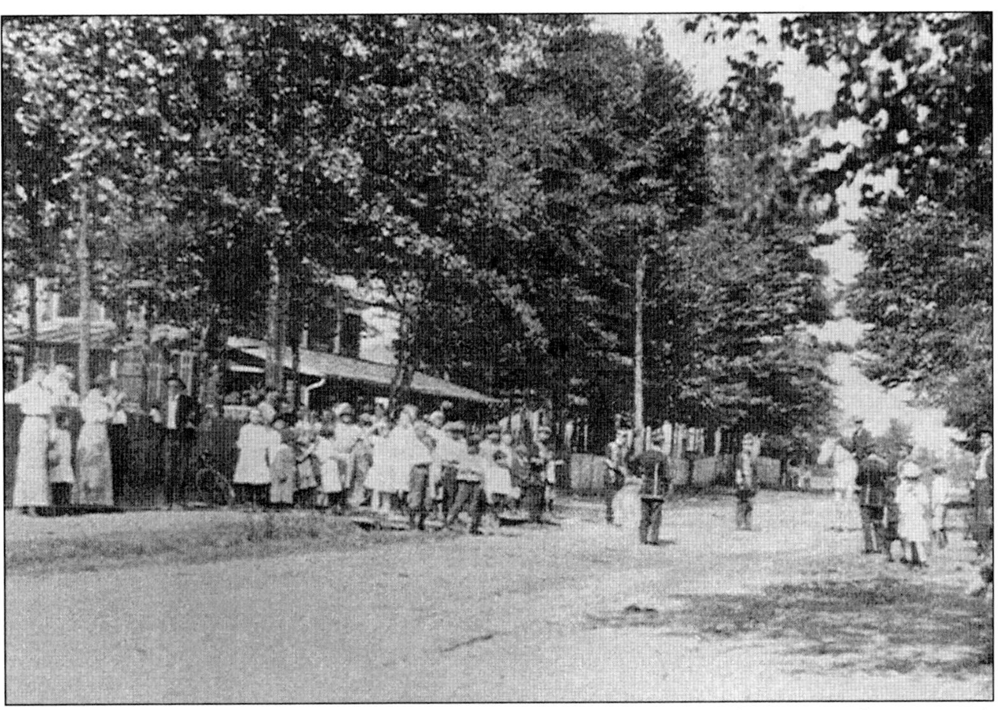

Main Street had a few lamp posts equipped with oil lamps that were lit every night. Livestock ran loose in the street and often one had to walk around an old sow resting on the dirt sidewalk. Most yards had no fences to keep livestock out, and the sidewalk was between the yards and the drainage ditch on the street's edge. By 1910, the yards were fenced. This Main Street scene shows the residents awaiting the arrival of a circus parade in 1912. (*)

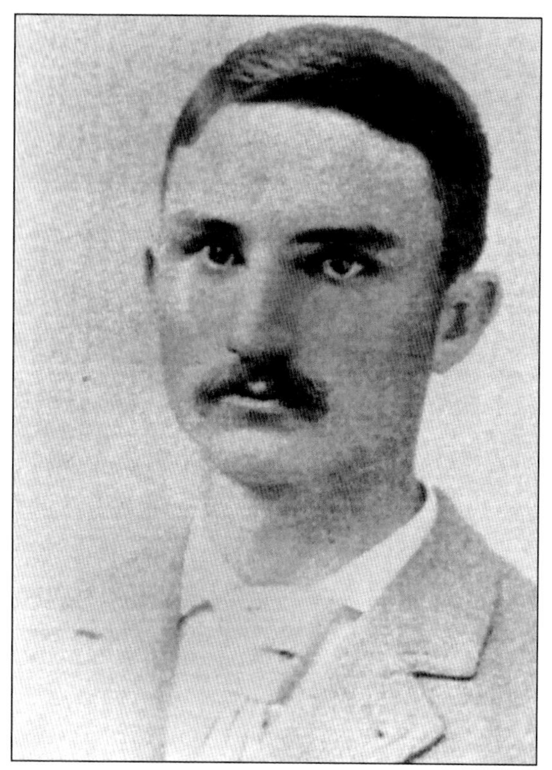

Surry Parker was born in 1866 and "planned, owned, organized, and appropriately named Pine Town [in 1893]," says Elizabeth Parker Roberts in her book *Family and Friends, Pine Town, North Carolina.* Parker is pictured here at about age 35. Parker began designing and building steam logging machinery around 1893. He died in 1942 at the age of 76. (*)

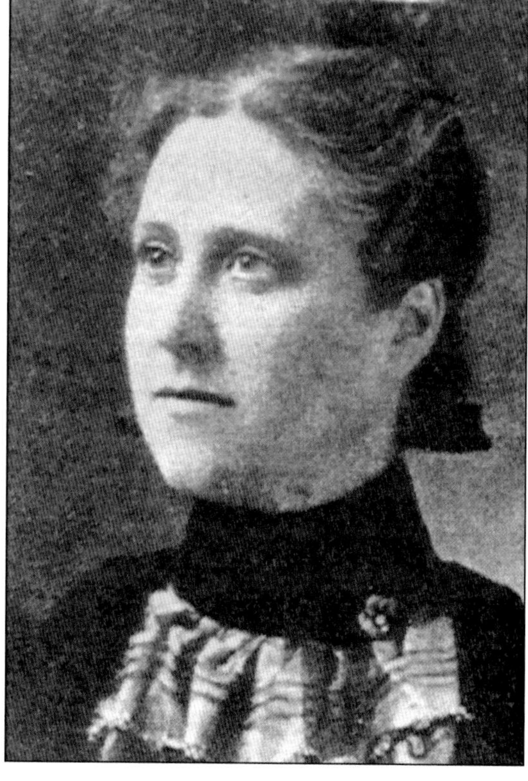

Mary Shepard Odam Parker was born in 1872 and had two sisters and a brother. Her mother died at age 35 and her father died at age 43. Mary then became the head of her family. She was Surry Parker's second wife, his first wife having died at an early age. Mary was valedictorian of her class at Suffolk Female Institute and remained to teach until her two sisters finished college. (*)

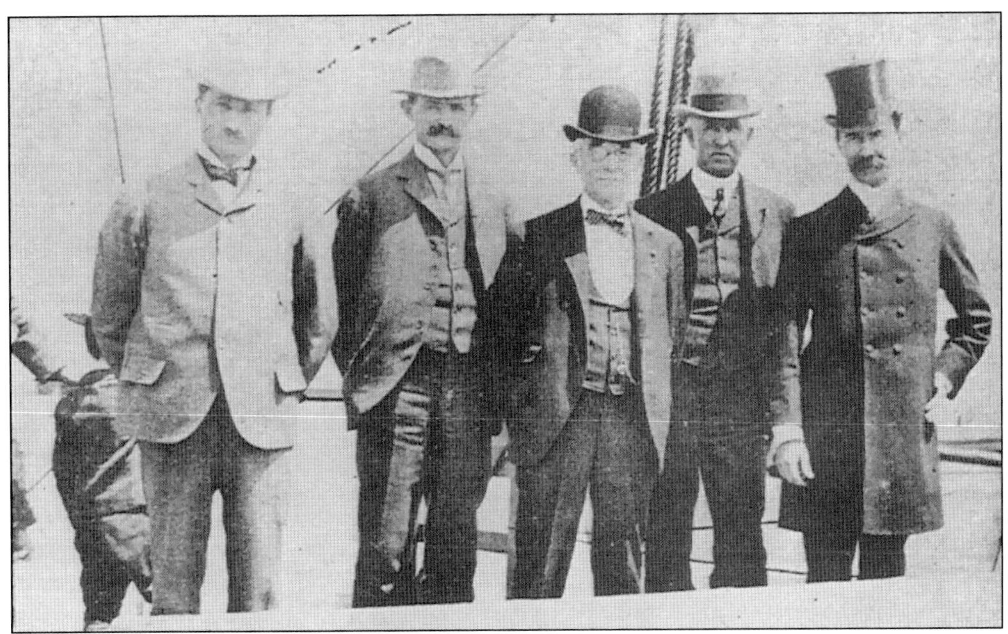

In 1904, the Atlantic Seaboard Coastline Railroad opened a station on Gladden Street in Washington. The company officers gathered for the opening, from left to right, are Surry Parker, R.S. Cohn, ? Cheney, William M. Whaley, and Judge E.A. Armstrong. (*)

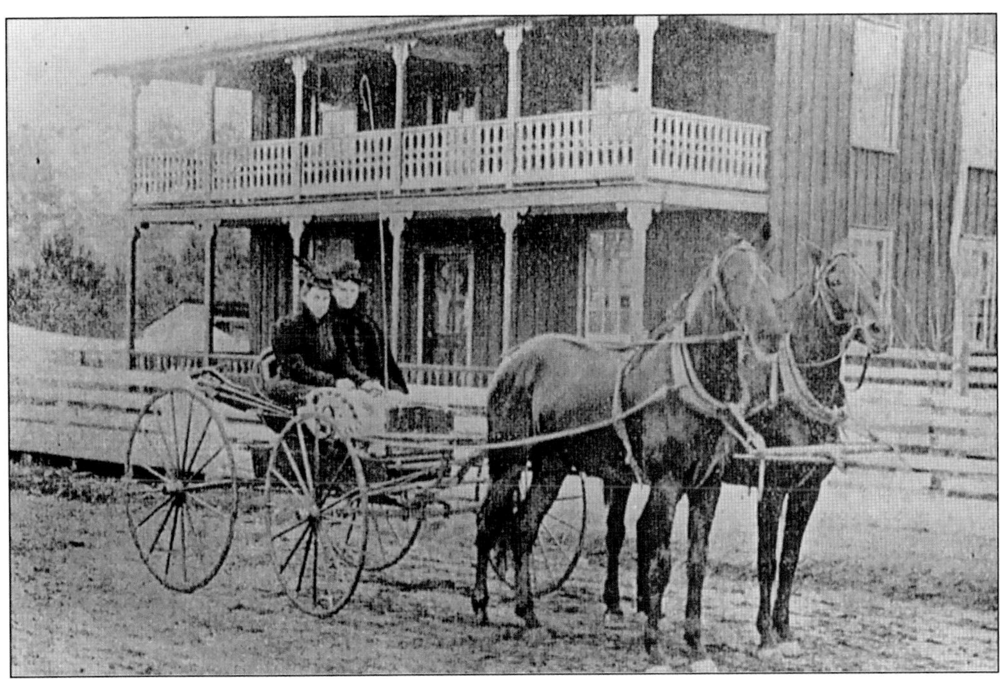

The Pine Town Hotel was a fine Victorian two-story inn built by Surry Parker for the "drummers" (traveling salesmen) and for the bachelors who worked in his office. The hotel had a double-trimmed porch adorned with Victorian curlicues. The hotel's first cook was Mrs. Nelms, a wonderful cook with a special old-fashioned chicken salad recipe the Parker family continues to pass down from generation to generation. (*)

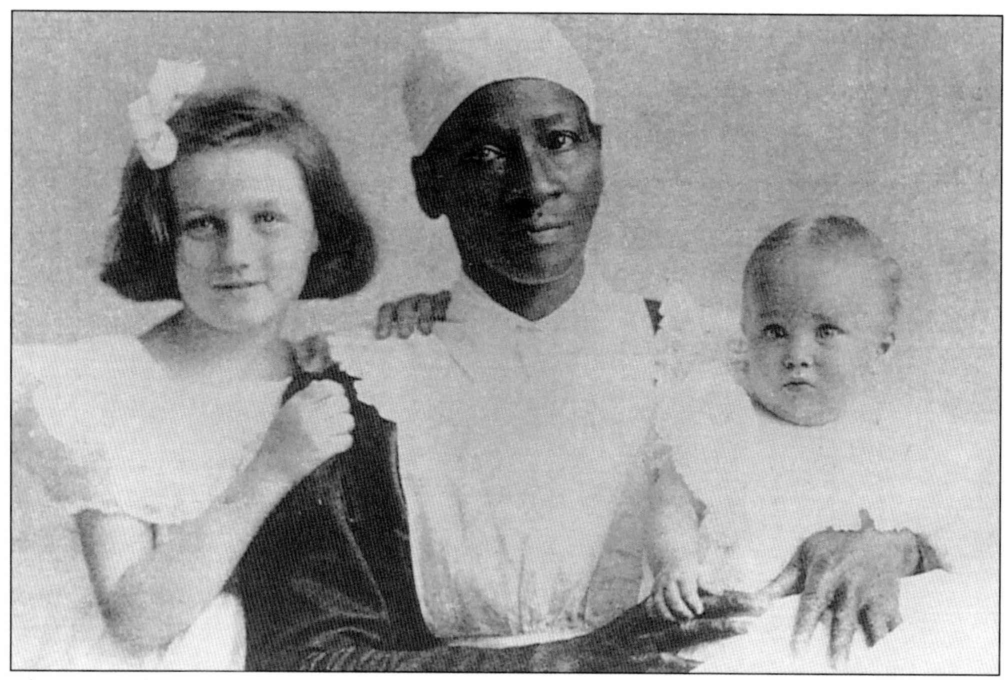

This is Caroline "Mammy" Robinson (center). Mammy wet-nursed Isabel Parker (on the left, shown at age eight, and baby Emmy (right). Mammy once accompanied the Parker family to Atlantic City. (*)

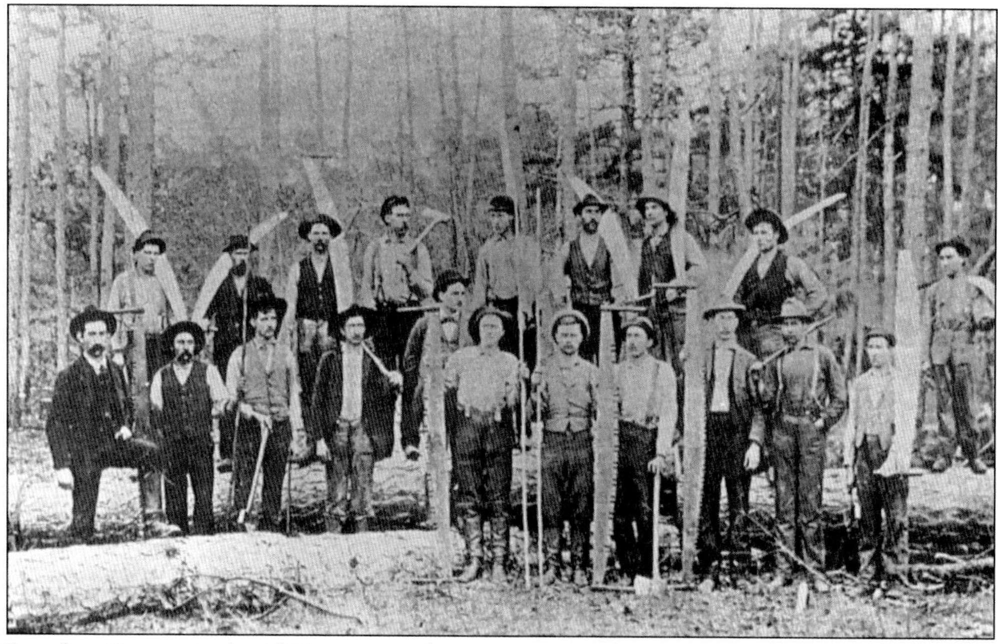

Beaufort County in the 1880s was mostly virgin pine timber country. Every little town had a lumber mill, but Washington was the shipping center of the industry for this area. Pine Town developed around Surry Parker's machine shop, where he designed and built his own logging machines. This is Parker's Pine Town crew of loggers who gathered for a picture on May 1, 1897. Surry Parker is the man in the center wearing a derby hat. (*)

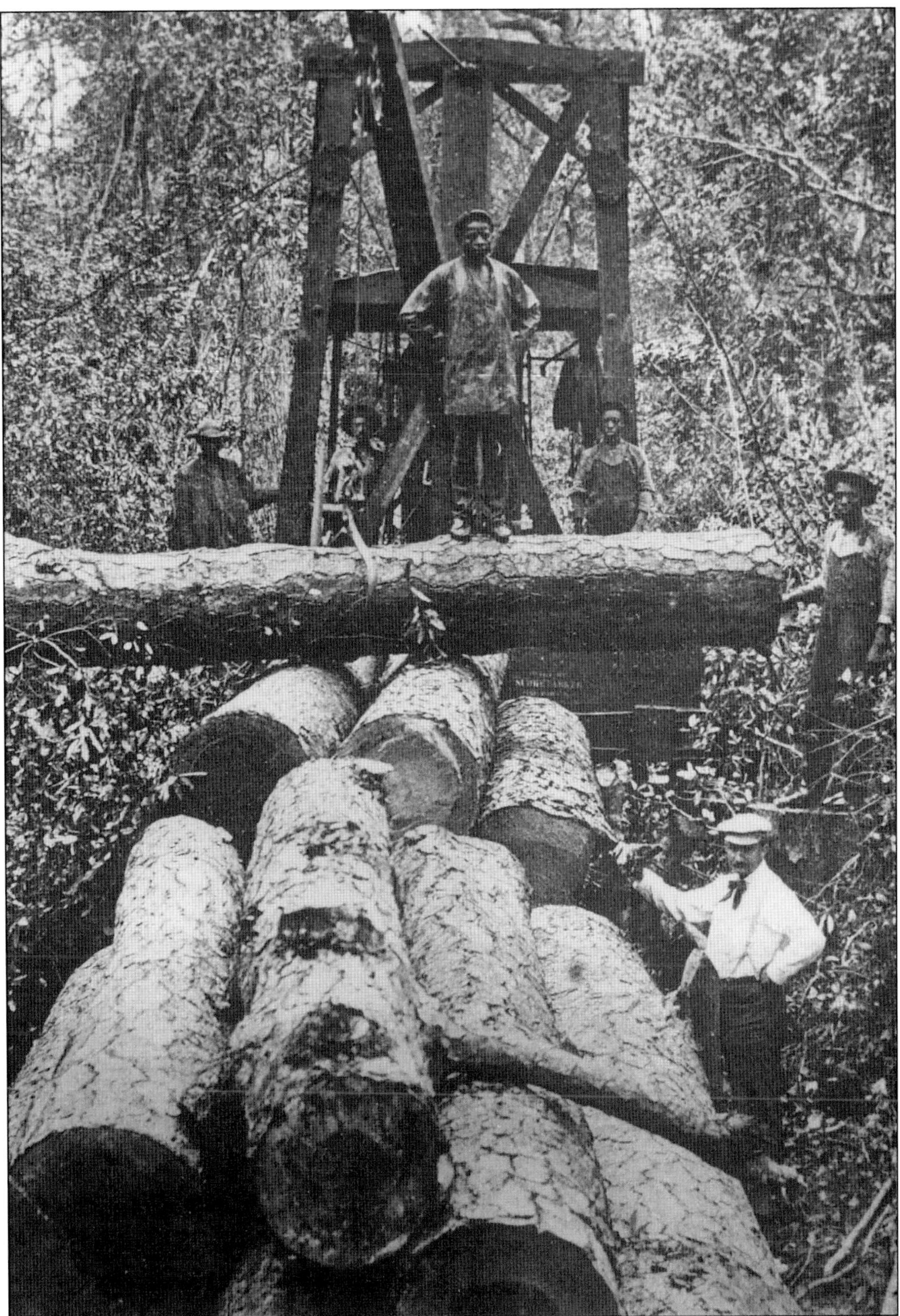

Surry Parker was known far and wide for his ingenious designs of logging machines. Here, Parker (in the white shirt) stands next to one of his machines working deep within a swampy pine tree region near Pinetown. (Postcard courtesy of Oden's Store.)

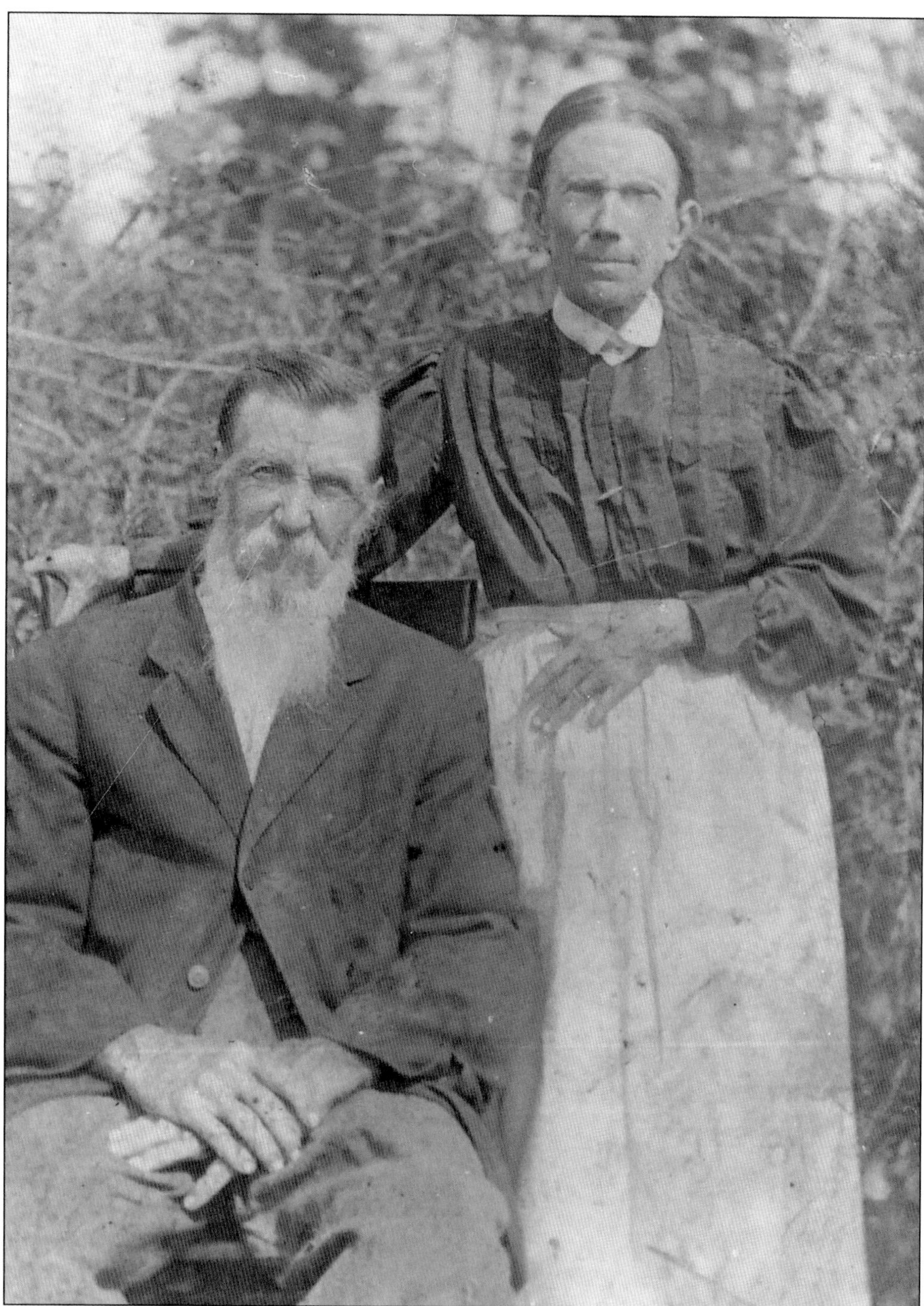

John William Jordan Sr. and his wife, Mary Jane Baynor Jordan, were both born in 1845. They were married on November 10, 1866 and had seven children: Robert Caswell (born 1870), Ellen Vielena (born 1872), Mariah Victoria (born 1876), Katie K. (born 1879), Robert Adelaide (born 1882), Mary (born 1888), and John William Jr. (born 1890). (Courtesy of Jean Bowen.)

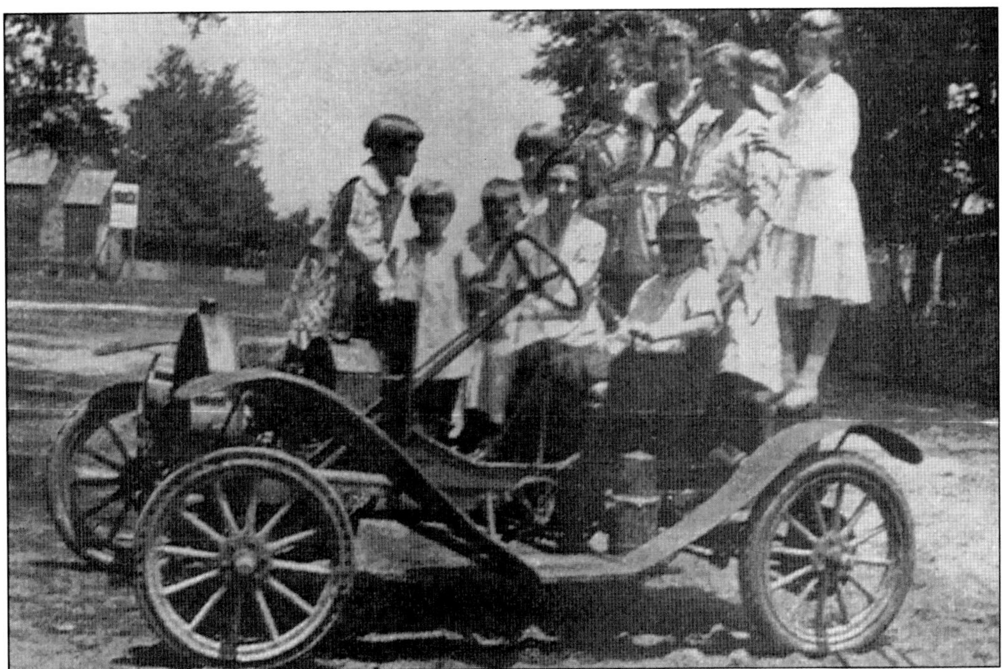

The Parker family owned one of the first automobiles in Beaufort County. The family pose in their Brush automobile, which Parker acquired to settle a debtor's account around 1910. The children nicknamed it "Baby Bullet." This handsome car had wooden spoked wheels with solid rubber tires. The motor hood was often left off to make it easier to prime the engine when starting. (*)

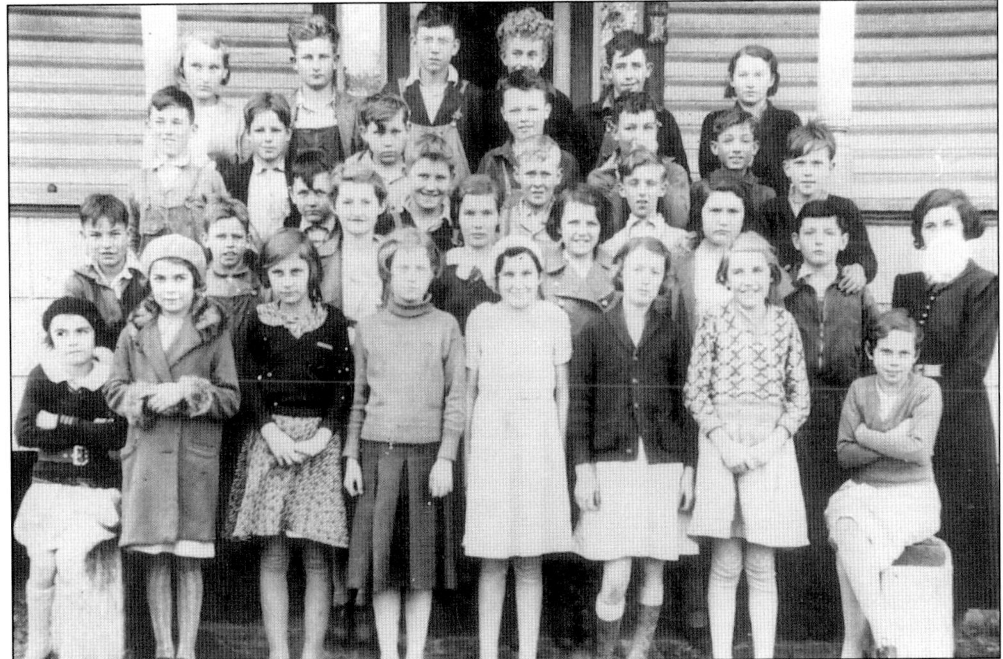

These are the students of Pine Town Elementary School around 1930 with their teacher Elizabeth Oden Elliott (in black, on right). (Courtesy of John Oden.)

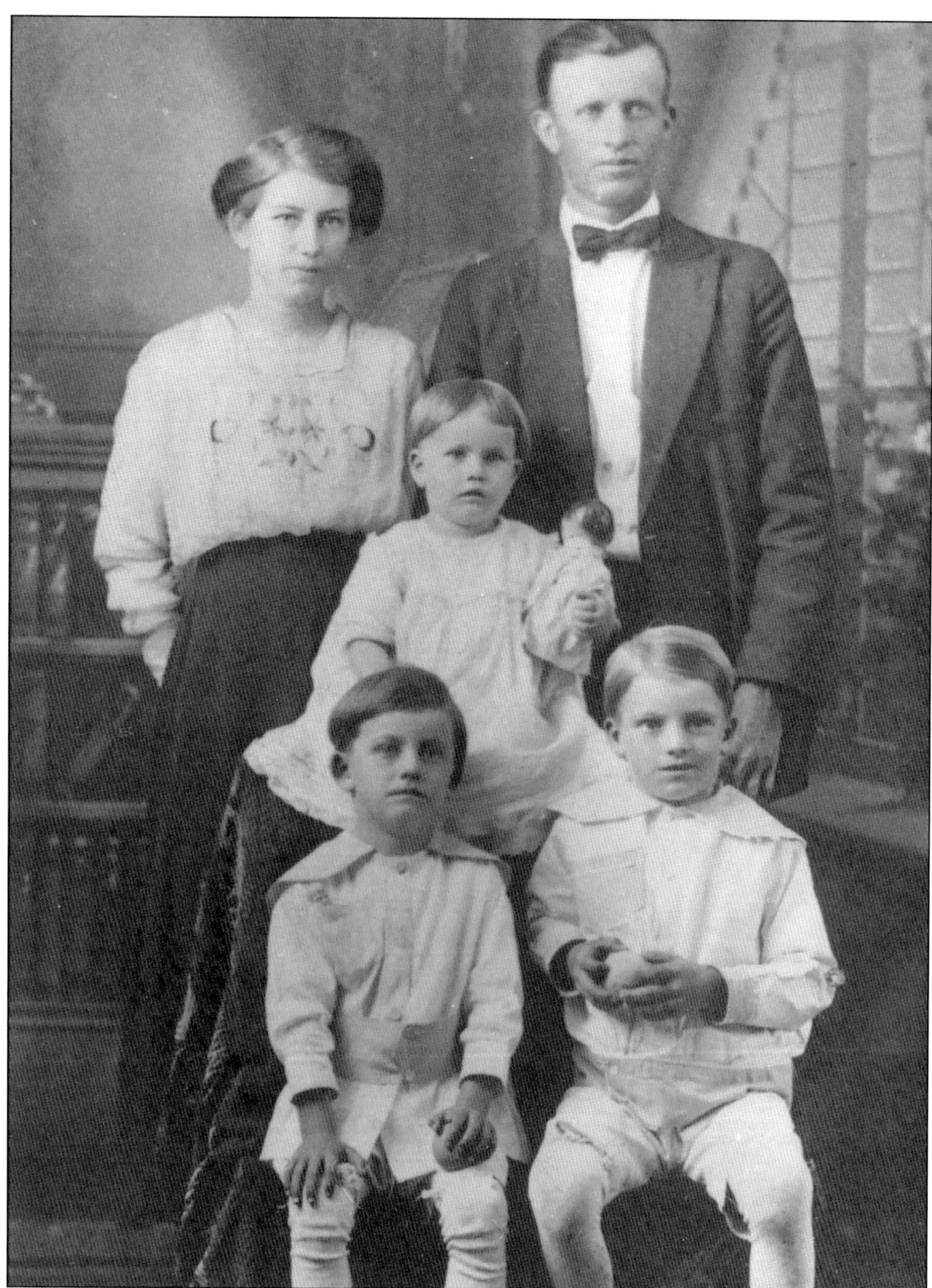

This photo of the John William Jordan Jr. family of Pinetown was taken around 1921. Jordan was a section foreman for the Norfolk Southern Railway in Pinetown until 1926, when he returned to farming. Pictured, from left to right, are (front row) Leslie William Jordan (born 1915) and Leroy Edward Jordan (born 1913); (middle row) Blanche Isabell Jordan (born 1918); (back row) Malissa Alice Bell Jordan (born 1899) and John William Jordan Jr. (born 1890). (Courtesy of Jean Bowen.)

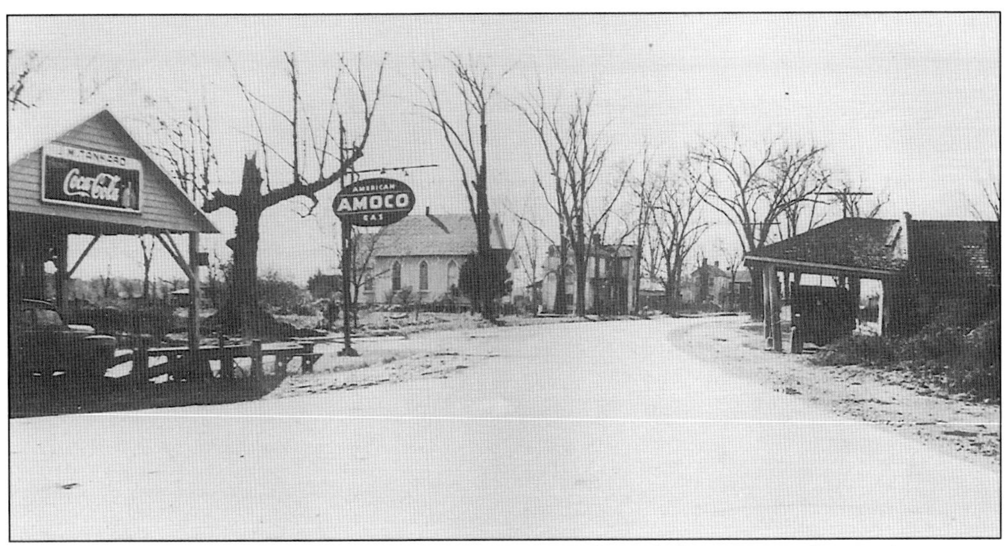

Around 1920, if you were traveling east on NC 264 and needed gas or got thirsty, there was a very quaint Amoco gas station at the intersection of Yeatesville Road and NC 264. It was the J.M. Tankard & Co. general merchandise store. This store had everything from stick candy and soda pop to gas caps. J.M. Tankard bought a larger piece of land on the opposite corner, and in 1935, he rolled his store—on logs—across the road. That fine old country store is gone now, but this 1940s picture shows the remains of the original store on the right, and the moved store on the left (looking west) with the old Cooper home in the distance. St. Matthews Church can be seen beneath the Amoco sign. (Courtesy of John Tankard Jones.)

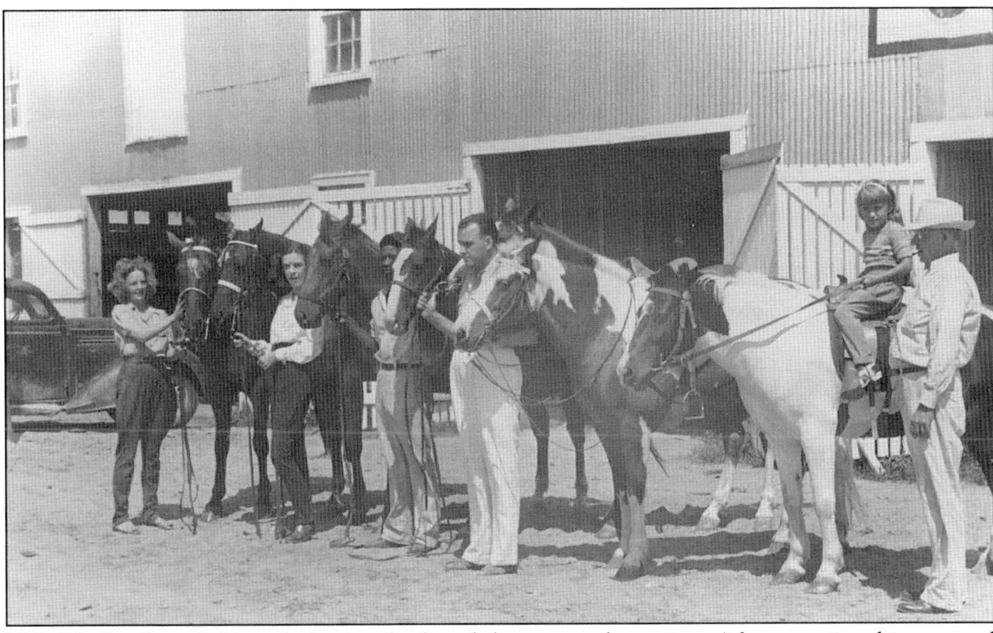

J.M. Tankard and his whole family loved horses and ponies. After moving his general merchandise store, Tankard put up a stable and feed store on the southwest corner of Yeatesville Road. Shown here, from left to right, are Lillie Tankard, Sarah Tankard, unidentified, Ralph Tankard, Ann Jones on the pony, and J.M. Tankard. (Courtesy of John Tankard Jones.)

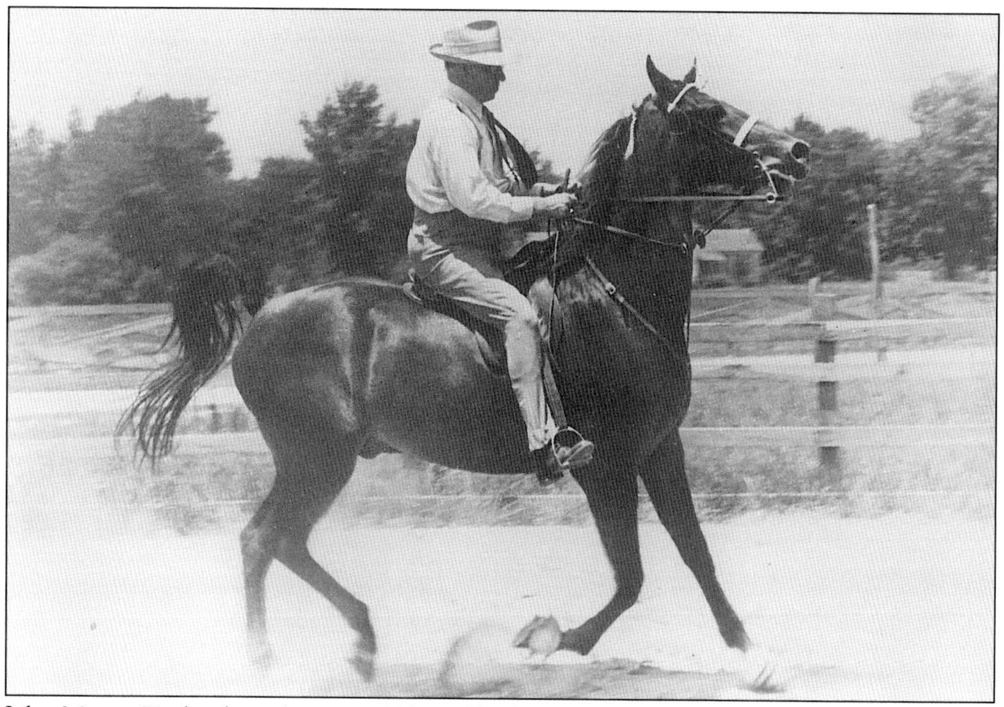

John Macon Tankard was born in 1883, and he lived until 1944. Here is J.M. at his best as he rides his favorite pony. Tankard was a dealer for the Pamlico Chemical Company of Washington. (Courtesy of John Tankard Jones.)

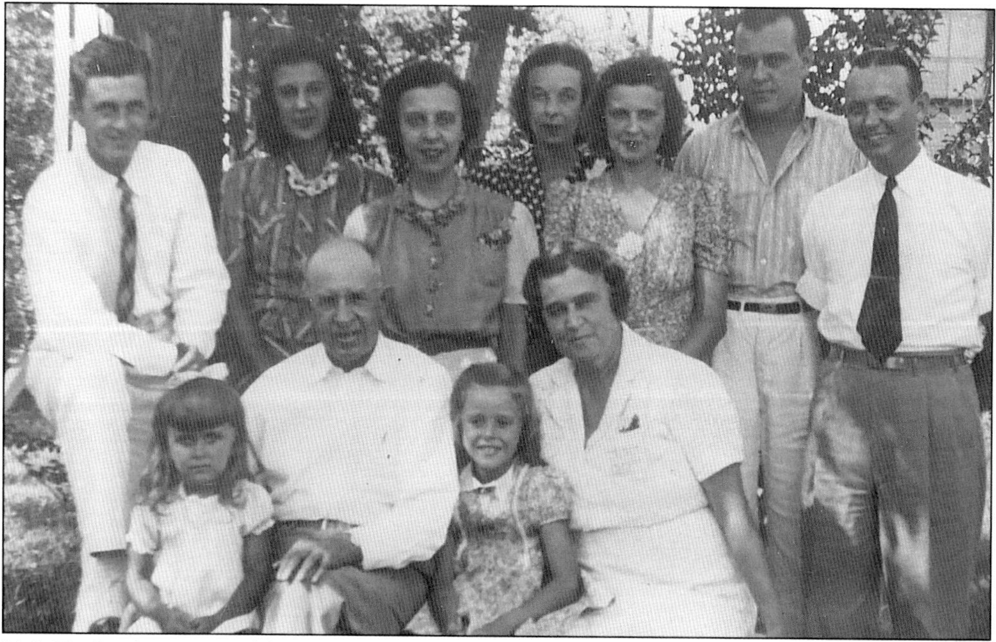

J.M. Tankard is pictured here with his family in 1938. From left to right are (front row) Ann Jones Forgey, John M. Tankard, Clarine Harris Aiken, and Mary Irene Tankard; (back row) Enever Jones, Ruth Tankard Jones, Helen Tankard Nixon, Sara Tankard, Irene Tankard Harris, Ralph Tankard, and Henry Russell Harris. (Courtesy of John Tankard Jones.)

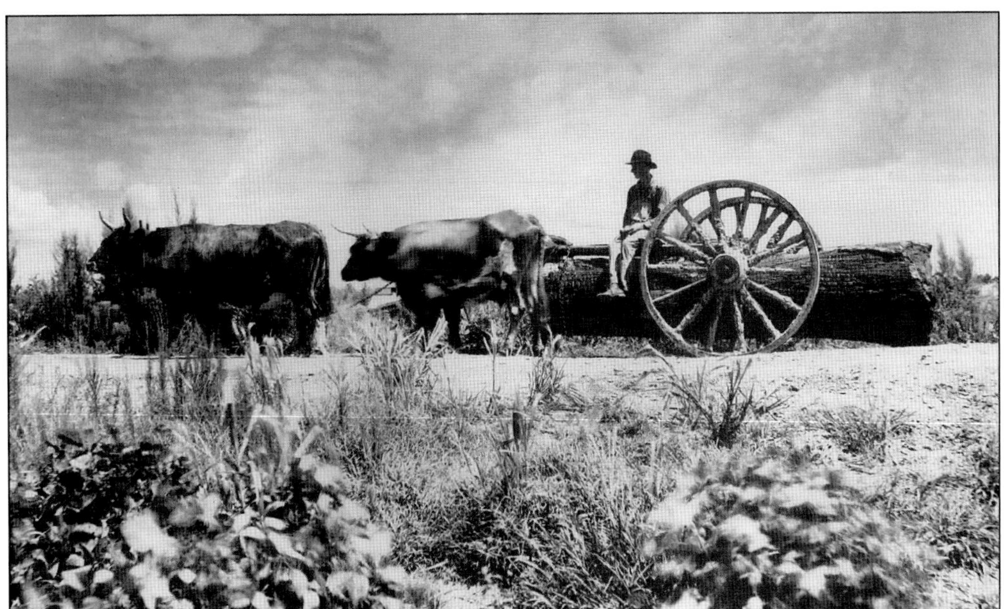

From 1890 to about 1925, in the Pike Road area near the Hyde County line, oxen were used to drag downed juniper trees on a "carry log." The trees were then loaded on barges and floated down a drainage canal to the Pungo River and on to Pantego Creek. The juniper trees were then cut into shingles for railroad shipment. (Courtesy of W. Mayo.)

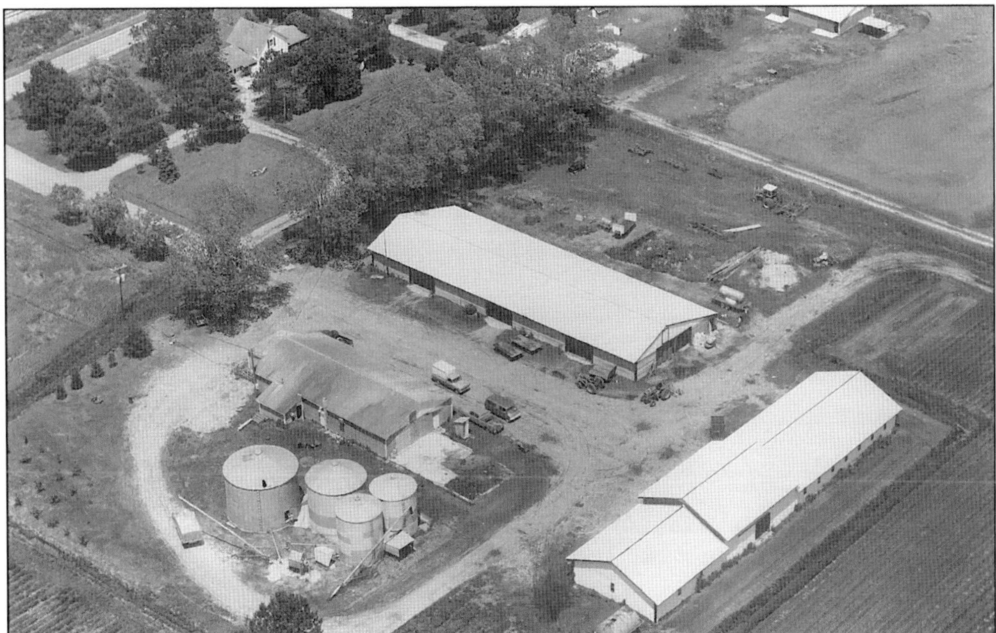

This 1978 aerial photo shows the 1,400-acre Terra Ceia Farms complex, owned by the Case Van Staalduinen family since 1948. These buildings handle every operation required for grading and sorting exotic flower bulbs to grain storage. The owners run a large mail order and internet catalog business and offer many unusual varieties of flower bulbs, such as cannas, tulips, day lilies, daffodils, peonies, and crocus. They also raise large amounts of cotton, corn, and soybeans. (Courtesy of Terra Ceia Farms.)

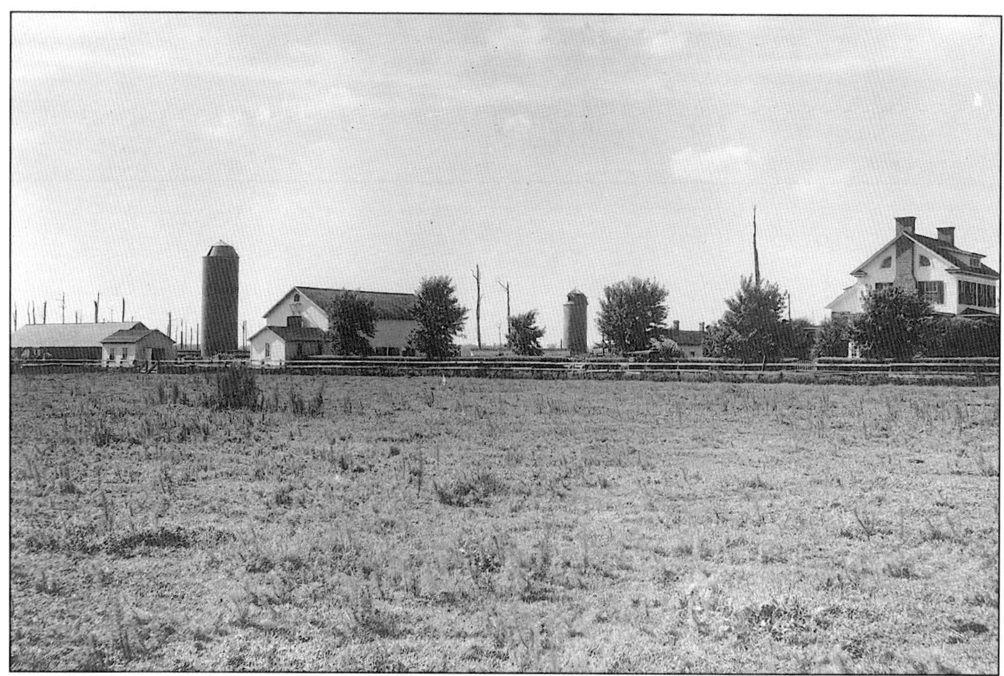

The Respess farm in Terra Ceia was one of the area farms that raised a large herd of beef-producing cattle in the early 1900s. They also had several large pins of hogs, along with the staple crops of corn and soybeans. Son Wallis Respess (1928–) took over his father's farm around 1946 and eliminated the herds and pins of cattle and hogs. Wallis retired a few years ago and built a brick ranch home about a half-mile south of his childhood home, which still stands. He recently sold the old homestead. (Courtesy of W. Mayo.)

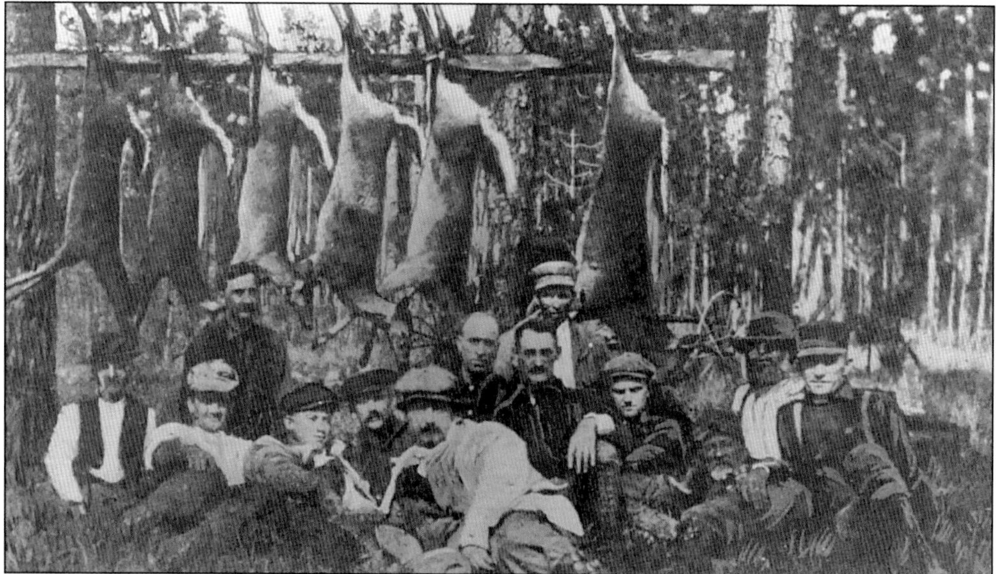

This picture was probably taken around 1900, when Beaufort County still had thousands of acres of timberland that supported bountiful wildlife. Although much of the land has been cleared since 1900, there are still many large forests that support game. Seasonal hunting by quota and permit is still very productive. (Postcard courtesy of Oden's Store.)

The following abbreviations were used to acknowledge the sources of some of the pictures contained within this book.

BCM — *Beaufort County* Magazine
DAR — Daughters of the American Revolution
HGML — Hazel W. Guildford Memorial Library
WDN — *Washington Daily News*
* — Surry Parker photos are courtesy of Vernetta Lang of Bath, NC. They were reproduced by permission of Elizabeth Parker Roberts, the author of *Family and Friends of Pine Town North Carolina 1893–1918*.

INDEX